Bringing *the* Arts *into* *the* Library

Edited by Carol Smallwood

Bringing *the* Arts *into the* Library

ala editions

AN IMPRINT OF THE AMERICAN LIBRARY ASSOCIATION

CHICAGO 2014

Printed in the United States of America

18 17 16 15 14   5 4 3 2 1

Extensive effort has gone into ensuring the reliability of the information in this book; however, the publisher makes no warranty, express or implied, with respect to the material contained herein.

ISBNs: 978-0-8389-1175-4 (paper); 978-0-8389-9471-9 (PDF); 978-0-8389-9469-6 (ePub); 978-0-8389-9470-2 (Kindle). For more information on digital formats, visit the ALA Store at alastore.ala.org and select eEditions.

Library of Congress Cataloging-in-Publication Data
Bringing the arts into the library / edited by Carol Smallwood.
    pages cm
  Includes bibliographical references and index.
  ISBN 978-0-8389-1175-4
  1. Libraries—Cultural programs—United States—Case studies. 2. Libraries and community—United States—Case studies. 3. Library outreach programs—United States—Case studies. I. Smallwood, Carol, 1939– editor of compilation.
  Z716.4.B675 2014
  021.2'6—dc23

                    2012027379

Book design by Adrianna Sutton in the Minion and DIN typefaces.
Cover image © echo3005 / Shutterstock, Inc.
♾ This paper meets the requirements of ANSI/NISO Z39.48–1992 (Permanence of Paper).

Contents

Foreword, by Molly Raphael   vii
Introduction   ix
Arts Acknowledgments   xi

PART I   LITERARY ARTS

1   **The Big Write-In** *A Collaborative Outreach Event for Writers during National Novel Writing Month*   STACEY R. EWING | 3

2   **Librarian as Teacher** *Teaching a Creative Writing Class in the School Library*   ROBERT CRAIG BUNCH | 11

3   **Poetry Corner** *Collaboration among Us*   SUE SAMSON | 25

PART II   VISUAL ARTS

4   **Adult Literacy Programs and Art**   SARAH NAUMANN | 37

5   **Displaying and Promoting Visual Art at the Nashua Public Library**   CAROL LUERS EYMAN | 47

6   **Utilizing Student Talent to Create Appealing Library Posters**   HEATHER PAYNE | 59

7   **Visual Arts in the Academic Library**   JENNIFER MAYER | 73

PART III   PERFORMING ARTS

8   **Developing Regional Heritage Music Collections**   SANDRA M. HIMEL AND LANCE R. CHANCE | 87

9   **Making Music Collections Come Alive**   GREG MacAYEAL | 97

10   **PML Players** *Theater Arts at the Patchogue-Medford Library*   JERI WEINKRANTZ COHEN | 107

PART IV   MIXED ARTS

11   ART: Art Revolution for Teens   HEATHER PIPPIN ZABRISKIE, NATALIE HOUSTON, AND VERA GUBNITSKAIA | 117

12   Children in a Research Library? *Creative Projects for K–12 Students at the Rakow Research Library of the Corning Museum of Glass*   REGAN BRUMAGEN AND BETH HYLEN | 129

13   Gilpin County Public Library Arts Programs LARRY GRIECO | 139

14   The Library as Canvas *Library Larry's Big Day* KEROL HARROD | 147

PART V   MANAGEMENT AND ADMINISTRATION

15   Art Works *Strengthening Downtown with Library-Arts Partnerships* ELIZABETH GOLDMAN AND SARA WEDELL | 157

16   Behind the Scenes *The Legal and Contractual Aspects of Booking Exhibits and Presenters in a Library*   NORA J. QUINLAN AND SARAH CISSE | 165

17   Collaboration as Outreach in the Twenty-First-Century Academic Library   ALLAN CHO | 175

18   Java City *Developing a Successful Cultural Center* JACK G. MONTGOMERY | 187

19   Raising Money to Support the Arts in Your Public Library FLORENCE F. CADDELL | 197

20   Where to Find Programming Ideas and Resources for the Arts Online ALA PUBLIC PROGRAMS OFFICE | 209

Contributors   215
Index   223

Foreword

JUST WHEN WE SEEMED to be virtually consumed by social networking, digital content, and technology applications in libraries along comes this inspiring and useful book, *Bringing the Arts into the Library*. To be sure, libraries have been viewed as cultural and educational centers in their communities for decades. Yet we recently have been so engaged in keeping our libraries current with technology that we may have overlooked just how much we have advanced in bringing the arts into our communities.

Libraries have long designated spaces for exhibitions and programming, but what we have seen in recent years is a genuine expansion in how these spaces are being reinvented and used. As new libraries have been designed and existing buildings renovated, many planners have recognized the value of including professional performance space with not just a stage and banked seating but also sound, light, and recording equipment. This is true particularly in larger communities.

Collaboration with community arts organizations has been a key factor in the success of cultural programming in libraries. These community arts organizations have recognized the penetration that libraries have in communities and neighborhoods. With libraries of all types being identified as the heart of their communities, arts organizations have joined with us to bring a wide variety of arts programs to many people who would probably never have experienced them because of location, cost, or other barriers. Since libraries enjoy a high level of trust and engagement with their communities, they often help arts organizations connect with new audiences. Libraries, in contrast, gain a valuable partner for expanding and enhancing their own programming. These library–arts organization partnerships are particularly important in exhibiting and celebrating local arts, strongly identified with diverse elements of the broader community.

Carol Smallwood has edited five other ALA anthologies, and in this compilation of real-world examples of arts collaborative programming, we see noteworthy programs from all types of libraries and a variety of successful programs serving diverse communities and populations. The value for our profession comes in reading these descriptions, which are full of ideas that can inspire us in our own environments to look beyond what we are doing now. The chapters include very practical advice and look at behind-the-scenes activities and the public components of the programs.

I often describe librarianship as a very generous profession. We willingly share our successes and lessons learned for just about everything we undertake. This is not necessarily true for other professions. Most of us feel very flattered when we introduce a program or service in our library and then watch others adapt it for their own environments and communities. We feel grateful to those who may have pioneered in a new area where we want to go. This book contributes to that generous spirit of sharing and building by offering a rich array of examples of how we can increase our contributions to helping our communities realize their aspirations through the arts.

Molly Raphael
2011–12 President
American Library Association

Introduction

WITH THE PREOCCUPATION of keeping up with technology, libraries may be perceived as no longer playing their traditional role as transmitters and centers of culture, of overlooking the visual and performing arts so necessary for a local community's quality of life. This anthology presents innovative ways to foster the arts even in times of cutbacks in staff and budgets: contributors provide concise examples that visual and performing arts are at the core of communities and that libraries play a central part in that.

Will Manley, in one of his commentary columns in *American Libraries*, observed that librarians must not just be seen as engaged with computer screens at library desks and not interacting with patrons. The twenty-five contributors to *Bringing the Arts into the Library* are engaged with their communities, actively support the arts, and are carrying on the tradition of libraries being cultural centers.

The twenty chapters written by school, public, academic, special, and library and information science faculty in the United States and Canada are arranged in four parts: "Literary Arts," "Visual Arts," "Performing Arts," and "Mixed Arts." Chapters cover various topics, including developing regional music collections, strengthening downtowns with library-arts partnerships, and raising money to support the arts in the library.

Anika Fajardo, online communications librarian at St. Catherine University in Minneapolis, noted, *"Bringing the Arts into the Library* is an affirmation of the role libraries can play in the arts, even in this time of technology overload."

The selection of chapters was difficult and many contributors had to be turned away because of space limitations, which makes a strong case that the relationship between libraries and the arts is currently alive and well. A balance was sought between the many forms of art and types of libraries to achieve the most comprehensive application for librarians.

Carol Smallwood, editor

Arts Acknowledgments

Mary Lou Andrews, technical help, Spring Mills, Pennsylvania

Dr. Kim Becnel, contributor, *Contemporary American Women: Our Defining Passages* (All Things That Matter Press, 2009)

Robin Bourjaily, certified Yoga as Muse facilitator, www.radiantomyoga.com

Vandella Brown, librarian and author of *What Is a Zawadi to We? A Poetic Story Celebrating Kwanzaa and Gift Giving* (Lumen-Us Publications, 2007)

Dr. James B. Casey, director, Oak Lawn Public Library, Oak Lawn, Illinois

Tom Cooper, director, Webster Groves Public Library, Webster Groves, Missouri

Mark Donnelly, winner of best playwright award in 2010 and 2011, Northport (New York) One-Act Play Festival

Martha Engber, author of *The Wind Thief* (Alondra Press, 2009) and *Growing Great Characters from the Ground Up* (Central Avenue Press, 2007)

Anika Fajardo, online communications librarian, St. Catherine University, Minneapolis

John Glover, reference librarian for the humanities, Virginia Commonwealth University, Richmond

Janet Husband, contributor, *Writing and Publishing: The Librarian's Handbook* (ALA Editions, 2010)

Jason Kuhl, library operations director, Arlington Heights Memorial Library, Arlington Heights, Illinois

Terry Ann Lawler, librarian, Phoenix Public Library, Phoenix, Arizona, and contributor to *Library Management Tips That Work* (ALA Editions, 2011)

Dahlma Llanos-Figueroa, author of *Daughters of the Stone* (St. Martin's Press, 2009)

Ann McCauley, former registered nurse, freelance writer, and author of *Mother Love* (CB Publishing, 2012) and *Runaway Grandma* (Madison Avenue Publishing, 2007)

Foster Neill, founder and editor of *The Michigan Poet*, http://themichiganpoet .com

Rebecca Marcum Parker, school district librarian, Kansas City, Missouri

Stacy Russo, electronic services librarian, Santa Ana College, Santa Ana, California, and author of *The Library as Place in California* (McFarland, 2008)

Part I
Literary Arts

CHAPTER 1

The Big Write-In

A Collaborative Outreach Event for Writers during
National Novel Writing Month   **STACEY R. EWING**

NATIONAL NOVEL WRITING MONTH (NaNoWriMo) was founded by a small group of writers in San Francisco in 1999. The goal of NaNoWriMo (or NaNo) is to begin writing a fifty-thousand-word (approximately 175-page) novel on November 1 and to electronically submit the completed word count to the official NaNo website (www.nanowrimo.org) by midnight on November 30. Over the past eleven years, NaNo has grown from a modest 21 participants in 1999 to more than 200,500 participants in 2010.

The mantra of NaNo organizers and participants is "quantity not quality." NaNo is all about fighting and overcoming the inner critic and getting the words out and down on paper, so that after November 30, the true editing process can begin. The beauty of NaNo is that it is not just for seasoned writers; anyone can participate, which makes this an excellent opportunity for beginners to give writing a try while receiving encouragement from others participating in the event.

So as not to stifle the creative spirit, the official rules of NaNo are few: write a novel of fifty thousand words or more, between November 1 and November 30. Participants must be the sole author and may not use previously written prose, although NaNo allows the inclusion of outlines, character sketches, research, and citations from the works of others. To get credit for reaching the fifty-thousand-word count, participants must upload their completed novel to the NaNo website between November 25 and 30.

NaNo seemed like the perfect opportunity around which to craft an event for library outreach to writers, especially since we had the perfect space and the right atmosphere for writing—and what better inspiration than to be surrounded by a building full of books!

PLANNING OUR FIRST NaNoWriMo EVENT

While planning the first NaNoWriMo event at the University of Florida's (UF) library, I researched NaNo and consulted the website (www.nanowrimo.org) to locate the NaNo writing group closest to Gainesville, Florida. I was pleased to find that Gainesville had its own NaNo writing group and contacted the municipal liaison, the NaNo title for someone who officially organizes NaNo groups in his or her hometown, to see if she would be interested in collaborating on an event.

We met and discussed my idea of hosting a write-in event in the InfoCommons area of Library West, the humanities and social sciences branch of the University of Florida's George A. Smathers Libraries. The primary goals of the event were to foster the creation of new literature in the library, to promote both the UF Libraries and National Novel Writing Month, and to bring together writers from the University of Florida and the local Gainesville writing communities to provide a networking opportunity for the members of those groups. We decided that we would try a "final push" writing event on November 29, 2007, and provide space, refreshments, and computers to those who would like to join in and work on their final word count from 5:00 P.M. to 1:00 A.M.

The municipal liaison helped identify and invite two local published writers, Sandra Lambert and R. Michael Burns, to come give motivational pep talks on writing. Both writers spoke about their methods for overcoming writer's block, their experiences participating in past NaNos, and the process of getting published. Their sessions during our event were approximately thirty minutes long, with the last ten minutes reserved as a question-and-answer period. We scheduled their talks two hours apart to break up the evening and to give the event participants a pleasant intermission from writing.

In preparation for the event, I used a free online wiki program by PBworks to track the checklists, assignments, brainstorms, and communication for the event preparation. The wiki allowed me to easily assign projects to volunteers and to streamline the event-planning process by creating an online collaborative checklist.

Although many of the attendees brought their own laptops or netbooks, we reserved several desktop computers adjacent to our event space. Anticipating heavy laptop usage, I borrowed several power strips and extension cords from the libraries' facilities department to provide ample and convenient power for all participants. We staggered the power throughout the event area, and everyone was able to plug in and keep their mobile devices charged.

At 1:00 A.M. (the closing hour of Library West), we still had ten participants hanging in there and working on completing their word count. We even had one participant submit her fifty-thousand-word novel to the online NaNo submission form for verification that night, with cheering from attendees crowded around her computer screen watching her hit the "Enter" key.

PROMOTION AND MARKETING

During the first NaNoWriMo event at UF, I had a zero-dollar budget. Therefore, creative thinking led to creative advertising ideas. Electronic marketing was an effective method that also extended the reach of the information. We publicized the event on the main UF Libraries' homepage and events calendar, in both the UF Libraries and Library West Twitter accounts, as well as on the Library West InfoCommons blog. We created a PowerPoint slide advertisement and posted it on the large annunciator board in the very busy Marston Science Library as well as our own Library West's annunciator screens located in front of each computer at our active circulation desk area. We were also able to add a slide to ResTV, one of the university's television channels that broadcasts UF events in all the residence halls and dorm rooms. We forwarded event information to the UF English Department via its departmental electronic discussion list, and our libraries' public information officer submitted our event details to the university's weekly e-newsletter, the *Gator Times*.

Our library's public relations administrator also designed a template for a poster and flyer that allowed us to reuse the design each year, necessitating only the change of dates and times, thereby saving us the energy of re-creating a poster every year. All flyers and posters were printed in-house, and the Gainesville NaNo group assisted in posting flyers around town while we took care of posting the information at key locations on campus, such as in the student union and in all the dining halls.

A donation request asking for coffee and treats was sent to the campus Starbucks Coffee Company; Starbucks gave us two gallons each of caffeinated and decaffeinated coffee along with various coffee-cake samples. The library provided a large electric carafe to heat water for the tea and hot chocolate donated by UF librarians and members of the Gainesville NaNo group.

To meet our goal of promoting the UF Libraries and National Novel Writing Month, we set up a display table of books from our library's collection to present materials we felt were supportive of the writing process and books on the craft of writing, biographies of famous writers, as well as several books on baby names to help inspire character development. This allowed participants to browse a small selection of the library resources available to them while taking a break from writing. We also set out promotional brochures on library services offered by UF Libraries and the Alachua County Public

Library. We provided table space for the local NaNo group to set up its own NaNo poster-board display to advertise the group and the history of NaNo. The display tables were positioned at the entrance of the event space and next to the refreshment table to maximize foot traffic as participants entered and exited the event space and paused from their writing. Many curious UF library patrons who were not participating in the write-in stopped by to look at the displays, so there was a nice bit of advertising for all parties represented.

PARTICIPANTS COLLABORATING AND NETWORKING

Since the first NaNoWriMo event, participating groups have included members of the Writers' Alliance of Gainesville (WAG), students from the University of Florida and Santa Fe College (English literature and creative writing students, as well as students in other majors who write as a hobby), Gainesville NaNo group members, NaNo participants with no affiliation, students from the local high schools, and usually one or two people from the Gainesville community not participating in NaNo but who want to hear the speakers and talk to participants for advice on getting started on writing for pleasure. At all four of the events we have hosted so far, the diversity of the participants' backgrounds has helped foster a creative and inspiring writing environment. The attendees have been excited and have spent time networking with other participants and various local writing groups.

USING EVENT FEEDBACK

Feedback for this event (and subsequent events) has been overwhelmingly positive. We put out a very simple and informal questionnaire asking attendees whether they thought the event helped promote National Novel Writing Month, whether they learned anything new about the UF Libraries, whether they would like us to hold this event again the following year, and whether they had any suggestions or comments about the event. The first three questions received 100 percent yes answers, with approximately 75 percent of attendees submitting a completed questionnaire. Many thanked us for holding the event, and comments were all positive, with most noting that it was fun and helpful to meet other writers, and many requesting that we do it again the following year. I used the wiki to record the participants' suggestions and to make a running list of things I thought worked really well, what could be improved, and what needed to be done differently the next time.

One of the things we decided to change for subsequent events was the hours. The 5:00 P.M. to 1:00 A.M. time frame during our first event made for a long night, and although we still had ten participants hanging on until the bitter end, participation dropped off drastically and quite noticeably after 10:00 P.M. For this reason, the following year we decided to change the event window from 5:00 P.M. to 10:00 P.M. This worked so well that we have continued with the same time frame ever since. Because we had reserved our event space for the entire evening, participants were able to continue working in the same space after the "official" event ended at 10:00 P.M. We also decided that the speakers, games, and refreshments were too distracting for a "final push," because some participants were rushing to finish their word count before the deadline the following day. The following year we moved the event to the middle of the month and called it "The Big Event," so that we could carry on with entertainment during the evening.

USING TECHNOLOGY TO BRING PUBLISHED AUTHORS TO THE EVENT

We also added technology to the mix the following year. Since our budget did not allow us to pay for authors' travel expenses, we used the free online chat program Meebo, which allowed us to invite speakers from outside of the Gainesville region. The municipal liaison was able to embed a chat widget into the Gainesville NaNo WordPress site. We were originally going to embed it in our libraries' web page, but it worked better using the local NaNo group's site, because users could more easily log in to the chat forum instead of worrying about a UF network login.

The chat technology proved a crucial step in the development of the event. Local participants at the event could choose to watch the live chat on the sixty-one-inch screen in the event space, to follow along on their own laptops, or to completely ignore the chat (given the silent nature of instant messaging) and continue their writing undisturbed.

Knowing that the majority of the participants in 2007 had been writing stories in the science fiction, paranormal, and urban fantasy genres, the following year I wrote to several nationally known and published authors in those genres to see whether they would be available to chat with our participants via Meebo. In 2008, we were able to set up chats with Ann Aguirre, who lives in Mexico City, Mexico; Jeanine Frost, from Southwest Florida; and Ilona Andrews, who at the time was living in North Carolina. I asked whether they would be willing to do a thirty-minute chat session, reserving the last ten minutes for a question-and-answer session. We had to be careful in scheduling and advertising, since Ann Aguirre was located in the central time zone. In addition to the writers participating online, the Gainesville NaNo municipal liaison identified two local published authors whom we invited to speak in person: Marjorie Abrams (M. D. Abrams) and Pierce Kelley. Every hour during that event we had a fifteen- to twenty-minute talk going on either online or in person. The talks were staggered so that in-person chats could be sandwiched between the online chats, and Ann Aguirre, in a different time zone, anchored the spot for last online guest speaker.

It has been surprisingly easy to persuade authors to volunteer to be online guest speakers. Social networking makes self-promotion much easier, and today most authors are highly accessible through their blogs, Twitter, and Facebook pages. I send an e-mail describing the details of the event along with a polite request asking whether the author would be interested in joining in and "speaking" to our participants via online chat. All the authors we have contacted in the past four years (including J. V. Jones, J. C. Hutchins, and Mur Lafferty) have been excited to participate and willing to freely donate their time and share their experiences.

Communication with the authors was essential, given tight scheduling, potential technology issues, and different time zones. The municipal liaison obtained permission from each author to post edited transcripts of the chats on the Gainesville NaNo website.

IMPROVING THE EVENT

In the years following our first NaNoWriMo event in 2007, I tried to make the event even more fun and engaging for participants. In 2008, as a donation to the libraries, I purchased books written by each of the guest speakers, and at the end of each chat session and in-person talk we held a "word war," a contest in which participants tried to write as many words as they could in ten minutes. Once the time was up, we collected the word count from each participant (on the honor system), and the winner won a copy of the book by the author who had just spoken in person or online. In addition, both authors who were present autographed their books, and Ann Aguirre offered to personalize the winner's copy of her book and include a galley copy of the sequel if the winner mailed her the copy of the book he or she was writing. All the authors were very friendly, very interested in promoting their work, and very encouraging to all the NaNo participants by offering great advice on writing, editing, finding an agent, and getting published.

In addition to the books we gave away, I created commemorative NaNo pins using the library's button maker and small NaNo icons freely available on the NaNoWriMo website to help promote the month. Municipal liaisons also receive a certain number of free NaNo stickers and postcards each year to share with local groups, so we were able to use some of these items as fun giveaways and consolation prizes for the word-war contestants who did not come in first place. We also used some of the UF Libraries' promotional items, such as branded pencils, sticky notes, and InfoCommons stress-relief squishy balls.

Every year since 2007, I have been compiling a slide show in conjunction with the Gainesville NaNo group to play on the sixty-one-inch monitor throughout the event when author chat sessions are not taking place. These slides include quotes by authors, photo excerpts from a great Salon.com blog article about authors and their writing spaces or studios, photos of books, photos designed like inspirational posters, and more. Over the past several years our slide show has grown from fifty slides to more than two hundred. We also slip in slides to promote the UF Libraries' resources and services available to both UF affiliates and community users.

A large portion of the slide show consists of excerpts from past "idea jars." Each year, the local Gainesville group puts together what it calls the idea jar, an empty jar next to a stack of blank paper slips. During the event, NaNo participants can take a break from writing to add an idea or pull a slip from the jar for random inspiration. Ideas can be names, places, or things, but they are most often leading sentences or prompts, such as "She was horrified to find that her skirt had been caught in her pantyhose as she walked through the restaurant back to her table," or "The sun was setting quickly," or "A freak storm blows up the power to your scene—characters must continue their work in the dark." Everyone contributes to the jar throughout November, and the following year the funniest and most interesting ideas are culled and added to the slide show.

At our first NaNo event, one of the participants brought a little handful of fortune-cookie slips to keep by the idea jar for inspiration. I have actually been keeping my fortune-cookie slips for the past twenty years, so now I bring in my large jar of fortunes for participants to use as a fun source of writing ideas.

"Jailing the Inner Critic" has been another great way to help keep participants focused and engaged. Each year the Gainesville municipal liaison brings a paper "jail" that she created out of a large clasped envelope with slots cut out to represent the bars of a jail cell. This is placed in the center of the room near the idea jar and fortune-cookie jar along with crayons. At the beginning of the event, participants are encouraged to draw a quick representation of their "inner critic" with the crayons and place that drawing into the cage for the duration of the evening, or if they like, the municipal liaison holds on to them until the end of the month. This is a fun way for participants to take a break and a nice exercise in putting the inner critic at rest so that a blocked writer can again write freely.

Budgeting for this event has remained very low. After the 2007 event, we decided to put in a small $50 funds request to our libraries' public relations and marketing committee for a fruit platter and granola bars as a healthy alternative to the donated Starbucks coffee cake. I hope to secure additional funding to supply prize novels in the future.

As we approach the fifth anniversary of our NaNo event, I see it as drawing the arts into the library and making my job more relevant to the community.

CHAPTER 2

Librarian as Teacher

Teaching a Creative Writing Class in the School
Library   ROBERT CRAIG BUNCH

IN MY EIGHTEENTH YEAR as a librarian (and my first at Hamilton Middle School in Houston, Texas), I was willingly drafted to teach the second semester of a yearlong creative writing class. I credit Barbara Valentine and other teachers at Hamilton Middle School and various elementary schools whose diverse talents and teaching styles surely whipped up the unique gusts of inspiration that frequently threatened to blow me away.

Hamilton, a public school in the Houston Independent School District, pulses with 1,400 students who are not always easily contained within the cramped classrooms of a building that dates to 1919—thus the decision to hold the class in the spacious library. My students were a mix of high achievers recruited to our vanguard program from across the city and students from the Houston Heights neighborhood. The library offered far more space, access to books, and (eventually) computers than any standard classroom. It was also the physical heart and metaphorical brain of the school's campus.

A small number of sources became key prompts, especially the issue "Parties" of *Two Lines: A Journal of Translation* (Center for the Art of Translation, 2003) of non-English poems and their contemporary English translations. We looked only at the non-English source poems, which ranged from Italian and classical Japanese to Uzbek and Finnish. Although my students and I had no knowledge of these languages, we were not quite clueless. The length, arrangement, and layout of lines and stanzas; imagined affinities of sound and rhyme; and the occasional visual aid, such as a Japanese woodblock print, were sufficient to elicit thoughtful and thought-provoking "translations" that I would have thought far beyond the linguistic and imaginative capabilities of sixth and seventh graders—often, too, the work sounds like that of sixth and seventh graders; there is charm and honesty in that. From a library book on ancient Egypt, the hieroglyphics of a tomb relief prompted a handful of extraordinary lines. A challenge from Ray Fenwick's hilarious graphic masterpiece *Hall of Best Knowledge* (Fantagraphics, 2008) provided another successful prompt.

While "translations" provided a touchstone to which we frequently returned, other successful prompts included a walk outside to contemplate what we would "never see again"; stories and vignettes inspired by stickers (also a favorite reward); abandoned photographs, postcards, and other ephemera; a version of the surrealist game exquisite corpse using index cards taped together accordion style; a discussion titled "What Is Art?"; and a vignette or story each student created from an artwork-a-day calendar. Throughout the semester, I photocopied promising work for possible inclusion in an end-of-course anthology. My wife, Delana, and I read, debated, laughed, winnowed, and word processed our way through the work to get it down to one hundred pages, a selection of which follows. As I promised them, each student was represented by at least one work in the anthology.

The following selections are very lightly edited—for the occasional misspelling or lack of subject-verb agreement, and for virtually nothing else. I retained creative spellings and punctuation, layout, and handwritten quirks in the writings' word-processed, anthologized final product. I attribute my students' impressive vocabulary, diction, syntax, and wordplay to their aforementioned teachers, to lots of reading in the short lives of most, and to a willingness to excel and to please. I fed them a steady diet of verbal and written praise (and crazy stickers from a book); where they made a genuine effort, I could almost always find something worth praising. Students completed these assignments in a single class period, often in thirty minutes or less and almost always handwritten. Occasionally, a journal entry represented a revised or, more likely, unrevised class assignment.

Most days I read aloud what I considered the best work, usually without attribution—because that was the preference of most students. Only one regularly volunteered to read her own work aloud or to have me read it aloud. Some, I am convinced, saw little merit in their own efforts. A most eloquent thought arrived on an index card submitted by the student Sandra Gonzalez in response to the very first assignment: "Writing is a beautiful way to express yourself when you don't have the bravery to talk. When you write, your thoughts flow out like water, and before you know, you know what's bothering you."

Born of the chance encounter of a bookmark and a wrongly oriented page on a copy machine, the prompt for these quickly rendered but deeply felt words became an abstract image (later dubbed "L") for my young students to

An abstract image (dubbed "L") used as a writing prompt at the Hamilton Middle School library

"translate." It was stapled to poems in Italian, Russian, and Japanese. Despite my best efforts, I could not determine the author of the unsigned last entry; for the anthology, I changed emitted to admitted but have now reverted to the evocative original.

Writings Prompted by an Abstract Image

He took a piece of light and tried to spread it around the darkness that surrounded me—to brighten my day
—*Raven Aguas*

The boot . . .
it sits . . .
Never worn . . .
Never looked at . . .
Never been played with . . .
the only mark,
is a silver stripe . . .
of a piece of Duck tape
—*Michaela Baca*

A house of hope
in darkness.
   —*Rebecca Gonzales*

The open window,
My freedom path,
the light that shows me
darkness
wonder in a bottle
My open window.
   —*Hannah Davis*

This is an x-ray of
the robot's
leg.
he was emitted into the
hospital last night for a broken
leg.
We have run out of
tin foil for his cast.
Sorry.
   —*Anonymous*

Translations of an Ancient Japanese Poem and Its Seventeenth-Century "Faux" Parody

The first source poem is from Fujiwara no Teika's thirteenth-century anthology *Hyakunin Isshu*, which translates as *One Hundred Poets, One Poem Each*. Its faux version is from Yûsoan's seventeenth-century parody of the former, *Inu Hyakunin Isshu*. My students were only vaguely, if at all, aware of this. Nevertheless, they made shining use of stanza structure, humor, and the connotations of *poets* and *faux* (the latter a word we discussed).

Poets.
You see them everywhere,
in the street, in the stores,
in the salons.
But do you know who
they are?
Do you know how their
lives are?

Do you know them at all?
A hoax.
A trick.
It wasn't real, it was fake.
Fake as that man's watch, as
that girl's nose.
 —*Sandra Gonzalez*

Love
An unshattered heart
Hate
A shattered heart
 —*Raven Aguas*

One hundred poets:
Sitting in a room
telling their tales
each one different
no one's the same
but all end . . .
with one word . . .
fin
Faux Hundred:
not one hundred . . .
not fifty . . .
not twenty . . .
not ten . . .
but one.
 —*Michaela Baca*

The world
is falling
apart. Run
to the safest
place you
can find.
The war
will not
end. And
you cannot
stop it.
 —*Violeta Cisneros*

The Stars Sing
Let us offer up to the light
in our hearts
an old tale of a country awaiting
its awakening . . .
Our wishes become stars,
which we can see tomorrow . . .
My love, please wait for
me . . .
Araai = Red love
Let us shoulder the light
of the priestess' life
upon our gracefully dancing
wings of purity . . .
Go to sleep in the arms of
the one you love, who in
order for you to become a star . . .
Should not have been born
    —Tara Thompson

Yay, today is the marve festival! We are going to have cake, pizza, rice, chopsticks, egg rolls, and sweet-and-sour chicken.
There will also be kites and people wearing masks. The biggest part of the festival is when the big dragon comes out.
    —Raquel Vara

Nothing
to
write. Can't think of
anything.
Still
can't think
of anything.
    —Javier Castillo

Kiss the kitty
goodnight.
She loves you so
much, the kitty
does!
The rat went
up the clock.
    —Mercedes Tinney

A Japanese wood-block print used as a writing prompt at the Hamilton Middle School library

Writings Inspired by a Japanese Woodblock Print

A lovely evening. We all sit down and have lunch, rice on the floor, our small bowls filled with the sweet smelling stuff. We talk about the old times, of how we were young, of how we were powerful and brave soldiers that served our country. We are old men, with bad knees and bald heads. We have fat in our stomachs, and we are okay with it. We lived already, it is our time now to rest. We eat calmly and joyfully. We don't care. We lived.

—*Sandra Gonzalez*

The three little men in the houses came out and met up. They talked about the ancient scrolls and then they smoked some pipes and talked about their wives.

—*Graeme Campbell*

Asian men
one in PJ's

the rest are ninja
The ninja have a mission: kill
the PJ one . . .
but they are drunk friends!
  —*Michaela Baca*

Today I am going to teach you some karate after we eat rice with some
chopsticks on the floor. I am also going to show you how to write in
Chinese.
  —*Raquel Vara*

My friends and I,
We smoke you see.
We can't stop ourselves,
So we will die soon.
  —*Jade Klingler*

Guys sharing food at a Japanese buffet in Japan. They are enjoying the
moonlight which seeks through the transparent walls of the buffet.
Happiness spreads amongst their faces.
  —*Mercedes Tinney*

Chicken Fry
  —*Hannah Davis*

We gather up to sing.
  —*Jessica Cantu*

4 guys in a painting relaxing
  —*Stephanie Cortez*

It teaches about the ways of life, like not to drink beer.
  —*Gustavo Martinez*

A Story Inspired by Old Photographs

The prompts for the story exercise were packets of photographs, postcards, old
letters, advertisements, and other ephemera that I supplied. Although I intended
that each student do his or her own work, this particular group insisted on
arranging their photographs into a story in pictures, which they then wrote up

in parts. The library's nooks and crannies afforded this group of friends, or a close approximation, the inspiration to collaborate on more than one occasion.

Part 1
Storybook fairy tales have been with me all my life. My mother's silky voice guided me through my years. My father's rough but gentle hands helped me be all that I am. My childhood years were the best years of my life. The late nights playing outside with my brothers was the main thing I looked forward to during the school day. You couldn't imitate the love and joy that dwelled in my house. I grew up in it. I couldn't ask for a better childhood, and I wouldn't try. But childhood has to end, and it did all too soon . . . I grew up, and saw reality.
—*Rebecca Gonzales*

Part 2
It was a cold, windy day, the wind whipping my coat harshly. I strode down Bental, crossing onto Main Street. I kept my head down, the wind whipping at my exposed skin. I stopped, suddenly ramming into something hard. A strong scent of lavender, warm and secure, filled me, warming my heart. When I looked up, it happened so suddenly, I can't ever remember the transition. Those eyes. Bottomless, engulfing blue. The blue of the gentle ocean, sparkling, or the infinity of the clear blue sky, on a day when the sun hangs proudly in the sky. Her dark hair flew haphazardly around her tiny, heart-shaped face, making her appear delicate and strong at the same time. "It's Marney," she said, her voice clear and powerful. I knew at that moment that she was the rest of my life.
—*Nicki Loisel*

Part 3
Four years later and Marnie and I have two healthy children. One boy, one girl. Every summer we go to the family lake. This year was no different. Aaron dipped his toe in the water and looked back at Shiloh and Marnie. "It's too cold. I'm not going in." Shiloh rolled her eyes and rushed over to Aaron, pushing him in. Aaron splashed, we laughed, thinking he would be okay. Five minutes. 6. 7. 8. Aaron still wasn't coming up.

"We all jumped in, thrashing around. Weeds pulled Shiloh down and Jeremy reached after her. 1 minute. 2. 3. 4. 10. No matter what I did, it really hurts to know that I couldn't save them," whispered Marnie, tears strolling down her face.
—*Hannah Davis*

Part 4

"The funeral will take place on a Friday," one announced. "Oh, dear!" my mother-in-law Amelie cried. It had been only 3 hours since I saw my husband and 2 children drown. My face felt wet and clammy, and my eyes were red with pain. "Oh dear, it's okay . . . ," Grandma Amelie said to me. But it wasn't. My mind kept telling me *no*. What would I do? Why has this happened?

In another wrought of tears, I grabbed my gray knit and pinned up my hair. As I slipped on my black felted gloves, I realized that this would be the last goodbye. Amelie had been so kind in readying the food and guests. The pastor began to speak. "And Jeremy will be received into the arms of the lord, forever more."

—*Graeme Campbell*

Part 5

Many long years after the last member of the Price family passed, the man that started it all sits in heaven. He stays in the corner where no sunlight can reach or mock his sorrow. Questions still remain in Mr. Price's mind. What had he done wrong, why was he hurting so much, who was he without his family? All of his life, he had spent trying to turn his life around, but his fate hadn't spared him. Mr. Price was a little boy inside, clueless, innocent, and loving. Now, in that corner, Jeremy sits in the form of a boy, the wise boy who wanted more. This is who he was . . . without a family.

—*Isabel Jackson-Alvarez*

Lines Inspired by a Page from Ray Fenwick's *Hall of Best Knowledge*

Her laughter was sweet, and thick, and slow, like warm caramel, dripping slowly from a thin metal spoon. It enveloped my senses, bringing a lightness and warmth to my heart.

—*Nicki Loisel*

My voice box corrupted and a cackle burst up from my throat and whooshed out my mouth. And that's when this laughter happened. But somehow I was laughing in pitches! My laughter was cracking and cackling to the tune of my song—going to a high D to low C. It was so uncontrollable, and it almost sounded as if I was choking on something. My trachea was blocked with air and I seemed to feel dizzy. My head was pulsing as I continued to sing in an operative manner with a tad bit of a sore throat. How could I be laughing when my face was dead serious and humor was nowhere to be found? I held my hands against my throat and squeezed hard until a cccccccccrriccckk was heard from my voice and I dropped dead: the sound of dying from laughter.

—*Raven Aguas*

Laughter
crying, tears of joy.
Hysterically laughing.
Words spoken, and you explode.
The laughter spreads,
everyone around you
laughing.
Hysterical
laughter

—*Rebecca Gonzales*

Laughter
You pray to make her happy, to make her happy, happy, happy.
To hear her laugh, better than the harps of angels,
everyone tries to make her love them, love them, love them,
To be able to have a small chance every day,
to make her laugh, that laughter, laughter, laughter.
1%, 100% to see her dreamcloud teeth,
brightly, brightly, brightly, against her raw pink lips
against God's piano playing on E,
That's the key,
to being happy, happy, happy.

—*Claire Jordan*

Dear Fred,
It has been ages since I saw your gorgeous face—two days since I last wrote, & I am already missing you. I am sure that by now some slinky siren has stolen your handsome, beautiful, glittery heart. This letter is saddening me, but I must go further. I hope your selfless ways do not attract another woman. The way you walk & talk makes me shiver with joy, I hope nobody else thinks so too. I love everything about you, & yet I fear you do not feel the same. I am beginning to be cross, Fred, very cross. Now that I think about it, I can do better. Fred, I hate everything

you do, from the way you ride your bike to the way you chew. Fred, we are done!
I hate you,
Linda
P.S. No siren could ever fall for you!
   —Hannah Davis

My laughing was loud yet high. The laughter seized through the students around me. My laughter beautiful and song-like. Like a thousand shining crystals gleaming in the bright sunlight. My laugh was like a China Crystal glass shattering into many *******Dreams!*******
   —Mercedes Tinney

Classmate Sketches

Blonde hair tickles her cheeks. She keeps her head down, holding a secret. Never letting it go. She sketches silently, her innermost thoughts. Her green eyes move across the room, capturing each image. Her thin lips softly speak each word, like a question. Unsure. You never know what the girl in the corner is thinking. You just know that she's there, and she's watching.
   —Rebecca Gonzales

Her hair is black as the night sky.
But her voice is soft as a freshly bought
fur coat.
What is she thinking about?
Who is she writing about?
I don't know. No one knows.
We'll just have to wait.
Wait.
Wait.
Wait.
   —Dezarea Baxter

I will add only a few thoughts about other aspects of the course. Each student kept a journal throughout the semester. Some were prolific, and others languished. Some work seemed too good to be true, and sometimes it was. I frequently reminded students to put quotation marks around, and credit the authors of, song lyrics. Students completed journal entries almost entirely outside the classroom. My decision to limit journal entries in the anthology to two pages and a fraction from only three students reflects both the strength of the in-class writings and my reluctance to risk any chance of including work that was not my students' own. Finally, students compiled what each considered his or her best work into a final project—a book. Results ranged from the well crafted and prolific to the slapdash and minimalist. (Minimalism has its merits, though, as some inclusions in this chapter attest.)

In today's lean economic times, the school librarian, already a generalist, is increasingly called on to fulfill duties outside the traditional role of librarian. The school librarian's typical immersion in an environment and culture of books offers a superb starting point for innovative approaches to the teaching of creative writing, whether as for-credit courses or after-school clubs. In either case, I commend a course that privileges unconventional uses of texts and books as source material, honest praise, a minimum of revision, and creative approaches to letting students experiment with and find their own voices. There is a time and place for revision, but not at the expense of squelching authentic voices. I conclude with student Violeta Cisneros's "translation" of an Italian poem whose original sounds just might evoke "a joyous dance": The library is quiet. / We should not talk in here, / we shouldn't scream either.

CHAPTER 3

Poetry Corner

Collaboration among Us   SUE SAMSON

POETRY, LIBRARIES, AND COMMUNITIY provide an excellent symbiosis for establishing a dynamic that fosters poets, strengthens libraries, and builds creative community. At the University of Montana, Missoula (UM), the well-established and nationally recognized creative writing program hosts students, visiting professors of poetry, and notable faculty. The Maureen and Mike Mansfield Library has a long, established working relationship with the Department of English through its liaison and outreach program to build collections suitable for curricular integration, its hosting of the occasional reading, and its instruction in information literacy. The Missoula writing community flourishes with both new and well-published authors-in-residence, healthy local bookstores, multiple reading series, the Missoula Writing Collaborative, and the annual Festival of the Book.

In combination, these things became the perfect framework for donors, writers, librarians, administrators, and students to fund and foster the design and development of a library space for the creation, study, and reading of creative writing. The Poetry Corner was created like a poem: "spontaneously, individualistically, independently, with a flavor all its own" (Moffeit 1992, 61). Collections in the Poetry Corner include the works of select poets and authors whose contributions to the study and writing of poetry and fiction have affected the UM community and national literature. Since the grand opening of the Poetry Corner in 2006, the space has hosted the readings of visiting instructors, community writers, middle school writing camps, and graduate student thesis readings; it has fostered the successful acquisition of the archival manuscripts and papers of one of those poets; and it has established continued collaborations among the library, the creative writing program, and the writing community, including the annual publication of a new creative writing journal for undergraduate publication. This chapter describes the evolution of the Poetry Corner in the Mansfield Library, its original design and development, and the unexpected benefits that developed and continue to reverberate.

FUNDING, ADMINISTRATION, AND COLLABORATION

Space became available in a corner of the top floor of the library when an archives storage area was vacated. The area is a large room with glass walls on one side that open to the library and windows on the far wall that provide a narrow but lovely view of the campus. A new dean of libraries had been working with the UM Foundation Center to identify and attract donors. Collaborations between writing programs and libraries are well documented and natural. Since the UM Creative Writing Program is one of UM's flagship programs, the dean was enthusiastic about exploring opportunities to establish further connections.

When the Foundation Center identified a potential donor interested in supporting the value of literature and creative writing, the dean contacted the humanities librarian to explore appropriate options. The dean wanted the donor to have a designated space in the library that would cultivate opportunities for collaborative events and that would bring students, faculty, and community members to the library. The available space was perfect in terms of square footage but had the drawback of being located in the far corner of the top floor of the library in an area of the collection focused on the sciences. If we built it, would they come?

The humanities librarian crafted a prospective for the design and development of the Poetry Corner. Communication with the head of the English Department identified the possibility that poets with direct connections to UM and the creative writing program would be interested in donating their personal libraries to the Mansfield Library at a time when they needed to divest themselves of these collections. These potential donations would serve as the Poetry Corner's collection and would provide a backdrop of personal libraries that surrounded the poets as they wrote. The room had the potential to provide casual seating, study tables, and presentation space that could be easily adjusted to accommodate varying sizes and types of activities. In addition, there is an extended space outside of the room that creates a lobbylike effect and has the capacity for additional casual seating, extended audience seating, and space for refreshments or book signings.

The humanities librarian, Foundation Center officer, and potential donor viewed the space and discussed the ideas of the donor and how they could translate into the library space and the UM curriculum, and enhance the lives of students. The space was a mostly empty shell with a few shelving units against one wall and new carpet. We discussed furnishings, spatial arrangements, potential use, and how everyday students would have a space for quiet study and contemplation. After this meeting, the Foundation Center officer requested an estimated cost analysis, and the process was formally under way. After accepting the prospectus and cost estimate, the donor became an advocate and actually solicited donations for the project from a suite of family and friends. As a result, the donation came in slightly over budget and represented the combined donations of eight individuals. It was particularly fortunate that the library could now consider all these individuals as friendly to future communications with the library.

DESIGN AND DEVELOPMENT

Not unexpectedly, this part of the project was filled with equal parts of fun and frustration. It is an interesting conundrum that picking out the most appropriate tables, chairs, ottomans, fabrics, and paints builds enthusiasm and engagement, whereas actually getting all those tasks accomplished and furnishings purchased and installed requires stalwart resolution and creativity. The library, English Department, and Foundation Center established an open-house date to which the donors and dignitaries would be invited. The Poetry Corner had a deadline.

As the painting was completed and the shelving units installed to wrap the entire room, the first donation of books was received. It was a much smaller donation than originally expected, with a promise of more to come sometime in the future. Filling those empty shelves became a priority to create the library ambiance identified as essential by the donor. Creative writing serials were relocated to the Poetry Corner to provide a related and relevant collection that could then be gradually returned to its original location as the donations continued to arrive. Personnel in cataloging, acquisitions, and circulation were instrumental in facilitating this unexpected and short-term relocation. Their expertise, hard work, and good humor provided the developing Poetry Corner with its complement of volumes and levity.

The study tables and chairs were on order for months but were never actually designated for delivery. It is sometimes amazingly very difficult to spend money. Fortunately, the Poetry Corner's casual furniture was included in a larger purchase of similar furniture for another space in the library. This provided continuity in furnishings and upholstery across the library and savings as part of a larger purchase order. With the open house scheduled for two weeks away, two librarians partnered to go furniture shopping and provided the local market with an unexpected benefit. Four study tables and twenty-four matching chairs were delivered within two days.

The Foundation Center provided essential support for the open-house gala. An invitation list was created, and engraved invitations including a photo of the new space and a program of events were mailed. The invitees included the UM president and Foundation Center president, along with other dignitaries, including the group of donors as special guests. The program included the new interim dean providing introductions, a short presentation by the president, a response by the primary donor, and a poetry reading that included Montana's poet laureate, an English Department faculty poet, and both a graduate and undergraduate student selected by the creative writing program.

More than one hundred people attended the open house and set a record for attendance at a single library event. The outer lobby area adjacent to the Poetry Corner was filled with overflow seating. A portable wall was placed beyond the outer lobby with tables of food, providing an amazingly intimate setting within the confines of the top floor of the library. This very successful grand opening was a harbinger of the future of the Poetry Corner.

SERENDIPITY

Due in large part to the successful grand opening, other UM poets agreed to donate their libraries in the future. One UM poet also immediately donated an original work of art that hangs in the outer lobby area and a unique publisher poster that hangs inside the Poetry Corner. The original artwork was curated by the Montana Museum of Art and Culture and sent out for cleaning before being hung permanently in the library. This same poet and her writer husband subsequently sold their papers to the Mansfield Library Archives, further securing opportunities for quality research of original source materials in the area of creative writing and underscoring the value of collaborative alliances with poets, libraries, and community. This collection was processed, and an online exhibit, "Inextricable Fusion: The Poetry of Patricia Goedicke," is available as part of the digital collection of the Mansfield Library Archives and Special Collections.

Collections from four poets have been donated and received. These collections are reviewed for unique items that might be best located in Special

Collections and then are processed and added to the Poetry Corner collection. Individual items in the collections themselves are often signed copies of books, as well as personalized notes both from the authors and from the poets in whose library they resided, and these serve as a noncirculating collection to foster research and study.

During National Poetry Month, the Mansfield Library hosts the student reading Poetry for Lunch. This initially engaged upper-division students in the Creative Writing: Advanced Poetry class who were invited to read one of their own creative works and that of a poet who had inspired their own writing. The event is presented in the lobby of the library during the lunch hour to bring attention and focus to the process of creative writing and to give the students an opportunity for public reading experience. To complete the process of scholarship, the library publishes a chapbook of the poems read for the occasion and prints a formal program.

As a result of this activity, in 2008 student participants initiated and successfully established an undergraduate fine arts publication, the *Oval* (www.umt .edu/theoval/). This publication is now in its fourth year of successful operation. In addition to supporting printing costs, the library's annual Poetry for Lunch reading coincides with the release of each year's new issue of the *Oval* and includes select readings from the publication. The reading has moved into a presentation space as part of the library's evolving learning commons, and the backdrop for the reading includes huge posters that include the cover and pages of poetry from the *Oval* mounted on an expandable, portable display board.

These readings draw a solid attendance. Although some library patrons stop by as they enter or leave the building and hear the event taking place, creative writing faculty and students are regular attendees, as are entire classes that use the event as a classroom experience. One year, the teacher of a middle school class that was visiting campus the day of the reading asked whether her students could attend. The students' rapt attention to the entire event was an awesome part of the experience; individual students actually asked poets to sign their programs.

The English Department faculty who teaches the credit class Literary Magazine Studio for the publication of the *Oval* also works closely with a local high school creative arts publication. Students from UM mentor high school students through the publication of their own literary magazine, the *Aerie Big Sky* (www.mcps.k12.mt.us/portal/Activities/AerieBigSky/tabid/2511/), and their own poetry reading. The dynamic of drawing students into the campus and into the library for the creative writing experience further establishes the community-campus connection, with the library at its center.

Both the publication of the *Oval* and the reading event garnered attention from the award-winning advertising campaign sponsored by the UM

Admissions Department. They captured clips from the Poetry for Lunch reading and interviewed students and the humanities librarian, with a plan to craft another aspect of campus life that would attract new students. This video resides on UM's YouTube Channel and places the library in a very collaborative role for student engagement.

BUILD IT, AND THEY WILL COME

This corner location on the top floor of the library in the midst of the science books has become a popular study location. Students were quick to locate this special place in the library that provides them with quiet study and isolation. Public relations relative to the Poetry Corner initially hinged on the gala grand opening, sponsored by the Foundation Center and widely publicized through a combination of print and media outlets and direct invitations. Local reporters and media covered the gala, which was then disseminated in local publications. This established a broad base of interest in and knowledge of the Poetry Corner across campus and in the community. Subsequently, the hosting of events in the Poetry Corner has garnered more attention to its potential use and has certainly established word-of-mouth communication that has been an integral component of its publicity. It is not uncommon for the humanities librarian or the library administration to receive contacts requesting use of this space for a wide range of activities.

Although the room is not a classroom, one of the most popular uses that developed is for faculty to request the Poetry Corner for class use when their students will give presentations or lead discussions. This provides the students with a more casual and user-friendly environment and provides a library setting for thoughtful debate, critical thinking, and information sharing. The English Department uses the Poetry Corner for specific events, including its award ceremony for student poet and fiction writers of the year. These events pack the room and often require overflow seating into the outer lobby. The Missoula Writing Collaborative, connected to the Department of English, hosts a summer writing camp for middle school students and schedules two weeks of sessions that are held in the Poetry Corner in the afternoons. Four years after the grand opening of the Poetry Corner, a photograph of a young writer engrossed in the process of writing a poem, seated at one of the study tables, and surrounded by the collection of books was sent to the donor. The library has adopted this location for meeting space and presentations.

The Poetry Corner did not occur as a spontaneous, one-shot event. It developed during the course of years as part of traditional liaison librarian activities—meeting with faculty, supporting faculty research initiatives, providing reference assistance, collaborating on collection development, providing consistent information literacy instruction, and coordinating learning outcomes and assessment. In addition, the humanities librarian is a writer as well and is connected with the creative writing program in support of teaching and readings. All these contacts provided the groundwork for the subsequent development of the Poetry Corner.

The Poetry Corner is unique in its ability to build on a juncture of community donations, a campus commitment to and expertise in creative writing, and a library administration rich in collaborative innovation. Even without all these elements, libraries can and have optimized collaborative events in celebration of poetry and the creative process. National Poetry Month began in 1996, and while readings are certainly not new to libraries, the breadth of documented events sponsored by and reported in the library literature are certainly creative. At the time of the third annual National Poetry Month, Higashi (1998) reported on eighteen systemwide events sponsored by the Seattle Public Library that included staff and community read-alouds and open-mic sessions; readings by local, national, and international poets; a group reading by children; and the writing workshop Words from the Heart. Other branch libraries had poem-a-day display boards; exhibits of a local photographer accompanied by poems; and readings placed directly in the path of patrons, often in the lobby, so that patrons would happen upon poetry while entering.

The Galway Public Library in New York sponsored a social history project that culminated in the public performance of a story quilt of a community's stories in homegrown poetry (Cuffe-Perez 2008). Using poetry to market the library and its literary resources, an academic library formed the Rooftop Poetry Club and sponsors an array of events that have "attracted new patrons and proven itself an invaluable forum for the campus writing community and an asset to the entire college" (Forrest 2006, 28). The Hostos Community College in New York hosts a website for its literary magazine *Escriba!/Write!*, a cross-campus collaboration.

IN SUMMARY

For those interested in designing a library space that fosters creative writing, strengthens libraries, and builds creative community, first establish connections with individuals. An effective liaison librarian quickly learns that each faculty member or student with whom he or she interacts is a bridge to the next faculty member or student. Providing excellent instruction for one class translates to requests for more instruction in other classes. Effectively engaging students in class, at the reference desk, or as student employees builds trust and camaraderie for future engagement. Assisting a faculty member with his or her personal research builds a dialogue of respect and professionalism. Volunteering in community initiatives establishes important campus-community connections that expand the horizons of collaboration.

Second, these individual relationships will augment further collaboration with departments, administration, and community members and groups. While working in collaboration, always consider it a work in progress with the primary goal of outreach to students, faculty, and community. One of the biggest collaborative challenges in the development of the Poetry Corner was to successfully complete the donations of library collections from individual poets. Not surprisingly, each individual had his or her own personal narrative that both supported and occasionally interfered with the transfer of his or her collections to the library. This required consistent and careful contact throughout the process of acquisition, sometimes transferring from the original donor to a relative, friend, or executor. Although it could be recommended that a formal, signed document to secure the donation would facilitate this process, it can also be countered that each individual interaction needs to be measured on its own merit and based on the process of working together to the same end.

Finally, the successful development of the Poetry Corner was based on effective liaison outreach and administrative efforts at fund-raising. Since the Poetry Corner was built on collaboration, cooperative ventures between the library and the English Department and community have continued to flourish within both the spirit of and limitations of cooperation. Cooperation is defined as the process of working together to the same end. Changing personnel, evolving campus and departmental strategic planning, fluctuating student participation, and funding challenges all combine to form stressors to successful collaboration at any given time. By focusing primarily on student, faculty, and community engagement, it is possible to override short-term issues that interfere with problem-free event planning or on-time publication.

"Poetry is about sharing, about the expression of individuality, about celebrating the creative process" (Moffeit 1992, 68). This spirit of the creative process was an integral component to the uniqueness of the design and development of the Poetry Corner. Although each library is local, literature is defined as written works of lasting artistic merit, and poetry as a literary work in which special intensity is given to the expression of feelings and ideas by the use of distinctive style and rhythm. In this case study, poetry also serves as the common bond that fostered a commitment of donors, community members, campus and library administrators, librarians, and writers to unite.

References

Cuffe-Perez, M. "Story Quilt: Poems of a Place." *American Libraries* 39 (2008): 50–52.

Forrest, L. "Up on the Roof—With Poets." *American Libraries* 37 (2006): 28–30.

Higashi, C. "How to Plan a Moveable Feast of Poetry." *American Libraries* 29 (1998): 52–54.

Moffeit, T. "Poetry, Libraries, and the Community: The Pueblo Poetry Project." *Collection Management* 16 (1992): 61–69.

Part II
Visual
Arts

CHAPTER 4

Adult Literacy Programs and Art

SARAH NAUMANN

A STUDENT OF ART AND ART HISTORY, I found myself missing the creative element while working in the adult literacy program and studying for my MLIS. I thought, "If I miss being creative, maybe my students do as well." I began thinking of ways to incorporate art into the literacy program. I realized the students had to voice their interest in learning about art. What did they already know? Ultimately, would art enhance their literacy experience and literacy skills?

WHY DO WE NEED ART IN THE LIBRARY LITERACY PROGRAM?

- To increase self esteem
- To explore alternatives to traditional literacy teaching methods
- To inspire learning and creativity
- To enhance the student's learning experience

ABOUT OUR STUDENTS

Berkeley Reads Adult and Family Literacy program serves people age sixteen and older who test at eighth grade or below in reading, writing, or comprehension. This target population includes the at-risk, disadvantaged, low-income, underserved, and those from challenging personal backgrounds. Our specific clientele include those with mental health and learning disabilities, and those in substance-abuse recovery and rehabilitation programs.

THE PROGRAM

The idea for the Cultural Arts Literacy Program grew from conversations with the students. I discovered that the students had a great desire to learn about art and how it applies to their lives. Class discussions about art led to a group consensus that everyone wanted to visit museums and learn from what they saw. The students each expressed an interest in an art form that they had heard about. One learner said that he had always wanted to paint, but without instruction, he did not know how to start. Another learner said that when he was little he wanted to sculpt.

METHODS

People who study art learn how to express their ideas, and self-esteem levels rise with creative self-expression and experience. The combination of learning about art and creating art is both motivating and inspirational, and it contributes to the whole person in the form of cultural literacy.

SURVEY

The idea to introduce art and culture to our program seemed like a good idea, but I had to find out whether the students were interested in learning about art. I created a short survey and interviewed fifteen students whom I regularly tutored to discover whether the program would be practical. The survey questions were the following:

1. Have you ever been to a museum? If yes, when? If yes, did you enjoy the museum visit?
2. Using the main art themes found in the Bay Area art museums, I asked if the students knew about ancient, Asian, African, Jewish, and modern art. If the student was unfamiliar with the style of art in question, I showed them images from the museums' websites. For example, to explain modern art, I showed them images from the San Francisco Museum of Modern Art.

3. Have you ever created an art project? Tell me what you created—for example, did you draw, paint, or do sculpture? If yes, did you enjoy creating art?

4. Are you interested in learning about art? Are you interested in creating your own art?

The survey results were the following:

- Only one of the students knew about the art styles in the survey prior to the explanations: the student from Mali knew about African art.
- Fourteen out of fifteen students showed enthusiasm for attending museums and doing hands-on art projects.
- Thirteen of the students had never visited an art museum.
- Thirteen of the students had done some form of art in the past and enjoyed the experience.

TRIAL FIELD TRIP

To test the idea of a visit to an art museum and to see whether students would respond positively to the experience, we attended the free day at the Berkeley Art Museum and joined the docent tour offered that day. We were able to walk to the museum from the Berkeley Public Library. Although the museum advertised a free day, I wanted to make sure it would be OK to bring a group of ten adult students; I contacted the museum before our visit and received permission to visit and to attend the docent tour. This communication with museum staff opened up a conversation about our learners and how the docent might decide to discuss the art.

Students had mixed reactions to the art. One student, normally a quiet type, was prolific in his interpretations of the art. He was so inspired that we took a smaller group for a second trip a month later on the next free day to revisit the art. He wrote about his experience and freely discussed his new-found passion. Other students enjoyed the visit and wrote about their experience. One student felt intimidated about her lack of knowledge of art; she felt unable to express what she saw in the paintings.

On our walk back to the library, the students shared their life stories. Although I had already done my interviews and determined that most of the students had never been to a museum, a few students told us how much they enjoyed the visit and that this was their first museum experience. As we passed by the University of California's Berkeley Stadium, one student remarked that he had never been to a sporting event such as a basketball or baseball game. (We kept this idea in mind, and I later wrote to the San Francisco Giants and got free tickets for the students to attend a local Giants game.) Bringing the group together outside of our traditional classroom brought about a new sense of community. Students bonded with one another and with us. After this trial run, we knew the art museum field trips would be a success.

GRANT PROPOSAL

The idea to create the Cultural Arts Literacy Program was initiated by a grant-writing course I took in my MLIS program at San Jose State University's School of Library and Information Science. We were to find a library-related project that needed funding and write a grant proposal. I chose to create the Cultural Arts Literacy Program and to fund it. I submitted the grant proposal to Bay Area Library Information System (BALIS) during a call for proposals for the BALIS Innovations Fund Program in 2008. My grant was funded, and we were able to plan for six museum trips and six art classes. I used the experience from the trial field trip in the grant narrative and included a group photo of us outside the Berkeley Art Museum.

THE CULTURAL ARTS LITERACY PROGRAM

Part 1: Preparation
Adult students prepare for their museum visit by researching the art they will learn about. They study books on art and view the museum's website.

Part 2: Museum Visits and Related Literacy Projects
Adult students visit Bay Area art museums, where they are introduced to multiple art forms from different cultures, such as Asian, African, European, Jewish, pre-Columbian, and Egyptian. The intention is to introduce a global and multicultural perspective to the students, which will develop the whole person through cultural literacy. The students come from diverse ethnic and cultural backgrounds, and understanding how world cultures relate to their lives and literacy will round out their total experience in the Berkeley Reads Adult and Family Literacy Program.

Berkeley Reads tutors work with students on literacy projects that are directly related to the Cultural Arts Literacy Program's activities. For example, students write about their museum visit and work with their tutor on spelling, punctuation, and sentence structure.

Part 3: Hands-On Art Class

Students participate in hands-on arts activities. As a follow-up to the museum visits, students create their own art. For example, a class in African art will accompany a visit to the Museum of the African Diaspora, a sculpture class will accompany a visit to the Legion of Honor, and so forth.

ART INSTRUCTORS: HOW TO FIND THEM

Artists are all around us. It is surprising how many talented people we work with; some of them are willing to teach art classes free of charge.

The first art instructor we hired works for a local museum's education department. Instructors at the museum teach art classes to children in Bay Area schools and gear the art classes to the subjects studied at particular grade levels. I asked whether they would consider teaching our adult students; this was their first request to teach adults, and they were delighted at the idea. The instructor came to the Berkeley Public Library and taught our students about African visionary artists. She also taught a course in pre-Columbian art. The classes were well organized and included slide shows, art materials, and instruction.

Berkeley Reads students also teach the art classes: one of our students is a painter and is trained as an architect in her country of origin. As a literacy student, she was able to relate to the students in a special way; she told them how creating art helped her with her self-esteem issues.

Another of our art instructors is an MLIS student who volunteers in our organization. She is a painter and offered to teach an art class free of charge. She specifically asked to attend the museum visit before teaching her class,

---

Guidelines to Keep in Mind

- Seek out and find partners with connections to the schools, who know the curricular needs of the district (e.g., education departments in museums and academic institutions; children's librarians in public libraries; school librarians, teachers, and curriculum directors; local arts organizations).
- Make your program fit local curricular standards.
- Customize presentations for your audience.
- Make the activity interactive.
- Market your successful programs.

which proved an exceptionally positive experience. Not only was she able to tailor her class to the art we learned about; she also bonded with the students on the field trip, and the students felt at ease and enjoyed the class more because of it.

In the future, we plan to hire library staff artists to teach art classes. We are exploring how we can share our experiences with the library community and the art world.

HOW WE MEASURE SUCCESS

The students are enthusiastic about their arts experience. They write creative stories, which we are compiling for a book, and they share their art in library exhibitions. Students are motivated to read and write, and the art they learn about inspires them. Literacy skills translate into larger life skills, and students take on their new roles as cultural literacy experts. Students share their newfound knowledge with their families and communities.

At the end of a six-month period, at least 50 percent of the students who have participated in the Cultural Arts Literacy Program will have exhibited a difference in pre- and post-knowledge of art and will be able to use this in their daily activities.

MANAGING THE CULTURAL ARTS LITERACY PROGRAM

Management of the program includes the following:

- Keeping track of budget, which includes Bay Area Rapid Transit (BART) costs and museum fees
- Communicating with the museum and arranging payments, discounts, group visits, and docent time
- Making attractive posters to share with students, tutors, and literacy staff
- Finding art teachers by talking to artist friends and coworkers, telling them about the program, and asking whether they are willing to teach a class free of charge
- Getting donated supplies from local art stores or purchasing supplies, or using materials available in the library or bringing materials from home; for example, for one exhibit, we used books from the library, and for another, we brought glittery objects from home, such as gold wrapping paper and Mardi Gras beads.

- Reserving meeting-room space with library administration; since our library's main meeting room space is highly used, the art-class schedule has to be coordinated with the literacy coordinator, art instructors, and the library administration.
- Enrolling students, as well as discussing the field trip and art class with students, creating a sign-up sheet, and reminding students in person and by phone to ensure attendance
- On the day of the field trip, meeting students in front of the library, walking to BART as a group, participating in the museum tour or gallery visit as a group, enjoying bag lunches at a local park, and returning to the library as a group
- On the day of the art class, arriving early and placing directional signs in the library, assisting the art instructor with setup, participating in the art class (students often need encouragement and having literacy staff in the art class is recommended), and taking advantage of the informative and fun art classes
- Working with the literacy coordinator, who also attends all field trips, on program details and attends all field trips (and having fun curating the library exhibits!)

GETTING PAID

I do a lot of the program work during my literacy classroom hours, when I am not busy tutoring students or teaching computer skills. For example, while at work I can organize museum visits and art classes and create flyers and sign-up sheets. Occasionally, I need to contact museum personnel from home. Because I work only eight hours per week at the Berkeley Public Library, juggling tasks is essential for success. I wrote myself into the grant as the Cultural Arts Literacy Program consultant, which means that the grant pays for any work done outside the literacy classroom, such as attending field trips. Grant funding is minimal; therefore, I have to be careful about how much work I do off-site.

EXHIBITING ART

I created a website for our program using a template from the Weebly website, which is free of charge and easy to manage: (http://culturalartsliteracy.weebly .com/). The website is a perfect venue for displaying student artwork and writings and for sharing our program with the library, literacy organizations, and art communities. Moreover, make sure to get photos of art museum visits, art classes, and student artwork to put on the website and use in exhibits.

It is necessary to schedule use of the library's display cases well in advance. Local community groups, artists, and library departments regularly use the cases. Each library branch has a different scheduling system; therefore, it is important to locate the person in charge of exhibits and coordinate with him or her. Once the exhibit is scheduled, I work with the literacy coordinator to curate exhibits. Because of the exhibit schedule and my limited hours, we have only a small window in which to install the exhibit. We prepare as much as possible in advance, but usually the exhibit comes to life on the day of installation.

Exhibits include program information, colorful signs, images of students and staff at Bay Area art museums, images of students creating art, and student artwork and writing. Using available resources from the library and from home, we create colorful, informative exhibits. To announce the exhibits, I contact the library administrative assistant to have our exhibit dates added to the library newsletter.

PARTNERS AND OUTREACH

To spread the news of our program and to participate in more arts communities, we communicate with art organizations and university art departments. Program partners are important for the following:

- Sharing information about what we are doing
- Getting discounts for museum visits
- Finding art instructors
- Applying for funding
- Finding support for our program and for literacy

LESSONS LEARNED

- One art instructor asked to attend the museum visit before teaching her art class. This scenario worked especially well. Not only was the art instructor able to tailor her class to the museum's themes; she also met the students, creating a bond with them that extended to her art class.
- Students love the art museum visits and art classes. Students who attended the earlier museum trips make a point to sign up for each new trip. Students gain self-esteem after attending one art class.

They get encouragement from the art instructors and one another, and they see their artwork exhibited in the library.

- We have to remind students that no prior art experience is required for the art classes, as they are nervous about attending.
- Students' literacy skills have improved as a result of student participation in the Cultural Arts Literacy Program. Their writing is inspired by the art they see and create.
- It is ideal for students to attend both the museum visit and the art class, as they are designed to work together. However, because of our students' life situations not all of them are able to attend both events. The students who attend both events make the connection between the two and understand the art class assignments more readily. Still, students enjoy the art museum visits and art classes even if they cannot attend both.
- We have found that it is best if literacy tutors attend field trips. Knowledge of the museum experience helps the tutors focus subsequent literacy sessions. Students are encouraged by the tutors' presence on the field trips.
- Informing the art museum tour department and docents of our students' learning and literacy levels is helpful, as docents can adjust the tour accordingly. Docents may not be aware that this is a first museum visit for some students or that a student is not familiar with a particular medium.

WORKING WITH A TIGHT BUDGET

- As a nonprofit organization, it is fairly easy to get free or discounted tickets for museums. Check the museum's website and telephone, or send an e-mail for more information. It helps to be persistent if you want to visit the museum on a particular date. Don't just wait for the museum staff to call or e-mail you back.
- Many organizations also accommodate programs such as ours who help people from low-income households and disadvantaged communities. Check the wording on their websites and find correlations with your group or organization.
- Some docent tours are included in the museum group visit, and others are offered for an additional charge. Hiring docents is a good idea and helps facilitate learning. We have also found that having a docent is not always necessary, as it is nice to explore the museum as a group and follow our own interests.

- Many artists are willing to teach free of charge, if it is for a good cause.
- Each of the Bay Area art museums has a free day. Other than for our trial run, we decided not to visit the museums on free days because of the high volume of museum visitors on those days. We wanted the students to get maximum benefits from the visit; therefore, we avoid days that might be heavily attended.

CONCLUSION

The Cultural Arts Literacy Program was created for adult literacy students. However, a similar program can be implemented for children, teens, adults, or seniors. There are quite a few grants for library and arts related activities. Even with a reduced budget, much can be achieved.

CHAPTER 5

Displaying and Promoting Visual Art at the Nashua Public Library

CAROL LUERS EYMAN

IF YOU'RE AN ARTIST who lives in or around Nashua, New Hampshire, and you want to exhibit in the Nashua Public Library, you'll have to wait three, maybe four, years. But when your time comes, as many as five hundred people will see your work each day; no one will take a commission; and you won't have to pay for advertisements, because you'll most likely get more press, at least locally, than you ever have before.

Inviting visual artists to exhibit in our gallery is a year-round collaboration between the library and the arts community. It's not the only way we reach out to artists—we also participate in a citywide partnership between artists and community organizations to produce an annual art walk. And thanks to the largesse of a Nashua businessman, our trustees are able to purchase art for display in the library and other public buildings.

ART EXHIBITS IN THE IMAGE GALLERY

We hold six exhibits a year in the Image Gallery, each of which features work by a local artist. Sometimes the exhibit includes multiple artists, from a college class, the Nashua Area Artists Association, or the like.

SELECTING EXHIBITORS

We don't adhere to a strict definition of *local* in selecting artists for the space, but usually the artists live in Nashua or a surrounding town. To ensure the quality of the exhibits, the library's media services coordinator previews the work, either in person, via slides, or on the artist's website. We require the artist to have a sufficient number of works to fill the gallery, and (when appropriate) we ask that the works be framed. If the artist has exhibited at the library in the past, we ask that the current exhibit consist of new works. And the artist must be willing to take responsibility for delivering the work to the library, hanging it (usually with staff assistance), and removing it at the end of the show.

We don't solicit artists to exhibit in the gallery; they come to us, usually after seeing other shows here. A downside to our long waiting list is that oftentimes when we contact artists a few months in advance to confirm their show, they seem to have disappeared. Either they've changed their phone number or e-mail address or they've moved out of town completely. In that case, we are usually able to call one of the artists further down the list to fill in at the last minute. But as a rule, we have found that it's best to give artists several months to prepare: to put the finishing touches on some of their works, to retrieve their sold works from current owners for loan during the show, to write up an artist's statement, and even to save a bit of money to complete the framing of their pieces.

HANGING SYSTEMS

Currently, we hang works on hooks nailed directly into the wall. Our goal is to eventually install a more professional hanging system, probably one consisting of a permanent horizontal track mounted near the ceiling. This track would hold inconspicuous vertical rods or cables, which in turn would have hooks or clips that hold the artwork. The advantage of this type of system is that it eliminates unsightly holes in the wall, and it makes it easy to reposition the art. You can also purchase theft-deterrent devices for these systems, which make it more difficult to steal the art because they require the use of tools that are not commonly available.

Some libraries exhibit art on panels of plywood, tackboard, pegged board, or fiberboard. You can purchase vertical legs into which you clamp the panels, and rods and hooks from which to hang the art. You can also get hinges to connect the edge of one panel to another, either flush or at an angle.

LABELING THE EXHIBIT

Something we have learned from sponsoring art exhibits is that a talent for painting or drawing does not necessarily equate to a talent for graphic art. So, to maintain the professional look of the gallery, our media services coordinator, Bruce Marks (a top-notch graphic artist himself), often creates the labels for the artworks. Artists usually post an artist's statement in the exhibit space, which Bruce may format for them as well.

We don't allow the posting of prices on the artwork labels, our philosophy being that we are an educational, not a mercenary, institution. However, we keep copies of the artist's price list behind a nearby circulation desk, which staff distribute on request.

SALES

We allow the artists to sell their exhibited works, but the transaction is handled privately between artist and buyer. Our staff doesn't collect any money, nor does the library take a commission on the sale. The buyer picks up the piece at the end of the show to avoid creating an awkward gap in the display space.

I know some librarians are of the opinion that the library should take a cut of sales, having provided publicity and exposure for the artist. However, expecting a commission overlooks the benefit of the show to the library and its customers. One of our goals in holding these exhibits is to promote the arts, and how can we nurture the arts without nurturing artists?

SECURITY

Unlike the van Goghs in Amsterdam or the Monets in Paris, the artwork in our library's gallery does not enjoy the constant scrutiny of museum guards. Although a security guard is usually on duty, he is responsible for the entire building and can't spend all his time in the Image Gallery. Unfortunately, in 2005 two small, framed pastels were stolen from one of our exhibits. We think they were taken just after closing time one night, when most patrons had left the library but some were still watching a film in our theater.

After that incident, we started using security devices detectable by our Checkpoint door system when hanging shows. We also had artists sign agreements stating that they understood the need to carry their own insurance to cover potential theft. We installed security cameras in several spots inside and outside the building, including the Image Gallery (although that sizable expenditure was prompted by other incidents in addition to the art theft). And we hung a convex mirror in the gallery that made it more visible to staff at a nearby circulation desk.

Sometimes an artist needs to remove a work temporarily during an exhibit. Now we always post a note on the wall—"piece temporarily removed by the artist"—to avoid alarming our staff.

OPENING RECEPTIONS

Most of our artists hold an opening reception in the Image Gallery. We ask them to provide the food (making an exception to our usual rule of no food and drink in the library), and we publicize the event. We don't assign a staff member to be present during the reception, but our security guard usually helps the artist with logistics like getting into the building through the back entrance, setting up tables, and moving furniture. Receptions usually last two hours and are held on a Saturday or Sunday afternoon.

PROGRAMS

Frankly, we haven't taken full advantage of the potential for programming around our exhibits. But one of our exhibitors, Yong Chen, who has illustrated *Finding Joy, A Gift*, and other books, gave a lecture in our theater on the process of publishing children's books. He also demonstrated his watercolor technique during an art walk.

PUBLICITY

The library writes a press release publicizing each exhibit and its opening reception. We send the release to local newspapers along with digital photographs of two or three items in the exhibit. Many of our artists have limited experience promoting themselves, so we work with them to put together the information needed for publicity. Sometimes we have to explain to them how to shoot and e-mail high-resolution photos to us, although in recent years most artists seem to be familiar with the process. If necessary, we take the photos ourselves. To gather information for the press release, I have found it helpful to have the artist complete a form describing the show and his or her background. The form asks the following:

- What will the exhibit consist of? Be as specific as possible and fill in the following where applicable:

  - photography
  - pastels
  - drawings

  - oils
  - sculpture
  - acrylics

  - watercolors
  - other (please describe)

- Describe items in the exhibit, including subjects, techniques, inspirations, etc.
- What is your background? Include schooling (if pertinent), previous awards and exhibits, length of time you have been interested in your field of expertise, and other information you think would be appropriate.
- Please include any other information you feel will attract a potential viewer of the exhibit when they read about it in the newspaper, such as your related hobbies, history of the collection, a particular item that is very unusual or of local interest, or an unusual technique you use in creating your works. If you have an artist's statement, please attach it.

Because our budget and staff time are limited, we leave it up to the artists to create postcards, flyers, or posters about the show if they desire them. We encourage them to promote the show through their websites and mailing lists as well.

PUBLIC TASTES

The exhibits that generate the most response are those with a local flavor. For example, Paula Super paints impressionistic landscapes and cityscapes. During one of her exhibits in the Image Gallery, someone bought her painting of Jeannotte's Market, a locally owned landmark convenience store in Nashua. The work remained in the gallery until the conclusion of the show, and soon another would-be buyer of the painting came along, and then another. To accommodate them, she ended up painting the store two more times. When even more customers expressed interest, she had prints of the painting made and sold them.

I can also tell that an exhibit is popular when viewers interact with the works. We saw many amateur photographers snapping pictures of the pictures in an exhibit of old-time Nashua photographs by the late local newspaper reporter Mike Shalhoup.

Marc Winnat's drawings of the old Hillsboro Branch rail line were closely scrutinized not only by local history fans but also by railroad hobbyists. In

Drawings of the old Hillsboro Branch rail line, by Mark Winnat, appeared in the Image Gallery at Nashua Public Library. Reproduced by permission of the artist

another exhibit, Winnat showed photorealistic urban landscapes: graffiti-covered buildings in Brooklyn, a dingy train platform, a freighter in a bleak harbor. Viewers were enticed to interact with the exhibit by the promise of finding a pair of glowing red eyes that the artist's statement promised was hidden in each painting.

The sculptures in an exhibit by Wayne Goulet were created entirely from recycled materials. One was a steel garbage can whose contents included a dismembered pair of Barbie-doll legs, originally sticking straight up out of a mound of trash. Over the course of the exhibit, however, they variously appeared crossed, splayed, or bent flirtatiously, depending on the mood of the viewers.

EVERYBODY WINS

The Image Gallery exhibits are popular with our customers. In a recent survey of our customers, 20 percent said that viewing art exhibits is one of the reasons they visit the library. Surprisingly, this figure was even higher than the 11 percent who selected "use library computers" as a reason they visit.

From my adjacent office I can witness visitors' delight when they first lay eyes on a new exhibit. The gallery exposes people who may not visit museums or art galleries to a variety of fine art, in a familiar setting, with free admission, where no one presses them to purchase anything. Sometimes we need to remind them not to touch the work—even when they're standing right next to a sign telling them not to. Sometimes people show up at a reception more interested in free food than in meeting an artist. But I've seen even these accidental gallery patrons gain interest, after a few words about why they're being treated to punch and cookies prompt them to take a look at what's on display behind the buffet table.

The library benefits from the exhibits as well. The art beautifies a central space in the building, without cost to the library. As I mentioned earlier, sometimes the artist will do a program for us—a demo or a lecture—at no charge, or even donate a piece of work to the library. And for the artist, the exhibit often leads to a sale or two, as well as free publicity in the newspaper and a one-person show to add to their credentials. Artists with little exhibit experience get a chance to learn some of the ropes—hanging, publicity, communicating with viewers and potential buyers—with help of staff who, we like to think, are friendly and supportive of them as they learn. With the library's long hours and heavy foot traffic, the artist's work gets more exposure than it would in any local art studio or gallery.

ART WALK NASHUA

Another major project the library works on with artists is Art Walk Nashua. Our Image Gallery becomes the center of attention in the building each year during this event, when local studios and galleries are open to the public for viewing of art, demonstrations, artist receptions, performances, and other events.

In 2005, several downtown artists and gallery owners, working with the downtown revitalization organization Great American Downtown (GAD), the city's community development office, and the Nashua Public Library, launched Art Walk Nashua as a way to increase awareness and appreciation of the blossoming art scene in Nashua. I served as chair of the art walk's committee for two years, but production of the event has since been taken over by City Arts Nashua (CAN), a nonprofit that promotes Nashua's artistic and cultural community.

The library is a logical partner in Art Walk: we hold ongoing exhibits of local art in our Image Gallery; we are home base for a privately funded art collection; and we have plenty of space for art demonstrations and musical performances.

ART WALK EVENTS AT THE LIBRARY

Successful events we've held in the library during Art Walk Nashua have included the following:

- Painting demonstrations by artists whose work is on display.
- Artist's receptions with live music. Often we move our piano into the gallery and a performer plays low-key jazz, pop standards, or new-age music. Acoustic guitar has also worked well, although I've found that vocalists tend to shift the focus away from the art and the artist and onto the musicians instead.
- A film festival—screenings were held throughout the weekend at three venues, including the library, chosen for its large-screen theater and high-quality projection and sound equipment.

Other events we've tried holding during art walks have been guided tours of the artwork on display in library and a local-author fair with book signings, readings, and raffles. Those flopped. No one showed up for the guided tour. Twenty or so local authors participated in the local author event, but only a handful of members of the public attended, and few authors sold any books. The location of the event—on the plaza in front of the library, removed from the usual traffic pattern for entering the building—may have given the impression that it was private and unrelated to the art walk.

OFFERING EXPERTISE AND INFRASTRUCTURE

The library, along with CAN and GAD, offers expertise and infrastructure support to the Art Walk Nashua committee. For example:

- We share our lists of media contacts to help with publicity.
- We have written grant applications.
- We recommend musicians to perform in art-walk venues, on the basis of our experience sponsoring concert series.
- We offer to serve as a pickup or drop-off site for signs, paperwork, raffle prizes, and the like, since we are open long hours, we're centrally located, and everyone knows where we are.
- We sometimes provide rooms for art-walk committee meetings.
- We serve as one of three or four starting points on the Art Walk Nashua map. City Arts Nashua advises art walkers to begin their day at these points, where there's plenty of parking and people can pick up maps and programs. We have a volunteer sit at a reception table to welcome art walkers and distribute these items as they enter the building.

EXPENSES

Aside from staff time, the library's art-walk expenses are minimal. City Arts Nashua charges us $50 to participate as a venue. For that, we benefit from the press releases and paid advertising of the event that CAN provides. We also receive signs to place outside the building that designate us as a venue. We might spend some money—usually less than $50—on refreshments for an artist's reception in our gallery, although usually the artist pays for that. Our expenses for performers run from $100 to $300.

BENEFITS

For us, working with the Art Walk Nashua committee has let us develop relationships with artists who might not otherwise use the library. Through their comings and goings, they get to know staff, see our facilities, and in general feel more involved in the library.

The number of people visiting the library specifically for the art walk during those weekends is usually between sixty and seventy-five each day. That's not as high as at some of the other venues, like the old mill building that houses twenty different studios and sees five hundred or more visitors during the art walk. But we consider any library event drawing sixty to seventy-five people to be quite successful.

THE BURBANK COLLECTION

A third way our library reaches out to artists is by administering a trust fund. In 1932 a Nashua businessman and lawyer named Leonard Burbank passed away. A lifelong bachelor who enjoyed painting landscapes, he left $5,000 from his estate to create the Burbank Fund. He specified that the money be invested for fifty years, after which the income could be spent for the purchase of works of living artists for display in schools, libraries, and other public buildings in New Hampshire. In 1973, control of the Burbank Fund was transferred to the board of trustees of the Nashua Public Library.

Although administration of the fund offered an opportunity for the library to reach out to artists, the evaluation and purchase of art was beyond the expertise of most of the trustees. When the fifty-year waiting period ended, the board appointed an advisory committee, comprising art collectors, art teachers, and representatives of the trustees and library staff, to recommend works for purchase.

The fund has grown to several hundred thousand dollars, which yields significant income to make purchases. At first, much of the money was used to create a collection of less-expensive artwork that circulated from the library. Some has been used to commission or purchase sculptures and paintings for display at the library.

BUMPS IN THE ROAD

Administration of the Burbank Fund has not been without its hurdles. Maintaining a vision and focus for the collection has been difficult. Although the collection was designated for display in a variety of public buildings, its de facto home has been the Nashua Public Library. This was not a problem when the collection was small, but now that it has grown, space is at a premium. No explicit provisions were made in Burbank's will for administrative or infrastructure expenditures that arise from the maintenance of an art collection, such as storage facilities, display cases, refurbishing, appraisals, and the like.

Wrangling the members of the advisory committee into consensus on what to purchase has been challenging, with one faction favoring purchase of works by local artists and another preferring to make less frequent purchases of more expensive art from national artists. The will's directive to exhibit the work in venues other than the library has been difficult to carry out, since the fund made no provisions for the funding of staff to arrange and administer such shows.

DEVELOPING A PLAN FOR THE COLLECTION

In 2005 the trustees hired a consultant to help them develop a long-range plan for the Burbank Fund. In addition to overseeing an appraisal of the collection, the consultant helped the trustees adopt a mission statement, vision, and criteria for adding works to the collection.

Of particular concern in developing the plan was how to deal with requests from community groups for funds for community arts projects, such as a downtown mural, outdoor sculptures, and a labyrinth and reflection garden. The consultant recommended no longer donating to such projects because it was often unclear who owned them and who was responsible for maintaining them.

HIGHLIGHTS OF THE COLLECTION

Serving as trustees for the Burbank Fund has allowed the library to exhibit quality artwork throughout the building. The prize piece of the collection is *View from Jackson Falls,* by the internationally renowned painter James Aponovich, a Nashua native with works in several major museums. Several original children's book illustrations—by Jan Brett, Trina Schart Hyman, and Marilyn Hafner—purchased by the fund hang in our Children's Room. A public kiosk by sculptor Jafar Shoja, reminiscent of Paris streetscapes, stands outside on the library's plaza.

CONCLUSION

These collaborations with Nashua's visual arts community have brought artists to the library and have given them a chance to express their creativity. They have exposed the public—buyers and browsers, sophisticates and naïfs—to fine art, stimulating their imaginations. And they have brought the Nashua Public Library a reputation as a prime cultural center in the city it serves.

CHAPTER 6

Utilizing Student Talent to Create Appealing Library Posters

HEATHER PAYNE

LIBRARIANS CREATE HANDOUTS for students for a variety of reasons. Sometimes they are customized pathfinders for a particular class we are teaching, but often they just provide information about the library that we want to share with students. Many pathfinders that I have seen are text heavy, and in my library, they have rarely been of any design merit. Moving pathfinders to posters for wide appeal on campus is an area in which we lack graphic design knowledge. Student feedback has been clear that if we could present information in a visually appealing way they would better receive it.

We do not have a graphic designer on staff at the library; however, we do have graphic design and illustration programs at the college. The idea of collaborating with students on a project was not new to us. We had a very successful collaboration with students from a web-design class who helped build the look and feel of our website. As a result of this project, we were realistic in our expectations of both outcomes and challenges in working with students. When an instructor in the Illustration Department approached us about doing a project in her class, we eagerly accepted the proposal.

The students in the class were in the first year of the program. First-year students do not have many opportunities to work with a real client. The library provided a good solution for the instructor. We could provide the client project and act as the client. Students could have their first experience working with a client in a controlled environment. Because the library was an internal client, this diminished the apprehension that students face when working with their first external client.

THE CREATIVE BRIEF

The project was going to be a poster. It was up to the library staff to determine the subject of the poster. A contact librarian was chosen who would serve as the liaison among the faculty, the students in the class, and the rest of the library staff. The first step was for the library staff to create a creative brief.

A creative brief is a brief overview of the expectations or needs of the client. Students studying graphic design are familiar with the creative brief, and presenting material in this way gives them a familiar work platform. The Information Architecture Institute, a nonprofit organization that offers education, resources, and tools on information architecture, has a creative brief form that you can download (http://iainstitute.org/tools/).

In our project, the students received the following creative brief:

Client: College Library
Problem: Students are not aware of our services at the start of their programs and/or throughout their programs.
Specific services we would like to see promoted:

1. "E-library" aspect—24/7 library access, the new website, databases, communication (e.g., Facebook, texting)
2. Physical library—quickest, easiest way to get information, collection highly specific to program

Target audience: All students in all programs
Placement of posters: Housing, computer labs, elevators, café, student lounge, and information plasma screens

The instructor reviewed the creative brief and approved it. We knew we could not assume that all the students in the class would be familiar with the library, so our next step involved collecting some resources for the students to use to understand their target audience (for the specific resources that we provided to the students, see appendix A). In addition, we encouraged them to do their own research. We were surprised that a number of them came into the library to interview fellow students and staff members, another important reason everyone on staff needed to be involved in the project.

INTRODUCING THE CONCEPT AS A CLIENT

Only the librarian chosen as the contact went into the first class. It was important for her to establish herself as a client and to restrict questions to only those relevant to the assignment. The way she asserted herself as a client involved coming prepared with a creative brief that the instructor had seen and approved. She dressed in business attire. She sat at the front of the class but off to the side and took notes. She presented the idea and then responded to students' specific questions. She emphasized that she was an internal client but that the library should be viewed as a real client. Students whose work met the library's needs would have their work displayed across campus.

The instructor provided the students with a project sheet (outline) that clearly outlined the expectations of the assignment, the due dates, and a grading rubric. They were graded on their research, thumbnail concepts, and the composition of the final poster (for the project sheet, see appendix B). The project had a possible forty-eight points that could be achieved, and the project accounted for more than half of the student's final grade in class.

After the librarian's initial visit, the students had three weeks to develop a concept and submit thumbnail sketches to the instructor. The instructor then assisted the students in determining which concept they would develop into the final poster. Once their concept was approved, the student had two weeks to produce a poster for the library staff to review.

CRITIQUING STUDENT WORK

One week before final submission, three librarians came to the class. The students were to present their poster and to explain their concept. The librarians were there to critique the posters and provide the students with a real-life experience of talking to and then listening to a client.

This interaction was the most challenging part of the process. For many of the students, it was the first time they had ever presented their work to anyone. Many of them were nervous, and criticism had to be softly delivered. Students had varying responses to the critiques. Most of them accepted our suggestions and ultimately worked them into the final poster. However, a few were sold on their own idea and were uninterested in the client's point of view. This was an interesting experience for us. It was one of the reasons the instructor had used internal clients like us, but it was something we had not expected.

The librarians involved in this project were fairly comfortable with critiquing work, which is important for any project like this to be successful. There are a number of resources online that can provide you with information on how to critique work. You might also work with the instructor of the class you are going to work with. Many instructors have their own resources to teach their students how to critique one another's work. Marvin Bartel, on his website Successful Art Class Critique (www.goshen.edu/art/ed/critique1 .html), offers a form to use in critiques that provides a nice overview and structure for commenting on student work.

SECOND TIME AROUND

The initial project was successful for us. We ended up with three very nice posters that we placed in many locations on campus. The library staff worked with this class a second time. A new creative brief was used that provided students with two different problems they could choose from:

Problem 1: We want students, faculty, and staff to be aware of alternate ways of communicating with the library and librarians. The library would like to see an increase in patron communication through Facebook messages, posts, and instant messages, mobile texts, and instant messages (Meebo) through the library website.

Problem 2: Another important feature that we feel is not promoted enough is the library's DVD collection. Therefore, we would like to create an effective and enticing poster that advertises the DVD collection and consequently increases the circulation/checkouts of DVDs.

The other parameters (e.g., target audience, poster placement) remained the same.

The second creative brief had a clear objective, which led to a more successful project. The broader the topic, the more potential there is for students' creativity to wander from the desired outcome. We found that the posters produced by the second class were more uniform in their message. This allowed us to see various graphical representations of the same message. For us, it provided a better product, since our interest was more in the graphics than in the message itself, which we could edit and change if necessary.

LESSONS LEARNED

Students in the first through third quarters may not have skills with computers or even traditional media that are where they need to be for the students to finalize their concept. You might end up with a whole class of great concepts but none that is executed well enough to use on campus to represent the library.

Timing of the critique of the projects was almost too late. The students had very little time to respond to client input, especially if conceptual changes needed to be made. The contact librarian expressed that she would have liked to have been involved in the selection of the roughs and then had the preliminary poster due date backed up a week so that students would have had two weeks to work on changes.

Class dynamics have a huge impact on the success. After doing this project with two classes, we realized that the way students coalesce (or don't coalesce) in a class can have an effect on the project itself. A class that has some students who are excited by the project can lead to better designs. Internal competition is also a result of the students in the class. If you have a few competitive students, the other students tend to put forth more effort.

Do you have a lot of design constraints? Our only requirement was to use the library logo as is and to refrain from obscene language, gestures, and so on. The more freedom the students have, the better.

If students are your audience, have students weigh in on the designs. We had our student workers vote on the designs. Our first choice was not their first choice. Sometimes it is hard to separate what appeals to you from what will speak to your students. We have learned that what we find aesthetically pleasing is not always in agreement with what our students like to see.

Finally, our experiences have suggested that when you are trying to create graphics that will reach students, the students produce great material. It becomes more challenging when you are trying to create graphics to reach an audience that is not students. In those cases, it might be best to find students who are near the end of the program so that you have students who have more developed skills in dealing with clients.

Overall, both projects were successful for us. Each class produced one or more posters that we used (see pages 64–67). However, there are a few considerations one should make before deciding whether having students provide graphic work is a viable option:

- Is there a school in the community that has a graphic design, illustration, or other graphic arts program?
- Does the library have someone on staff who can allocate time to the instructor and class?
- Are there other members of the library staff who are willing and able to provide good critiques of student work?
- Does the library have a clear objective for the project?

If you are able to answer yes to these questions, I encourage you to see what opportunities might exist for you to collaborate with students. I am confident that you will find doing so an enjoyable and rewarding experience.

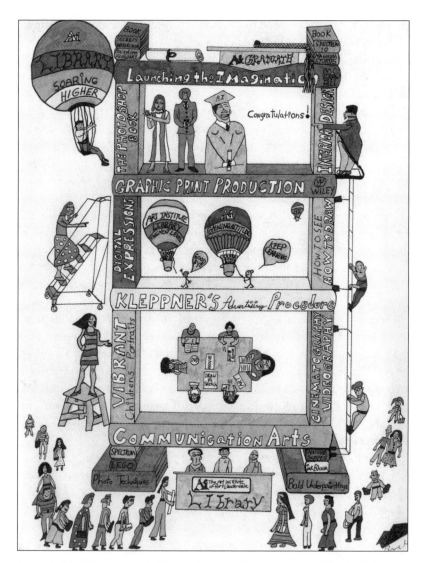

A poster by Bruce Hammond hung in classrooms, hallways and elevators on campus to market the basic services of the library. Reproduced by permission of the artist

A poster by Chris Figueroa was positioned in community areas on campus to promote the library's Facebook presence. Reproduced by permission of the artist

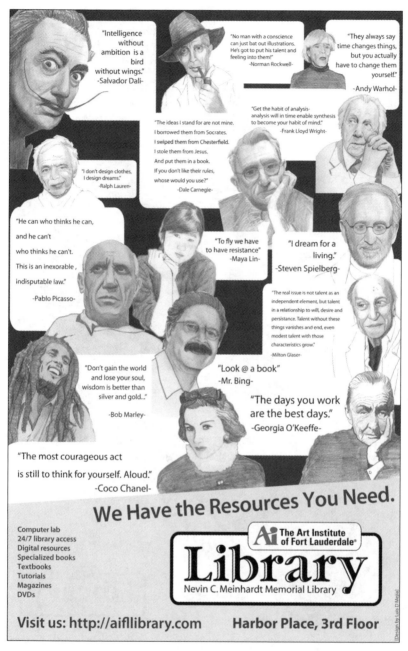

A poster by Luis D. Mejia featured the extent of resources in the library, as represented in famous quotes, including one from a faculty member at the college. Reproduced by permission of the artist

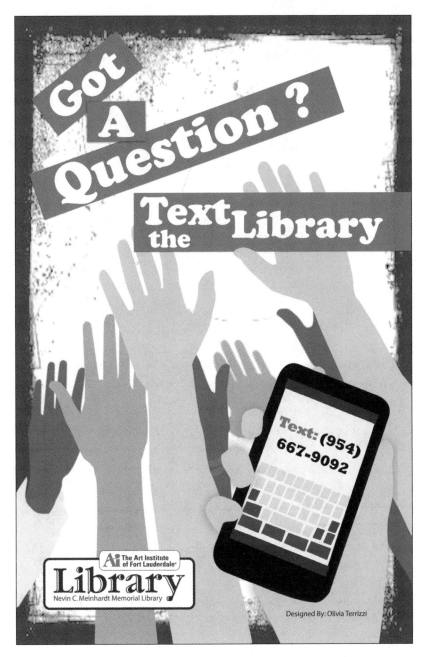

A poster by Olivia Terrizzi was placed in computer labs on campus to introduce the library's new texting service. Reproduced by permission of the artist

APPENDIX A: RESOURCE LIST PROVIDED TO STUDENTS

INDUSTRY INFORMATION

BOOKS

Dowd, Nancy, Mary Evangeliste, and Jonathan Silberman. 2009. *Bite-Sized Marketing: Realistic Solution for the Overworked Librarian.* Chicago: American Library Association.

Fisher, Patricia H., Marseille M. Pride, and Ellen G. Miller. 2009. *Blueprint for Your Library Marketing Plan: A Guide to Help You Survive and Thrive.* Chicago: American Library Association.

Kies, Cosette. 2003. *Marketing and Public Relations for Libraries.* Lanham, MD: Scarecrow Press.

Mathews, Brian. 2009. *Marketing Today's Academic Library: A Bold New Approach to Communicating with Students.* Chicago: American Library Association.

Weingand, Darlene E. 1998. *Future-Driven Library Marketing.* Chicago: American Library Association.

WEBSITES

ACRL Marketing Minute. www.facebook.com/marketingminute (accessed March 22, 2011).

ALA Store—Library Posters, Bookmarks and Library Science Books from the American Library Association. www.alastore.ala.org/ (accessed March 22, 2011).

Library Success: A Best Practices Wiki. www.libsuccess.org/index.php?title=Marketing (accessed March 22, 2011).

Marketing @ your library. www.ala.org/acrl/issues/marketing (accessed March 22, 2011).

Marketing Your Library. www.marketingyourlibrary.com/2008/05/40-marketing-tips -for-academic.html (accessed March 22, 2011).

ARTICLES

Dodsworth, Ellen. "Marketing Academic Libraries: A Necessary Plan." *Journal of Academic Librarianship* 24, no. 4 (2010): 320–22.

Hallmark, Elizabeth K., Laura Schwartz, and Loriene Roy. "Developing a Long-Range and Outreach Plan for Your Academic Library: The Need for a Marketing Outreach Plan." *College and Research Libraries News* 68, no. 2 (2007): 92–95.

APPENDIX B: ASSIGNMENT AS PRESENTED TO STUDENTS BY THE INSTRUCTOR

Assignment: You will create a poster for the Art Institute's library. The actual purpose for the poster will be determined and announced by the client. The client will be using this poster throughout the school and dorms. If your creation is selected, you will become a published artist/designer.

PROCESS

STEPS 1–4 are due next week at beginning of class! We are losing a class due to Memorial Day

PLEASE e-mail me drafts, studies, etc., along the way.

1. BE A SPONGE, which means "get smart fast" about the industry you are about to design for. Read and take notes from the material provided to you via the handout "Academic Library Poster Resources." Interview friends and classmates to get primary information. Observe students using the library and not using the library.
2. TAKE NOTES (simple bulleted lists are fine) AND list all the research resources you read, viewed, or consulted (use proper citation formatting for this, that is, MLA). Follow the "Give Credit Where Credit Is Due" document. You will be handing your NOTES in for grading.
3. Within your NOTES from outside sources, INCLUDE notes from your own THOUGHTS (visual ideas or worded ideas) that pop out as you work at being a sponge.
   a. Example: reading that an accident occurs every 40 minutes in the US due to DUI, a visual idea popped to depict a grid set up as circular clocks, the hands of the clocks show the progression of time (every 40 minutes) and the face of the clocks show a different DUI accident.
4. AFTER being a sponge, develop 8 new ideas in thumbnail form that address the problem the client is having.

STEPS 5–7 are due at beginning of class, Week 10!

PLEASE email me drafts, studies, etc., along the way.

5. Show your work up to this point to your teacher for thumbnail approval.
6. Take your one approved thumbnail sketch and work it up into the 3 stages of compositional development (i.e., 4 line and/or shape compositions, 3 grayscale studies, and 3 color studies)
7. STOP at this point and we will decide on Week 10 about going to FINAL FINISH.

GRADING FOR BEING A SPONGE: 16 POINTS = 100%

Criteria	A = 4 points	B= 3 points	C = 2 points	D = 1 point	F= 0 points
Followed the process and due dates	PROCESS, as outlined above perfectly followed.	Minor misses in following the PROCESS as outlined above	Somewhat follows PROCESS as outlined above.	Major misses in following the PROCESS as outlined above.	PROCESS not followed
Note taking	Notes from more than 3 sources AND notes from ideas generated from source material included	Notes from 2 or 3 sources AND notes from ideas generated from source material included	Notes from 2 or 3 sources BUT NO notes from ideas generated from source material included	Notes from 1 source with or without ideas generated from source material included	No NOTES
Recording Sources (citation)	All sources cited using MLA standards	Most sources cited using MLA standards	Some sources cited using MLA standards	Few sources cited using MLA standards	No sources cited using MLA standards
Type and number of sources	Evidence of more than one primary and more than one secondary source	Evidence of one primary and more than one secondary source	Evidence of one primary and one secondary source	Evidence of either primary or secondary sources, but not both	No evidence of primary or secondary sources

GRADING FOR THUMBNAIL CONCEPTS: 12 POSSIBLE POINTS = 100%

Criteria	4 points = A	3 points = B	2 points = C	1 point = D	0 points = F
Quantity	8 thumbnail sketches	6–7 thumbnail sketches	5 thumbnail sketches	1–4 thumbnail sketches	No thumbnail sketches
Quality	All concepts different, well thought out and well sketched	6–7 different concepts, well thought out and well sketched	5 different concepts, well thought out and well sketched	1–4 different concepts, well thought out and well sketched	No different concepts, well thought out and well sketched
Directions followed	All directions followed correctly	Most directions followed correctly	Some directions followed correctly	Few directions followed correctly	No directions followed correctly

GRADING FOR COMPOSITIONAL STUDIES: 20 POSSIBLE POINTS = 100%

Criteria	4 points = A	3 points = B	2 points = C	1 point = D	0 points = F
Line/shape composi-tions	4 different contour line and shape compositions	3 different contour line and shape compositions	2 different contour line and shape compositions	1 contour line and shape composition	0 contour line and shape composition
Grayscale studies	3 different value studies	2 different value studies	1 value study	½ of one value study	0 value studies
Color studies	3 different color studies	2 different color studies	1 color study	½ of one color study	0 color studies
Quality	All compositions are finished and demon-strate strong understand-ing of design principles.	3 compositions are finished and demon-strate strong understand-ing of design principles.	2 compositions are finished and demon-strate strong understand-ing of design principles.	1 composition is finished and dem-onstrates a strong under-standing of design principles.	0 composi-tions are finished and demonstrate strong under-standing of design principles.
Directions followed	All directions followed correctly	Most directions followed correctly	Some directions followed correctly	Few directions followed correctly	No directions followed correctly

Reproduced by permission of Diane Sammet (2011)

CHAPTER 7

Visual Arts in the Academic Library

JENNIFER MAYER

THIS CHAPTER DISCUSSES a variety of ways that academic librarians can partner with both student and professional visual artists to encourage and support artwork in the library. Included are tips on purchasing student art, hosting temporary art exhibits in the library, hosting a library art invitational with local artists, and commissioning a permanent art piece for the library. The chapter also makes recommendations about working with facilities aspects, legal issues, and how to promote the artwork via various public relations activities.

STUDENT ART PURCHASE AWARDS

One way to support and promote student work is to get involved with the student artists on campus, such as through shows sponsored by the university art museum or art department. If there are student shows that offer pieces for sale, create a budget so that your library can sponsor a student art purchase award, preferably every year. Presenting the award at the museum awards ceremony both recognizes student artists and gives the library visibility. At the University of Wyoming, an upper-level art student created an oil painting, which the library purchased at the 2010 student art show (fig. 1). The library has since commissioned the student artist to create a companion piece.

Student artist Gabrielle Reeves received the University of Wyoming Libraries Studies Art Purchase Award in 2010 for her oil painting *On Road*. *Photo by Nancy Marlatt*

TEMPORARY EXHIBITIONS

If your library does not have the budget to purchase student artwork annually, consider hosting temporary exhibits and installations of student work. Talk to your art department faculty and student art organizations and offer the library as a space for temporary exhibits. Temporary installations can include both two-dimensional and three-dimensional pieces (e.g., paintings, prints, book arts, sculpture). Two University of Wyoming sculpture students collaborated to create the work shown on page 75, which is on extended loan to the library. The library can host exhibits for one or two weeks or for as long as the artist wishes to loan his or her work.

It is a good idea to contact other campus departments beyond the art department to see whether they have items they wish to loan to the library for temporary exhibition. For example, the Geology Department may have some visually appealing fossils, bone casts, rocks, or other items that would create a visually engaging and educational display. Other potential campus departments that may be interested in loaning work may include photography from the Journalism Department, the American Studies Department, or photos from departments that sponsor a study-abroad program.

Perpetuate, a collaborative work by Dakotah Konicek and Anna Konkel, is on extended loan to the Coe Library at the University of Wyoming. *Photo by Nancy Marlatt*

In addition to student artists, local artists are important to mine for art-work in the library. A local artist could be affiliated with the university's Art Department or other department, the university art museum, or a free agent who lives in the community. One way to encourage local artists to exhibit at the library is to host a library art invitational: form an art selection committee (appendix A provides a sample call for publications). Be flexible; allow for art-ists to submit work for consideration in any medium (provided that you can accommodate it) and to submit multiple pieces. After the deadline, meet with the other selection committee members to decide which works to include in the library art invitational. Notify the artists of the timeline to fill out any contractual paperwork and when they should bring the pieces to the library. A yearlong exhibit leaves enough time for the pieces to gain exposure in the building and to be enjoyed by patrons.

If the works on display will be offered for sale, include the price on the art labels, so that those who frequent your building are aware that the pieces are available for purchase. If your library has the funding, purchase some of the works from the invitational so they become part of your permanent art collection. At the conclusion of the year, pieces either can be returned to the contributing artists or picked up by the buyers, and you can start the entire process again to host the next library art invitational.

Another means of finding artwork, especially if hosting an invitational is not possible, is to visit local art galleries. Community art shows and arts-and-crafts fairs should be taken into consideration as events where art purchases can be made.

ART COMMISSIONS

Commissions, or contracting with an artist, are another way to bring art into the library. Funding options may include a private donor from your library board or another donor. Some states have "art in public buildings" legislation that allocates a percentage of new construction costs to purchase artwork for a state-funded facility. If your state does not offer such a program, and you are planning a new library building or renovation project, investigate setting aside an allocation from the building project for public art. Even one piece of public art makes a huge difference to the atmosphere of a building.

If you have funding options and want to investigate commissioning an artwork for your library, partner with your campus art museum or the university's Art Department to see what contacts they have in the art world. If possible, identify and connect with a well-known regional or national artist to commission the piece. Meetings should be arranged and held at the library with the artist to discuss the library's interests, space, and budget, and then again to view preliminary sketches and specifications of the piece. You will need to meet with your legal office to review contracts and physical plant staff to review hanging and installation logistics, if necessary. After the contracts are signed and the work is complete, you will set up the details of the installation, dates, needed equipment, and personnel. Local art students may be interested in helping install the piece if it is large and requires multiple hands. Document the installation of the piece with video and photos so you have a record of the event. Finally, host an artist talk and reception at the library—preferably in front of the piece.

FACILITIES AND PHYSICAL SPACES

Facilities and physical space issues are important to contemplate when installing artwork. Public collaborative spaces, quiet study spaces, reading rooms, library coffee shops, and even office suites are all appropriate possible locations to exhibit artwork. As you amass your art collection, you will be able to rotate pieces throughout the building. Remember to include wall or other labels to accompany the work with the artist's name, title of the piece, year,

Sculpture students help artist James Surls with the installation of Rolling Flower, which was commissioned by the University of Wyoming Libraries in 2009. *Photo by Nancy Marlatt*

and any other relevant information, such as purchase award year if applicable. For installations, ask the artist to include a one-page artist statement to be posted close to the work. Depending on your university's or college's policies, you may incur costs from the physical plant to hang artwork or to patch and paint walls after temporary exhibits, so plan to budget for that expense if needed.

Another option for art in the library is to host rotating photography exhibits. You first need to identify a large wall space and to purchase and install a hanging rail system to be able to easily change out exhibits. In addition to hosting the exhibit, offer a library space for the photographer to give a public talk about his or her work. Other possibilities for rotating display space include movable panels. Display cases may be difficult to work with, as items would have to fit in a fixed sized space, and the work is not as accessible to the viewers.

LEGALITIES

The legal aspects of exhibiting and purchasing art are an involved and important part of the process. The first step is to create an art exhibit guidelines document for sharing with interested artists. A guidelines document example appears in appendix B. The guidelines document may include the following:

- Library space available for exhibits
- Selection process policy
- Exhibition procedures, such as who is responsible for the transport of work, whether lenders must sign a risk waiver, who is responsible for the delivery, the installation and deinstallation (your university may have a policy that indicates the university's physical plant must do this work)
- Promotion

A necessary companion document to the guidelines is a legally binding loan agreement, such as the art loan agreement, release, assumption of risk and waiver of liability, which is provided in appendix C. If your university does not already have a form available for this purpose, you will need to create one and have it approved by your university's legal office. A legally approved waiver signed by the lending artist will absolve the library of any legal and financial implications should the loaned artwork be stolen or otherwise damaged. It is vital that lending artists sign the waiver; but in my experience, no work has been stolen or damaged during several years of hosting art in our library. If you are concerned about theft, talk to your physical plant staff about secure ways to hang works, or put a book security strip on the back of the artwork.

PUBLIC RELATIONS

Promoting art in the library is a crucial part of the public relations process; otherwise, people who do not frequent your building will not know about your art collection and exhibits. Avenues to entice outside audiences include the usual places where your library conducts promotion, such as in your library's blog, newsletter, or social networking sites. Contact local nonprofit art organizations, tourism boards, or visitors' centers, as they often create community art maps, and you will want to ensure that your library is listed as an art destination. Offer art tours in the library to interested classes and to campus and community boards and groups. Your campus and local newspapers are other outlets for articles and photos to increase awareness about the art in your library.

There are other ways to promote the art in the library. You might interview artists from whom you purchase work, and make streaming audio and video interviews available on your website, with the artists' permission. Another way to promote art from within the library is to use cell-phone audio tours. For a minimal fee, you can contract with a company that provides this service. You record your own messages about the artwork, from either your office or your personal phone. Once your message prompts are complete and activated, you need to create signage that provides art viewers with a number to call on their phones to listen to your recorded message about each piece. Cell-phone audio tours are frequently used in art museums, and they are a quick and easy way for interested patrons to learn more about the art in your library.

Finally, an attractive "art in the library" web page or blog that showcases images of the artwork in the library, along with a map of where the artwork can be found, is helpful in a number of ways. The University of Wyoming's Art in the Libraries site (http://uwlib5.uwyo.edu/blogs/libarts/) is one example of this type of web page. An interactive web page of your library art is useful to patrons, so they get an overview of what you have and where it is, and they know where they can go to experience the art in person. Faculty may want to use an "art in the library" website to support a class exercise related to art or images. Also, an art website is helpful since it is serves as an attractive inventory of all the library's artwork.

Think of who you can partner with to make art in your library a reality: the campus Art Department, the university art museum, student groups, the library administration, a special projects librarian or other colleague, and local artists and gallery owners are all potentially valuable partners. Hosting exhibits and related talks sponsored by various departments and programs on campus builds relationships. Art is a way to connect students, the university, and the community at large to the library.

APPENDIX A

COE LIBRARY ART INVITATIONAL

The University of Wyoming Libraries are seeking proposals for pieces of art to be loaned to William Robertson Coe Library, the flagship library of the University of Wyoming. Recently remodeled and expanded to more than 250,000 square feet, Coe Library offers artists the opportunity to place their work in a very visible, significant building in the heart of the UW campus. Coe Library is a dynamic center for students, faculty, and visitors to campus, and records more than 440,000 visits each year.

ARTIST SCOPE OF THE COE LIBRARY ART INVITATIONAL
This invitational is limited to established local artists.

SUBJECT SCOPE OF THE COE LIBRARY ART INVITATIONAL
Subject matter should have a general appeal to all ages and backgrounds. Artists should also understand that Coe Library is a public facility and not an art museum.

DURATION OF LOAN FOR THE COE LIBRARY ART INVITATIONAL
UW Libraries request a twelve-month loan period for each accepted piece, with the option of a twelve-month renewal after the initial year. Accepted loaned pieces must be on display in Coe Library no later than August 20, 2010.

INSTALLATION DATES FOR THE COE LIBRARY ART INVITATIONAL
UW Libraries would like any accepted loaned pieces to be installed from August 1, 2010, to August 20, 2010. This installation date allows both artists and UW Libraries to have the loaned pieces on display before the UW Fall Semester begins. UW takes responsibility for hanging the art, but the artist is responsible for physically delivering his or her piece(s) to Coe Library.

TERMS OF SALE DURING THE COE LIBRARY ART INVITATIONAL
Ideally, UW Libraries request that all loaned pieces remain on display in Coe Library for the entire year. After six months, the artist has the opportunity to sell any loaned piece during the invitational, giving UW Libraries first right of refusal. Artists should arrange a predetermined price with UW Libraries, in the event UW Libraries wish to purchase the piece. Since no commission would be involved with these loaned pieces, UW Libraries would expect a price reflecting that discount.

RISK MANAGEMENT FOR LOANED PIECES DURING THE COE LIBRARY ART INVITATIONAL
Unless the artist has elected to maintain his/her own insurance, the university will insure pieces wall-to-wall under its Risk Management Policy. See the CONDITIONS STATEMENT for limitations and details.

TO SUBMIT A PROPOSAL OR FOR ADDITIONAL INFORMATION

Proposals should be submitted by July 1, 2010, and must include all of the following:

- artist name
- medium
- size/dimensions of piece(s)
- title of piece(s)
- year of creation for piece(s)
- cost of piece(s)
- images of piece(s) proposed for Coe Library Art Invitational

Artists are encouraged to contact UW Libraries prior to submitting a proposal. To submit proposals or to request additional information, please contact University of Wyoming Libraries Administration, care of David Kruger. David can be reached via phone (307) 399–7347 or email tseliot@uwyo.edu.

Selections for the Coe Library Art Invitational will be announced by July 15, 2010.

PROSPECTIVE SPACES FOR LOANED PIECES

GRAND STAIRWELL: LEVEL 1

- Base area at the foot of these steps would nicely accommodate a sculpted piece. This is a high-traffic stairwell.

SIDE WALL, MAIN CORRIDOR CENTRAL: LEVEL 2 (MAIN FLOOR)

- This broad corridor wall leads from the new building to the Alma Doke McMurry Reading Room on the west end of Coe Library. It has some visibility from the rotunda in the new building.

END WALL, MAIN CORRIDOR WEST: LEVEL 2 (MAIN FLOOR)

- This dark wall in the west building lies at the end of the main corridor and is visible from the rotunda in the new building.

SIDE WALL, MAIN CORRIDOR WEST: LEVEL 2 (MAIN FLOOR)

- This light wall is located just outside the Alma Doke McMurry Reading Room.

ILLUMINATION STAIRWELL, LEVEL 3

- Located near the IT lab balcony, this area also features ceiling illuminations that flow through multiple colors. Walls are a metallic blue.

Additional locations are also available. Consult UW Libraries for further information.

APPENDIX B

The University Libraries supports hosting art exhibits by University of Wyoming students, faculty, and staff. The artists gain a visible location on campus to display their work, and the Libraries benefit in aesthetic terms.

SPACE
- Wall space is available, as well as some display cases (measurements = 60" long, 28" wide, 6" tall) which are also used for library displays. Floor space and a modular cube display are additional options.

SELECTION PROCESS
- The Libraries reserve the right to decline the display of any proposed artwork without cause.

EXHIBITION PROCEDURES
- The lending artist (lender) is responsible for the transport of the artwork(s) to and from the Libraries. Please include signage for each artwork (artist's name, title and date of the work, and artist's statements are welcome).
- The lender will be consulted regarding where the art will be displayed, and the lender will provide an inventory of works of art to be displayed. The Libraries will determine the final exhibit location.
- The artwork will be displayed for a finite, negotiable amount of time. Items will remain on display for the entire exhibition period.
- The university physical plant will mount wall-hanging exhibits (UW Regulation 2-178).
- More than one artist's work(s) may be exhibited at the same time, depending on available space.
- Lenders must sign the risk waiver before works may be exhibited.

PUBLICITY
- The library will promote exhibits, for example, on the library website or in the newsletter.
- The lender (and professor) is encouraged to publicize the exhibit.

CONTACT INFORMATION
For questions or further information:
Jennifer Mayer, 766–5578, mayerj@uwyo.edu, Fine Arts Reference Librarian
1/19/00, rev. 1/13/06 jm

APPENDIX C: ART LOAN AGREEMENT, RELEASE, ASSUMPTION OF RISK, AND WAIVER OF LIABILITY

UNIVERSITY OF WYOMING LIBRARIES

This agreement and Assumption of Risk is made this _____day of ____, 20__, by and between the University of Wyoming Libraries and _____ (Lender).

1. The lender wishes to loan to the UW Libraries the following works of art:

_____

_____

_____ to be exhibited in accordance with the UW Libraries' Art Exhibit Guidelines for a period of _____ , starting _____ and ending _____.

2. The Lender understands and agrees that his/her works of art are loaned and will be exhibited at his/her own risk and that the UW Libraries, University of Wyoming, its employees and volunteers shall not be responsible for theft, vandalism, fire or other damage to the works of art.

3. In consideration of being allowed to loan works of art to the UW Libraries and have said works of art exhibited, the Lender hereby assumes all risks associated with the loaning and exhibiting of Lender's works of art and agrees to hold the University of Wyoming, its trustees, employees and volunteers harmless from any and all liability, actions, causes of action, debts, claims, or demands of any kind and nature whatsoever which may arise by or in connection with the loaning and exhibiting of Lender's works of art. The terms hereof shall serve as a release and assumption of risk by the Lender, heirs, estate, executor, administrator, assignees and for all members of Lender's family. I understand and agree to the above Agreement, Assumption of Risk and Waiver of Liability and I have read the UW Libraries Art Exhibit Guidelines.

_____   _____

Date   Printed name of Lender

_____

Signature of Lender
1/18/00jm

Part III
Performing Arts

CHAPTER 8

Developing Regional Heritage Music Collections

SANDRA M. HIMEL AND LANCE R. CHANCE

WORKING IN RHYTHM

This chapter provides general guidance to librarians developing a collection of local heritage music, using the Cajun and Creole Music Collection (CCMC) as a specific illustration. The CCMC is part of the Archives and Special Collections Department at Edith Garland Dupré Library at the University of Louisiana at Lafayette (UL Lafayette).

Syncopated rhythms, a cappella singing, call-and-response, clapping, and foot stomping are elements found in Louisiana Creole and Cajun music. Rhythm and feel are essential in learning and playing these indigenous musical forms. Playing and learning the music as part of a whole or together is also fundamental, whether with a band, a local community group, or family and friends (Louisiana Folk Roots 2010, 12).

Correspondingly, it is necessary to work together and provide support as part of a larger whole in order to develop and preserve musical heritage collections. Many participants are needed. The story of the development of the Cajun and Creole Music Collection is a story of collaboration. It encompasses collaborative efforts among library departments, between the library and the university, and between the library and the musical and cultural community at large.

BRIEF HISTORY AND DESCRIPTION OF THE CAJUN AND CREOLE MUSIC COLLECTION

Cajun and Creole musicians have been recording on major commercial record labels since 1928. Despite the importance of Louisiana Cajun and Creole music to the local culture, to the university, and to the state, few efforts had been made to collect and archive commercial recordings of this music at Dupré Library before 2002. Legendary musicians and ambassadors of Cajun and Creole cultures were awarded honorary degrees and titles by the university, yet the library did not own many recordings by these and other revered and influential musicians. Many recordings are now out of print. Further, some recordings and related historical materials on this area had been donated or sold to libraries outside of Louisiana. Accordingly, the library recognized the urgent need for retrospective and continued collection and preservation of these recordings and music-related materials. Local institutions should preserve such rich cultural treasures with local origins and make them accessible to current and future generations.

The CCMC was a collaborative effort from the beginning. Several librarians decided to seek grant funding to build a comprehensive collection of Cajun and Creole music. The library was eligible to submit funding proposals to the Louisiana Board of Regents during the 2002–3 fiscal year. With approval from the library administration, several librarians prepared and submitted a grant proposal. The library received a Louisiana Board of Regents Support Fund Traditional Enhancement Grant award in the amount of $90,487.00. The grant project, titled "To Preserve Cultures and Nurture Generations: Building a Collection of Cajun and Creole Music at the University Library," covered a three-year period from 2003 to 2006.

The stated goal of the proposed project was to further the university library's role in cultural education and preservation. The project would create a foundation on which to build a premier comprehensive collection of commercially recorded Louisiana Cajun and Creole music. Objectives included the following:

- Acquire a collection of audio and video recordings to begin the foundation work.
- Preserve archival copies to support and protect the musical heritage of South Louisiana.
- Provide access and promote use of recordings to university students, faculty, and researchers for needed curricular support and enhancement of scholarship.

- Provide (noncirculating) access and promote public use of recordings to the general public to educate, entertain, and foster new artistic creations.
- Publicize and promote the collection and Dupré Library's service and preservation efforts to attract support and donations.
- Work toward similar goals of cultural education and preservation to foster collaborations in the university and community.

Major project activities included identifying and purchasing current and rare recordings; providing bibliographic access (e.g., cataloging of materials, web page design); purchasing equipment and supplies; consulting with scholars and musicians; and engaging in publicity and promotion. Grant investigators purchased equipment for preservation and digitization projects, public listening and viewing workstations, and storage of the recordings. Personnel also purchased archival quality supplies, such as record sleeves; storage boxes; and cleaning solutions to protect, clean, and preserve the recordings. The grant also provided funding to hire student workers and a graduate assistant.

As the first grant project neared completion, CCMC personnel realized the need for additional resources to continue cataloging activities. In 2006, the library applied for and received a $29,456 grant award from the GRAMMY Foundation's Gulf Coast GRAMMY Foundation Archiving and Preservation Grant Program. The Cajun and Creole Music Collection Cataloging and Accessibility Project enabled the library to hire two graduate assistants and to continue extensive original and copy cataloging for the CCMC.

Thus, the CCMC developed from an existing basic collection of two hundred commercial recordings to include nearly nine thousand items. This expanding collection of primary and secondary resources includes commercial and noncommercial recordings, published and unpublished research materials, as well as unique and/or rare archival materials. The CCMC has two components, an archival collection and a public listening collection. The content and scope of the collection represents the music and musical cultures of Louisiana Cajuns and Creoles by covering their diverse histories, developments, influences, genres, and styles.

COLLABORATIVE SERVICES, PROJECTS, AND RELATIONSHIPS

As stated earlier, many participants are necessary in building a collection of local music. It is important to cultivate relationships, to foster artistic creations, and to support similar endeavors. This is especially true when the collecting is retrospective. For the CCMC, participants include library and university departments and personnel, state agencies, cultural organizations, individuals and groups from the local community, musicians and artists, researchers and authors, record companies, and private businesses and organizations.

The librarians working with this special collection have knowledge of and appreciation for Louisiana's musical cultures. They share a conviction that the material must be collected, preserved, and made publicly accessible. As other librarians involved with local music collections have argued, this conviction is an essential and primary requirement for success (Epstein 1967; Hathaway 1989).

Like many small and medium-sized libraries, Dupré Library has neither a music librarian nor a music cataloger position. However, existing library personnel and departments provided services and expertise to the initial grant projects and continue to contribute to the ongoing work. Participating departments include administration and development, archives and special collections, reference and instructional services, cataloging, acquisitions, and systems administration.

LIBRARY COLLECTION DEVELOPMENT AND ACQUISITIONS

When building an indigenous music collection, selection and acquisition processes need to be adaptable, which often requires collaboration within and outside the library. Also, as collections mature and expand, changes or additions in workflows, procedures, and policies may be necessary.

One of the first responsibilities of developers of this type of collection is to know the characteristics of the music being collected and, therefore, to understand its origins and history. Local musical cultures may have diverse and complex backgrounds. For example, "Cajun music is the product of creolization. Cajun music is a blend of German, Spanish, Scottish, Irish, Anglo-American, Afro-Caribbean and American Indian influences with a base of western French and French Acadian folk tradition. *Zydeco/zarico,* the most contemporary expression of black Creole music, and its precursors, *la-la* and *juré,* developed from the same set of influences with a heavier dose of Afro-Caribbean rhythms and styles" (Ancelet 1989, 1).

Librarians should expect the complexity of the music's history to affect selection decisions. Will the collecting be comprehensive and extensive or selective? Which musicians and performers, musical genres and styles, languages, time periods, record labels, formats, and media will be included or excluded? For the Cajun and Creole Music Collection, librarians adopted a collection development policy to address such questions. General categories of materials selected for the CCMC include the following:

- Audio recordings
  - commercially published musical recordings
  - unpublished and/or noncommercial musical recordings
- Video recordings
  - documentaries and motion pictures
  - instructional and educational videos on musical performance and dance
  - unpublished and/or noncommercial productions
- Other archival and research materials
  - published monographic and periodical materials
  - unpublished materials including letters and business papers
  - photographs, posters, newspaper clippings, pamphlets, and other ephemera
  - artifacts and other memorabilia

The collection of audio and video recordings contains both analog and digital formats. Analog formats include 78 rpm, $33^1/_3$ rpm (LP) and 45 rpm records and eight-track, audiocassette and VHS tapes. Digital formats include CD, DAT, DVD, and CD/DVD (dual media).

Librarians selecting and acquiring local music should refer to more than just standard collection development tools. During the initial grant proposal process, CCMC project investigators used various selection resources to create a wish-list database of recordings to be acquired. These resources included discographies, bibliographies, biographies, music and film catalogs, and artist and vendor websites. These sources continue to provide guidance and information. Also, from the beginning there was an emphasis on communication and networking with researchers and musicians to learn about new releases, rare and out-of-print recordings, and sources for acquiring these. As the project moved forward, investigators created a separate CCMC acquisitions database of purchases, donations, and transfers from within the library.

Because of the specialized and rare nature of the recordings and other materials, a library collecting local music should consider diverse acquisitions sources. In addition to standard library vendors, CCMC coordinators purchase items from wholesale and retail music outlets in Louisiana; online auctions; and local, national, and international music publishers. Librarians selecting for the CCMC make shopping excursions across Louisiana to sites that range from company warehouses to personal collections in garages and historic Louisiana recording venues. Frequently, the conditions demand immediate intervention to save endangered and unique items.

There are unique challenges and issues associated with the cataloging, classification, and organization of indigenous and ethnic musical genres and styles. With Cajun and Creole music, one challenge involves the assignment of subject headings. The author and musician Ben Sandmel (1999) notes the innate limitations of terminology and categories when assigned to traditional music or a hybrid musical style such as zydeco. The historian and author Ryan Brasseaux (2009, 3) explains: "Cajun music is woven of many strands. . . . Cajuns filtered the cultural and musical systems—overlaid for centuries in Louisiana—into an intricately nuanced and wholly creolized expression that eludes stringent categorization." When Library of Congress subject headings are insufficient, catalogers may find it appropriate to use keywords in a cataloging record note field or to use local subject headings. Additionally, libraries may submit subject-heading proposals to the Subject Authority Cooperative Program.

Another consideration when working with indigenous or ethnic music may be language. For the CCMC, Cajun and Creole French song titles and personal and corporate names present additional challenges in descriptive cataloging. For instance, Louisiana French geographic or place-names within song titles are often not recognized as proper nouns by those unfamiliar with the region and therefore are not capitalized. Library subject specialists with knowledge of the Louisiana French language and Louisiana musical history collaborate with cataloging personnel in the review and editing of catalog records.

Every library must determine cataloging policy on the basis of available resources and skills. Librarians working with the CCMC provide extensive descriptive and subject cataloging for original and copy cataloging records. Whether providing minimal or extensive cataloging, it is essential to document procedures and policies.

Librarians should explore different classification schemes based on the purpose and content of the collection. *Music Classification Systems* by Mark McKnight is an excellent manual for librarians working with music collections. The CCMC's lead coordinator created a customized and homegrown classification system based on the Alpha-Numeric System for Classification of Recordings (ANSCR). For the CCMC, the filing arrangement is alphabetical, then chronological by individual artist, performer, or group name, or by record publisher name in the case of various performers, compilations, and anthologies.

LIBRARY PUBLICITY AND PROMOTION

It is important to promote and publicize any special collection to encourage support, usage, and donations. The CCMC coordinators work with the library publicity committee and university public relations and media services to promote the collection and related activities. This has resulted in articles and announcements in university, local, and state newspapers and periodicals and an appearance on a local television news program. In September 2005, the library held an open house to present the collection. At the state level, the winter 2007 issue of *Louisiana Libraries* featured a cover photograph of CCMC recordings. Librarians working with the collection created and staged the photograph. Other creative collaborations by librarians include the design and creation of a logo and brochure and presentations at several conferences. The CCMC coordinators delivered presentations at annual conferences of the Louisiana Historical Association, the Louisiana Library Association, and the Association for Recorded Sound Collections.

PARTICIPANTS IN THE UNIVERSITY AND THE COMMUNITY

Any type of library creating or building an indigenous music collection can benefit from cooperative efforts with individuals and organizations outside of the library. Also, grant funding agencies usually encourage such relationships and projects. The following sections provide examples of collaborations between the Cajun and Creole Music Collection librarians and the university faculty and staff and the community at large.

EXAMPLES OF UNIVERSITY COLLABORATIONS

The CCMC supports related programs such as the Francophone studies doctoral program, the Department of English folklore concentration, and an undergraduate minor in Cajun and Creole Studies. The CCMC coordinators work with the holder of the Endowed Chair in Traditional Music in the School of Music. The university is planning a degree program and center in traditional music.

The library works closely with the Center for Louisiana Studies, the Center for Cultural and Eco-Tourism, and the Cajun and Creole Folklore Archives. In collaboration with these centers, the library has submitted a proposal to the university administration that would create a shared research and listening facility for the study of Cajun and Creole folklore and music.

The UL Lafayette Friends of the Library purchased a one-year underwriting package with KRVS, the public radio station at UL Lafayette, to promote the CCMC. The writing of the ad copy was a collaborative effort between personnel from KRVS and Dupré Library. An announcement aired once a week between local and National Public Radio programming times. In addition,

KRVS provides periodic public service announcements and updates about the CCMC and Dupré Library. The station also donates event and promotional posters to the library.

The UL Lafayette Office of Development and the UL Lafayette Foundation work with the library to identify and contact potential donors. The library requested and the university established a foundation account for gifts and donations to the CCMC. The CCMC demonstrates UL Lafayette's active support of local musical cultures. This, in turn, facilitates communication with interested donors.

EXAMPLES OF COLLABORATIONS WITH BUSINESSES AND ORGANIZATIONS

The library negotiated with the Louisiana recording company and studio Lanor Records to purchase selected historical and archival materials and equipment. In May 2010, Dupré Library purchased a collection of archival business files, ledgers and correspondence, photographs, office equipment, textile artifacts, and historical recording equipment. Lanor Records is one of the oldest recording studios in Louisiana. Lanor label recordings continue to have international popularity.

The CCMC personnel assisted Exhibits Etc., a nationally recognized music museum exhibit design firm, in working with Modern Music Center and J. D. Miller Recording Studio in Louisiana. The firm requested materials for the creation of a multimedia exhibit at the J. D. Miller Recording Studio Museum.

The CCMC coordinator participates and volunteers at the Louisiana Folk Roots' Dewey Balfa Cajun and Creole Heritage Week annual program, sponsored in part by the Louisiana Division of the Arts and the National Endowment for the Arts. Membership and participants in Louisiana Folk Roots and its programs are international in scope. This event provides opportunities for development and promotion of the Cajun and Creole Music Collection. During 2011, the library, along with other university departments, was involved in local events of the Grand Réveil Acadien (Great Acadian Awakening), a gathering of Acadian descendants.

The CCMC librarians met with personnel from the Louisiana Endowment for the Humanities regarding the online encyclopedia of Louisiana history and culture, KnowLA. The administrator of the Louisiana State Archives Research Library offered to refer donations of Cajun and Creole music recordings received by that institution to the CCMC.

EXAMPLES OF COLLABORATIONS WITH MUSICIANS, RESEARCHERS, AND INDIVIDUALS

The CCMC librarians provided reference assistance for the staff of *American Routes*, a radio program distributed by Public Radio International and hosted by Nick Spitzer. Spitzer and his staff relocated to Lafayette after Hurricane Katrina in September 2005. He acknowledged the CCMC, Dupré Library, and UL Lafayette on the episode titled "After the Storm IV: Thanksgiving," which aired nationwide through affiliate stations on November 23–29, 2005.

The CCMC coordinators digitized and transferred the analog cassette-tape recording of Marce Lacouture's *Sunday Gumbo* to CD format. Lacouture, a singer-songwriter, sold the rare item to the library with the request that the library provide her with digital copies of the recording. Lacouture owns copyright of the recording. The library made two digital transfers, an archival copy and a copy for listening and patron use.

Jerry Embree, a New Orleans–based musician, audio engineer, and director of Abita Music Company, invited the library to partner as a participating repository in two GRAMMY Foundation grants. These grants funded the digitization of radio program transcriptions produced by Embree. Embree's first digitization project covered *The Creole Gumbo Radio Show*. The second project covered *South to Louisiana: A Cajun and Zydeco Music Show (Hosted by Michael Doucet)*. Both programs featured Louisiana music and interviews and aired nationally on an independent National Public Radio affiliate network. Embree donated the original DAT master tapes, digital transfers on CD and DVD, and catalog data of programs and playlists. The library agreed to accept, preserve, and provide public access to this material.

The author Ryan Brasseaux researched and used record-label images from the CCMC in his books *Cajun Breakdown: The Emergence of an American-Made Music* and *Accordions, Fiddles, Two-Step & Swing: A Cajun Music Reader*, edited by Brasseaux and Kevin Fontenot. The CCMC coordinator attended a book signing and presentation at the Barnes & Noble in Lafayette for Brasseaux's most recent book, *Cajun Breakdown*. During the talk, the author referenced the CCMC and gave the coordinator the opportunity to provide information about the collection to the audience.

The CCMC is fortunate to have the assistance of volunteers, including students, individuals from the local community, and librarians. Some volunteers provide their time and work at the library, and others search flea markets and antique stores for rare recordings. Musicians, researchers, record company owners, and other individuals continue to donate recordings, photographs, costume artifacts, promotional realia, and offers of assistance and resources.

A COLLABORATIVE WORK IN PROGRESS

Indigenous and local musical genres have unique natures and environments. These characteristics resist the generalization necessary to construct a universal guide for librarians developing collections for these musical genres. Collaboration is fundamental and vital for collection, promotion, preservation, and the provision of access.

Today, as in the past, musical collaborations are part of the Cajun and Creole musical cultures. The CCMC librarians endeavor to create a history of collaboration for the Cajun and Creole Music Collection. Librarians working with the CCMC often receive words and acts of gratitude, encouragement, and inspiration from the creators, performers, scholars, preservationists, and others who share a passion for Cajun and Creole music.

Dupré Library will continue to demonstrate its commitment to cultural education and preservation and contribute to the university's role in the preservation and promotion of Cajun and Creole cultures.

References

Ancelet, Barry Jean. 1989. *Cajun Music: Its Origins and Development.* Lafayette: Center for Louisiana Studies, University of Southwestern Louisiana.

Brasseaux, Ryan André. 2009. *Cajun Breakdown: The Emergence of an American-Made Music.* New York: Oxford University Press.

Epstein, Dena J. 1967. "On Collecting Materials for Local Music Histories." *Notes (Quarterly Journal of the Music Library Association)* 24 (1): 18–21.

Hathaway, Edward W. 1989. "Developing a State Archive of Local Music Materials." *Notes (Quarterly Journal of the Music Library Association)* 45 (3): 483–94.

Louisiana Folk Roots. 2010. *The Dewey Balfa Cajun and Creole Heritage Week, April 16–23, 2010* (program booklet). Lafayette: Louisiana Folk Roots.

McKnight, Mark. *Music Classification Systems.* Music Library Association Basic Series No. 1. Lanham, MD: Scarecrow Press.

Sandmel, Ben, and Rick Olivier. 1999. *Zydeco!* Jackson: University Press of Mississippi.

CHAPTER 9

Making Music Collections Come Alive

GREG MacAYEAL

ONE WARM JUNE NIGHT in Chicago, two organizations joined to perform some rarely heard music. As Leo Sowerby's composition *Canticle of the Sun* played to a grateful audience, the concert itself resulted from a successful collaboration between the Grant Park Festival Orchestra and the Music Library of Northwestern University. A primary source needed to create the performance is held in the Music Library special collections, and this source proved essential to the concert. Connecting a library user to specific materials is imperative with special collections. Whether the user is a faculty researcher or a resident interested in local history, what one discovers in special collections cannot be found anywhere else. Frequently, our collections have interesting stories to tell, and by promoting their use, libraries, archives, and users will find new ways to connect. In particular, the music community can be well served in this manner. Individual musicians and music ensembles can expand their programming by looking for music that may not live anywhere but in a library special collections department.

UNFAMILIAR MUSIC

Attending a concert of classical music, especially one by a symphony orchestra, is many times a little like visiting a museum. Music that is routinely performed is often quite old and is likely to be authored by one of a handful of composers. The works of Mozart, Beethoven, and Schubert, for example, are commonly programmed and certainly loved by audiences. These are a few of the masters of classical music, and their music deserves to be heard. What is striking is how much music is not being heard, even music composed by a master. For a variety of reasons, it has become common for music organizations and performing ensembles to look only in shallow waters for their programming needs. As a result, only a small percentage of musical works are ever performed. Concert-going audiences are treated to the same pieces by the same composers year after year. The museum-like quality of many symphony orchestras develops from this approach to programming. Even so, in some cases an organization's survival depends in part on programming music that will be immediately recognizable to their audience when advertised. Hopefully, this recognition will generate a moderate and predictable amount of ticket sales. Symphony orchestras are increasingly financially reliant on the wishes of their audience. If an orchestra is a museum, then it is partly because many of us want it that way.

This is not to say that symphony orchestras refuse to expand their repertoire, but just that they are cautious. At risk of losing ticket sales, musical works that are unfamiliar or challenging because of their musical language are programmed very carefully. What such brave programming offers is the opportunity to develop new audiences and refresh the repertoire commonly heard in performance. This is the balancing act that symphonic music directors walk—how to engage new audiences and add newness to an orchestra's programming without alienating audiences who have been loyal and expect a degree of the familiar. Not all musical works will be successful in meeting the goal of the former without doing damage to the latter, and creative music directors diligently look for new works that can live in this tight space. To be clear, a new work is not necessarily newly composed, but sometimes one that is infrequently performed. Like art of all media, musical style will fall in and out of favor, and what will be newly heard to modern audiences may have been very well known to past audiences.

THE GRANT PARK ORCHESTRA

Based in Chicago, the Grant Park Orchestra (GPO) traces its roots to the Great Depression. James C. Petrillo, head of the Chicago chapter of the Federation of Musicians, created performance opportunities for out-of-work union members. His events, called the Grant Park Concerts, evolved into what is now experienced every summer in Chicago—the Grant Park Music Festival. Each year between June and August, Chicago's beautiful new lakefront Millennium Park is host to the orchestra, and large crowds typically pack the pavilion. To this day, all GPO concerts are free, and the organization claims to be the nation's only free, municipally funded orchestra. It is highly regarded and well known for adventurous programming. A 2004 nomination for a Grammy award serves as evidence of the high musical quality.

The GPO frequently performs unusual or little-known repertoire. As the organization tries to strike that balance between familiar and unfamiliar repertoire, it consistently programs music that other orchestras will not approach. Over the 2009–10 seasons, the GPO performed notable but less frequently heard composers, including Lutoslawski, Kernis, and Rautavaara. The GPO conductor, Carlos Kalmar, holds that since the Grant Park concerts are free, he is able to be more adventuresome in his programming.

A SPECIAL PERFORMANCE

In 2009, the orchestra leadership was looking to create a theme for a new recording project and subsequent performance. Ultimately, after kicking around several ideas, they selected the theme of early Pulitzer Prize–winning compositions. Three works were chosen for the project: Aaron Copland's popular *Appalachian Spring: Suite*, William Schuman's *A Free Song: A Secular Cantata*, and Leo Sowerby's *Canticle of the Sun*. Copland won the Pulitzer in 1945, Schuman in 1943 (the first Pulitzer awarded in music), and Sowerby in 1946. Once the music had been selected, GPO staff needed to acquire usable copies of the score and parts. In most circumstances, the publisher of a given composition rents performance materials to the orchestra, but in the case of Sowerby's *Canticle of the Sun*, the publisher did not own anything the GPO could use. By contacting the Leo Sowerby Foundation, the GPO was directed toward a *Canticle* source.

CONNECTING TO A COLLECTION

The Northwestern University Music Library (in Evanston, Illinois) is among the nation's largest music libraries. Its collection includes nearly three hundred thousand volumes of books, printed music, sound recordings, and journals, and it is recognized internationally for its extensive holdings of twentieth-century and contemporary music. The library's mission is, of course, to support the teaching and research needs of the university, but with special collections, the Music Library serves the needs of researchers from around the world. Many times interested users are in fact our neighbors in Chicago.

Among the Music Library's special collections are musical manuscripts and other primary sources. Music of the twentieth century is of particular collecting importance, and the library has acquired the archives of several important twentieth-century luminaries. In 1993, the Leo Sowerby Foundation donated a collection of materials by composer Leo Sowerby (1895–1968). Included is a manuscript copy of *Canticle of the Sun*. Upon learning of the manuscript, the GPO became quite interested in consulting this source, which appears to be the only extant copy.

A PULITZER PRIZE–WINNING COMPOSER

Born in Grand Rapids, Michigan, in 1895, Leo Sowerby found success early in life. In 1913, the teenage composer was fortunate enough to have his *Violin Concerto* performed by the Chicago Symphony Orchestra. Other notable achievements that came quickly in his career include the prestigious Rome Prize (1921), a three-year fellowship awarded by the American Academy in Rome. Upon returning to Chicago in 1925, he obtained a faculty appointment at the American Conservatory of Music. The following several decades were quite productive. In addition to his work as a composer, Sowerby became the organist and choirmaster at St. James's Episcopal Cathedral, located on Chicago's North Side. Perhaps his greatest acknowledgment came in 1946, when he won the Pulitzer Prize for music composition. The winning piece, *Canticle of the Sun*, received its first performance in 1945. The work is scored for full orchestra and chorus. Although many of Sowerby's orchestral works had been performed prior to 1945, after that year a steep decline occurred in performances of his orchestral music. The performance history of any given composition can be difficult to absolutely determine, but it appears that *Canticle* received only a handful of performances. Reasons for the lack of attention are not clear, especially considering the composition's initial reception. The well-regarded American composer Lou Harrison said of *Canticle*, "Mr. Sowerby has written an elevated cantata, with sustained workmanship and appropriate expression which should find ready admirers and performers."[1]

For whatever reason, *Canticle of the Sun* appears to have won the Pulitzer Prize and then immediately vanished from the repertoire.

WORKING WITH THE MANUSCRIPT

To realize the goal of performing the work, the GPO had the one choice of consulting the score held at Northwestern. Fortunately, the manuscript is in quite good condition. It is hand notated in ink and bound like a book, without any loose leaves. At 103 pages written for large orchestra and chorus, in a

Detail (woodwind section, opening measures) of Leo Sowerby's original manuscript for *Canticle of the Sun*

single movement that lasts almost a half hour, *Canticle* is a large manuscript and large musical work.

Having the manuscript score is important, but it is not enough to realize the work in performance. Each musician needs a part and the sheet music used during the performance, and the conductor needs a working copy of the full score. To create parts for *Canticle*, the entire score must be copied from the manuscript source and further transcribed. Any project requiring reproductions begins with securing permission to make copies. *Canticle* was completed in 1944 and still under copyright protection. With some research, the rights holder was identified. Music Library staff assisted in securing permission, and once secured, the staff proceeded to make a digital copy. A scanner using an overhead camera was used for this purpose, as it creates high-quality images with little stress to the manuscript. Still, the work of creating a usable version of *Canticle* did not end with mere scanning. In large orchestras, the job of preparing the music used for performance is usually the responsibility of the music librarian, and this was the case for *Canticle* as well. The GPO music librarian Michael Shelton describes the next steps: "Creating a score and set of parts for *Canticle* was an arduous task. First I needed to get a copy of the score, which was handwritten. [The Northwestern University Music Library] supplied clear copies of each page, which I enlarged and printed out. The score was . . . very legible and fairly easy to transcribe into Sibelius [music notation software that produces high-quality print copies]." Shelton further reports that he encountered ambiguities in how Sowerby wrote the music, sometimes omitting details required for an accurate performance: "In the end, I decided to stay with Sowerby's enharmonic choices. Once the score was put into Sibelius and checked for errors, it was possible to extract a set of parts. The parts also had to be proofed and corrected, a time-consuming job. During this process, I discovered several small errors in the original score. Sowerby occasionally left out an accidental or a dynamic, he was sometimes inconsistent in his articulations, and he was unclear with a few indications of muting."[2]

Finally, an edition of the composition that the conductor, orchestra, and chorus could use was ready. On June 25, 2010, the GPO and chorus performed *Canticle of the Sun* in Grant Park with a repeat performance the following evening. Because of the annual Taste of Chicago festival that was sharing the large lakefront park, the concert was moved to the adjacent (and indoor) Harris Theatre. The concert was titled "The Pulitzer Project." Critic of the *Chicago Sun-Times* newspaper Wynne Delacoma reported favorably on the June 25 performance, although she concluded the review: "A little triumphalism goes a long way." Cedille Records, a Chicago-based classical music label, recorded the concert and released it on CD in the summer of 2011 (*The Pulitzer Project*—CDR 90000 125).

Canticle of the Sun premiered on April 16, 1945, in New York's Carnegie Hall. As stated earlier, records indicate that the work received very little attention after having won the Pulitzer. Another performance of *Canticle* was perhaps long overdue, and fittingly, it occurred in Chicago. The partnering of the GPO and the Northwestern University Music Library resulted in a pleasing concert of an important work by a composer who called Chicago home. By partnering with a local music organization, the Northwestern University Music Library was able to highlight an important work as well as create awareness of the library and its collections.

CREATING A SPECIAL PERFORMANCE

Any library with special collections can have its own "special performances," each in ways unique to its collections. To paraphrase S. R. Ranganathan, library collections are to be used. Our job in the library profession is to help facilitate use. The following sections include a few thoughts on what we can adopt in theory and practice to help libraries let their archival and rare materials live.

MAKE CONNECTIONS—KNOW WHAT YOU HAVE

First, simply, know what collections you have. Public service staff, especially those working directly with special collections, should understand enough about the authors, scope, and general subject matter to be able to recommend collections to users who present themselves. In academic settings, knowing the research and teaching interests of the faculty will help make connections as well. The main access point to a given collection is many times the staff working with the collections.

Ideally, special collections need to be present in online public access catalogs and encoded archival description portals, and materials that are fully processed and cataloged will be found most easily. Good MARC records and detailed finding aids are traditional and expected routes to specific collections, even if used mostly by library staff. In an era of shrinking budgets, devoting staff time to developing good bibliographic data can be hard to justify. The ultimate goal is to connect the user to the collection, and incomplete records and bare-bones finding aids can still be of great help. In an "if you build it, they will come" sort of phenomenon, getting collections processed seems to bring out users. Build access points, even if they are not complete or up to a desired standard.

Promoting special collections through exhibits, displays, and publications is still effective. Allow the materials to tell their own story, and the best exhibits move far beyond old books in glass cases. Real scholarship can be created with exhibits. An engrossing narrative can be told through the documentary evidence of primary sources. Interest generated around one collection or item can be used to create interest around other collections and materials. There is a natural tendency for a good story to elicit inquiries about what else might live in special collections. Think about your collections, and ask what stories they tell.

BE A PARTNER, NOT A BARRIER

Staff Attitudes

Whenever materials are used, a threat of physical damage is created. This is of course true for all materials held in libraries and archives, but it is of greater concern when using rare and unique items. Finding the right balance between protecting the materials and assisting users can be challenging, but we need to remember that we want our collections to be used. In the case of music, it must be understood that music lives in performance, not on a dusty shelf. The music itself is what is communicated aurally from composer via performer to listener. The paper that contains notation is merely a set of instructions. Of course, it's incredibly important to preserve the paper, but what are we really preserving if the music is not performed? Use creates risk of physical damage, and some library staff are quite risk averse. For the collection to have any true meaning, it will connect with a user and live through his or her understanding and efforts. A collection is important only if it is part of a dialogue, and being part of a dialogue is worth any and all risks.

Even with fully digitized collections, most researchers will sooner or later need to contact a library staff member. In this regard, the staff becomes the face of the archives, collection, and library. We project our attitudes as we assist users, and when we keep the user's needs in mind, we can be sure to offer the best assistance to the best of our ability. Working with special collections can be time consuming and even tedious. What our users remember, and likely convey, is the service. We have a professional obligation to make sure that the level of service is high. Finding the right balance is key—the balance between protecting the collections and assisting the users. The payoff can many times be that we learn more about what we keep in our collections. It's also very exciting to be a part of a user's aha moment, and the gratitude reflected can be quite rewarding. Invest time in users of special collections, and they will often repay in full.

Assist Users in Their Goals

Library staff comfortable with the traditional reference interview may feel somewhat unprepared when dealing with the interview in the context of special collections. In providing access to rare and archival collections, many times we do not have the same kind of tools commonly found with generalized circulating collections. What library staff expect in terms of subject access, authority control, and reliable tools (e.g., catalogs, bibliographies) can be incomplete or nonexistent. The idea of original order can also make finding specific information difficult. The concept of original order dictates that materials in an archival collection are kept according to the organization of the collection's creator. The library or archive imposes as little as possible on the original order. This creates problems when creating or looking for access points. Additional problems with the reference interview arise when users are not local. Mediating an interview over a string of e-mail messages can be difficult, and the phone offers little improvement. Finally, adding to the difficulties already described, users at times can have prohibitively broad questions. A user once asked the Music Library for all letters related to vocal music in the correspondence archive of composer John Cage, a very large collection. By ultimately getting the user to focus on a few vocal works, the original information need became manageable. Through listening attentively, asking open-ended questions, and narrowing the topic, staff can help mold an information need into something that can be addressed by the extant tools that we have on hand. However, providing good service does get back to simply knowing what is in your special collections. Be patient in the reference interview, and be attentive to the user's questions.

Users will want copies, whether for their own personal use or for an upcoming publication or performance. Invariably, the need for copies leads to contending with copyright. Many times, special collections are unpublished, and this can further cloud an already-murky copyright picture. Library staff members have a professional obligation to understand copyright. If we do not become experts, we at least need to offer a path to answering copyright questions. Part of that will be helping users acquire permissions. Hopefully, information about a right holder (if there is one) is known, but many times it is not. Even seasoned researchers can become frustrated in this process. To assist library staff in navigating this landscape, the American Library Association and the Society of American Archivists offer a number of helpful workshops, webinars, and high-quality online tools. Library staff must restrain themselves from asserting that contending with copyright is outside the range of service. Library staff working in special collections must have a fundamental grasp of copyright law. Be a partner with the user in navigating the choppy seas of copyright.

TELL THE STORY

As stated earlier, one good success story will help generate interest. Not all libraries and archives have a public relations (PR) department, but for those that do, keeping PR staff informed is imperative. If you do not have in-house PR staff, be willing to devote some time to creating content for your website, blog, or other publications. Media outlets continue to look for human-interest stories, and it's not uncommon to see reporting relating to special collections. Stories involving users and materials coming together through the dedicated service of the staff use can help reinforce the position of a library in its community. Don't let the use of special collections end when a satisfied patron leaves the library. Be sure to tell the story.

Encourage staff working with special collections to make connections with staff working in other local libraries and archives. In Chicago alone, the music community is lucky to be able to take advantage of the collections of the Chicago Public Library, the Newberry Library, and the Center for Black Music Research, in addition to the collections held in colleges and universities. By creating a community of interested staff, libraries and archives can refer users to more appropriate collections and, in turn, can increase the visibility of their own collections.

CONCLUSION

Libraries and archives maintain special collections to preserve and promote human knowledge, and this is equally true for music collections. At times, this mission can seem abstract, and materials in special collections can languish in the shadow of more highly used general collections. In the case of music, it is important to remember it lives in performance. The users, or performers, are out there, and we have to connect to them.

Notes

1 Lou Harrison, review of score *Canticle of the Sun* by Leo Sowerby, Notes, 2nd ser., 2, no.3 (1945): 179.
2. Michael Shelton, e-mail message to the author, December 27, 2010.

CHAPTER 10

PML Players

Theater Arts at the Patchogue-Medford Library

JERI WEINKRANTZ COHEN

THE PML PLAYERS is the theater arts group of the Patchogue-Medford Library's Young Adult Department. Founded in 2005 by young adult services librarian Martha Mikkleson, the group provides an opportunity for artistic expression for teens from a variety of social, economic, and ethnic backgrounds. The Patchogue-Medford Library serves the communities of Patchogue and Medford on Long Island, New York. In PML Players, the teens work together to create, produce, and perform a variety of shows for younger children and their families. In the process, they build appreciation for theater and the arts. They also develop a sense of responsibility to one another and to the larger community. Activities include performing music and lyrics, scriptwriting, production, scenery design and building, and musical and theatrical public performance. The performances are often supplemented by displays of art, video, and photography by local teens. The program is offered at no expense to the participants or the audience.

ABOUT THE PROGRAM

The PML Players offers students in grades 6–12 an introduction to theater and practice in cooperative learning and team building. It is run on a shoestring budget, primarily by library staff with an artistic bent and experience in the performing arts. Support staff is brought in as needed and as the budget allows.

The teens prepare several shows and performances each year. In winter, a bilingual show is produced for El día de los niños/El día de los libros.

Summer productions are varied and feature music and performance for the general public. The last annual production is a Halloween show prepared and presented for younger children.

Each show involves hours of planning, writing, rehearsal, and stagecraft tailored to the particular production. For actors and musicians, there are usually two three-hour rehearsals weekly over the course of a period of two months (about thirty hours total for each group). An additional fifteen to twenty hours are spent designing and creating sets. Sets are planned to be minimal and, as often as possible, reusable.

In addition to the actual productions and displays, the library offers how-to sessions to help develop skills in stagecraft, performance, singing, music, and other related disciplines. Programs have been offered in puppet making, poetry, scriptwriting, and digital photography.

EL DÍA DE LOS NIÑOS/EL DÍA DE LOS LIBROS

The first production each year is in April for El día de los niños/El día de los libros, the Day of the Child/The Day of the Book. According to the American Library Association, El día de los niños is a celebration of "the importance of advocating literacy for children of all linguistic and cultural backgrounds" (http://dia.ala.org). The PML Players prepare and present a bilingual production for Spanish-speaking families. This involves rehearsals and preparation beginning in January. Rehearsals are held twice weekly in January, February, and March, and daily the week before the show, for a total of about thirty hours. The script usually starts with a bilingual folktale. Over the past few years, the teens have prepared both live productions and puppet shows. Since many of the teens taking part in this production are native Spanish speakers, they are able to ad-lib and pepper the show with Spanish words and phrases, making it all very natural and entertaining. Between eighty and a hundred people of all ages come to see this show. The production stresses interactivity: children in the audience are offered the opportunity to dance along or to prepare a small craft relating to the show.

SUMMER PRODUCTIONS

Summer is a very busy period for the PML Players, especially for the music ensemble, as they rehearse and prepare for a variety of public performances. Our summer productions have included family-friendly musicals, readers' theater and puppet theater workshops, as well as teen talent and band showcases.

Musician's workshops are key to the PML Players' summer season--the teens have a chance to hone their skills while school is out. More advanced students have an opportunity to help less experienced musicians. Instruments played and practiced have included flute, oboe, violin, clarinet, bass clarinet, trumpet, trombone, and piano. In a single and very busy summer, the music ensemble took part in three major productions: a readers' theater production of *Charlie and the Chocolate Factory*, *The Music Man* (produced in coopera-tion with another local library), and a local Labor Day celebration of the arts. Rehearsals are held twice weekly from the end of June until the end of August for performances.

For the past couple of summers, the library has coordinated an intense music camp, which meets for a few hours each day for a week. Separate camps are held for band, orchestra, and choral musicians. Participants in the music camps must have passed the New York State Student Music Associa-tion (NYSSMA) trials at level 3 or higher and are glad for the opportunity to maintain and improve their skills during the summer vacation.

In the library's Music Buddies program, the more advanced students (NYSSMA level 5) offer their assistance to middle school students who are at NYSSMA levels 1–4. This program has been a success summer after sum-mer. The younger kids improve their skills, and the older ones get some prac-tice and earn community service hours, which are required for high school graduation.

Approximately twenty-five teens participate in the music camp and Music Buddies programs each summer. We are extremely fortunate to have rehearsal space made available without charge by a music store located next to the library.

A recital at the end of the summer gives the teens the opportunity to show-case their improved skills for friends, family, and the general public. The teens develop the program and wear their concert dress. Last summer, the program featured several small ensemble pieces by the wind and string sections, fol-lowed by solos, duets, and trios. Innovative pairings included a brother-sister violin and flute duet and a piece for clarinet and voice. The library provides little more than the opportunity, encouragement, and sheet music.

The Patchogue-Medford Library is located on Main Street in the village of Patchogue on Long Island. Each summer, the village and the local chamber of commerce sponsor a series of outdoor events called Alive after Five. Main Street is closed to traffic, and stages, outdoor cafés, and crafts booths are set up to encourage people to come to the village. We take the opportunity of Alive after Five to present a variety of different performances. A teen talent showcase is held one week, and a teen-band showcase another. In the library, we often work on a puppet production based on familiar folktales to be pre-sented to the younger children.

All these summer activities bring in many teens as participants. Since several of the performances take place outdoors on Main Street, audiences often number in the hundreds. For next summer, we are planning to form a step team to march in the Fourth of July parade, increasing participation and audience even more. Step team practice will provide an opportunity for physical activity and performance.

NOT-TOO-SCARY THEATER

In the fall, the teens go back to school and to all their regular activities, which can make it hard to get them into the library for programs. The PML Players concentrate their efforts on preparing a Halloween production for presentation to younger children and their families. The production is called Scary Theater, but it is aimed at small children and young families. The teens prepare several short and not-too-scary skits, featuring acting, poetry, and music. The teen musicians perform as a pit orchestra, providing sound effects and appropriate music for the show. Sometimes the teens prepare an original script; sometimes the show is performed as readers' theater. There are usually between twenty and twenty-five teens who participate in preparing this show, including musicians, actors, writers, and stage crew.

Rehearsals are twice weekly, over a period of eight to ten weeks. About thirty hours of rehearsal time go into this show. Entire Saturdays are spent building and painting sets, and making costumes and props, totaling about twenty hours, depending on the production. Audiences of up to a hundred people fill our public meeting space for this show. Most years, the teens must present the performance two or three times to meet demand—some of the young audience members insist on sitting through several shows! Live theater is also a novelty for much of their young audience. One young patron, leaving the performance, said, "Thank you for the movie!"

SPECIAL PROJECTS

In addition to the three regular performances, the teens involved in PML Players have undertaken several special projects. One labor-intensive project was called One Community/Many Stories. This project was created in response to the murder of an Ecuadoran immigrant by a group a teens a few blocks from the library. One Community/Many Stories was a multimedia presentation of photos, graphics, music, and voice prepared over a period of four months. The dedicated teens conducted research; interviewed local district residents;

recorded music; created titles; and edited sound files using MP3 players, digital cameras, and free sound-editing software. Two performances were given. At the conclusion of each presentation, against a backdrop of the Statue of Liberty, four teens gave an emotionally charged reading of the poem engraved at the base of the statue, "The New Colossus," by Emma Lazarus.

IT'S ABOUT THE TEENS: PROVIDING AN EDUCATIONAL AND ENRICHING EXPERIENCE

Teen programs at the Patchogue-Medford Library, including PML Players, are developed to expand outreach efforts to underserved teens, plan for cross-generational programs, and expand volunteer opportunities for teens. The PML Players is only one of the after-school and school-break activities offered by the Young Adult Department of the Patchogue-Medford Library to complement what is offered in school. The program offers a supervised and productive environment for youth living in a community that is facing economic and social stress. All teens living in the library's service area and between the ages of eleven and eighteen are eligible and encouraged to participate. The PML Players gives them a means of self-expression and artistic growth, as well as a learning experience. The program is offered at no cost to the families, and the teens participating in the program receive community service credit, which is required for high school.

In many cases, the teens taking part in PML Players may have no other access to extracurricular arts and performance activities. Many of the participants have never been involved in theater production before. The participants include at-risk and latchkey teenagers who are in the library daily from the time school lets out until late in the evening. Local bilingual teens who are children of immigrants living in the community are encouraged to participate. The PML Players is inclusive. We believe that every teen has something to offer. Any teen who wants to participate can do so and has the opportunity to learn new skills and develop his or her talents. The teens are encouraged not only to develop their own skills but also to show off and to help develop the skills of others.

A major objective of PML Players is to involve the teens in all stages of the planning and delivery of PML Players programs. The Young Adult Department staff try to keep the developmental needs of adolescents in mind when planning programs, considering the Search Institute's forty developmental assets and Hart's Ladder of Youth Participation.

According to the Search Institute, their surveys have shown that the forty developmental assets have a major influence on adolescents and their behavior.

The assets are believed to reduce high-risk behavior and to increase positive behavior. The more assets teens have, the more likely they are to develop social competence and positive behavior and attitudes. The PML Players empowers the teens and sets boundaries and expectations, as well as providing a constructive use of time for the participants. Information on the developmental assets can be found at www.search-institute.org/developmental-assets.

Hart's Ladder of Youth Participation, also called the Ladder of Children's Participation, was originally created by Roger Hart for UNICEF in 1997. The top of the ladder is where young people and adults share decision making; the bottom rung is where adults manipulate young people. Achieving shared decision making and letting the teens initiate and choose the direction of the productions are among the goals of PML Players as a community program (for more information on Hart's Ladder of Youth Participation and descriptions of activities on each rung, see www.freechild.org/ladder.htm).

Program popularity is not always a deciding factor when we schedule programs, but we always consider the developmental and educational qualities. The goal is to give the teens a variety of programs that they can take ownership of and that teach them things they need to become caring, self-sufficient adults. Keeping them motivated and bringing in new members is a constant challenge.

The PML Players is designed to do more than teach theatrical and art skills. It also encourages team building and provides an enjoyable community service opportunity for teens to serve as role models while entertaining small children. The teens who participate in PML Players develop public-speaking skills and advance their language arts skills. The programming stresses development of feelings of competence and achievement, self-definition, and positive social interaction with peers and adults while offering a public venue for creative expression. The program is structured and has clearly defined expectations and rules of behavior. The teens know that the events and programs they develop are meaningful not only to themselves but also to the larger community. This is in line with the mission of the library, which states: "The Patchogue-Medford Library is dedicated to providing, facilitating and supporting the informational, educational, cultural and recreational needs of the community. The Patchogue-Medford Library, as a community resource, acquires, organizes and makes available books, non-print materials, electronic resources, programs and services to educate, enrich, entertain and inform."

When preparing for shows, the teens involved with PML Players work with supportive and positive adult role models in the library. Participants see that the community values them and their efforts as they are given useful roles in the community and perform as a service for others. The teens develop their productions in a secure environment with defined boundaries, and they are expected to meet the requirements and demands of the program. They have an outlet for creative activities, and they are engaged and motivated to achieve. A high value is placed not only on their creative talents but also on promoting support and respect for their peers and developing their sense of responsibility as part of the group. The teens are given the opportunity to plan and make decisions about the performances and are encouraged to feel that they have control over the program's direction. Working as a group, the members of PML Players become comfortable working closely with people of different socioeconomic and cultural backgrounds, and they develop negotiating and conflict-resolution skills. This results in their increased self-esteem; a sense of purpose; and a positive view of their achievements, capabilities, and futures.

ABOUT THE STAFF

PML Players is run primarily by Patchogue-Medford Library staff, led by librarian Martha Mikkleson. Support staff is brought in as needed and as the budget allows.

We are fortunate to have five full-time young adult specialists on staff, and we use discussions about program planning to bounce ideas off one another and to hone our ideas. We do most of our own programming, and we can really stretch our budget that way. In our department, we have staff members who can use their experience and education to help teens in their own artistic and theatrical endeavors.

Martha Mikkleson, the librarian who founded and runs PML Players, has training and experience in vocal and instrumental music, in dramatic and theatrical performance, and in graphic and fine arts. In many PML Players productions, especially in the summer and in those productions featuring vocal performance, Martha has able assistance in Jennifer Quirk, a part-time librarian. Jen has studied voice and vocal pedagogy and has performed as a soprano in two choirs. Assistance on set design and creation is provided by several of our very talented pages, who are willing to help paint and build whenever necessary. We have a new part-time librarian, who teaches dance. We look forward to her involvement in upcoming programs.

We have, over the past few years, had additional assistance from local college students. For two summers, we hired a student of vocal performance and conducting to lead the PML Players musicians' summer workshops. Digital video workshops have been led by a graduate of Patchogue-Medford High School who is currently studying video production at Five Towns College.

ABOUT THE COMMUNITY

The Patchogue-Medford Library is a school-district public library chartered by New York State in 1900 and is the New York State–designated central library for Suffolk County. The library is a 2010 winner of the National Medal for Museum and Library Service. In 2007, there were 408 programs for adults, 315 programs for young adults, and 760 programs for children, with a total annual program attendance of 30,020. More than 600,000 people enter the library annually to use its resources.

As a community resource, providing and supporting the educational, cultural, and recreational needs of the community is part of the Patchogue-Medford Library's mission. The PML Players program has been running continuously since 2005 with the support of the library administration and board of trustees. Funding for the PML Players is taken from the library's programming budget. Additional funding has been requested and obtained from the Friends of the Patchogue-Medford Library. The PML Player program activities have involved partnerships with high school teachers, a music store located next to the library, and the Patchogue-Medford Library's Children's and Parents' Services Departments. The Patchogue-Medford Library has also partnered with another local library to prepare and perform larger projects.

MARKETING AND COMMUNITY RESPONSE

The PML Players is marketed to our community year-round. It is publicized in the library newsletter, which is printed every two months and is mailed to everyone in our service district. Flyers and posters for upcoming auditions, programs, and events are put in the Young Adult Department so the teens can be aware of what is coming up. Flyers are also sent to the schools and are brought to any school meetings we attend with parents and teachers. We talk about the program when we visit the middle schools (there are three in our district) to talk about summer-reading programs. Word of mouth is probably our most effective marketing tool. The teens and families who have good experiences with the program publicize it for us by telling their friends.

Community feedback about PML Players and their performances has been very positive. Following the productions, feedback is requested from the participants, audiences, families, library staff, and the community. Exit interviews and wrap-up meetings have been the main methods of collecting feedback. The evaluations and responses have always been very encouraging. The teens are extremely appreciative of the recognition received.

We look forward to many more years of successful productions, providing enriching and educational experiences for teens and their families.

Part IV
Mixed Arts

CHAPTER 11

ART: Art Revolution for Teens

**HEATHER PIPPIN ZABRISKIE, NATALIE HOUSTON,
AND VERA GUBNITSKAIA**

The Orange County Library System's (OCLS) fifteen locations are spread over a thousand-square-mile area serving an urban population of more than one million residents. Our community is diverse in age, ethnic background, interests, and educational level. As Orlando's artistic community has grown, the city has taken steps to develop and promote the arts. It became necessary to create a unified agency focused on the arts, and the Orange County Arts Council was created in 2007 to respond to that need.

Several years ago, to emphasize its commitment to the artistic and cultural development of our community, the Orange County government conducted a study titled "The Status Review of Arts Education in Orange County." The status review assessed "the depth and breadth of arts education, both visual and performing arts, offered to all segments of the population." Announcing the study, the county chairman stressed "the profound impact of arts education on the learning ability of school children . . . [and that] education and participation in the visual arts, drama, dance, and music measurably improves children's readiness and ability to learn."[1]

Findings were compiled in an extensive final report.[2] Many successes were noted and analyzed, such as the fact that four art forms—music, visual arts, drama, and dance—were taught at schools. Some students were receiving instruction in more than one art form. More than 85 percent of students were involved in art education.

The study also identified several areas of concern:

- The majority of students participating in art classes were in elementary school.
- The number of students who received art instruction at public schools dropped significantly at the middle school level and dropped even further at the high school level.
- Not all forms of art were taught at every district public school.
- The shortage of qualified teachers at district public schools negatively affected chances to successfully implement art instruction. The student-to-teacher ratio decreased from 1:622 in music to 1:7,636 in dance. It was agreed that Orange County students do not receive art education on a nationally accepted level given the high student-to-teacher ratio.
- Not every student at every school had equal access to arts instruction. The report compared an elementary school that had 342 students with another one that had 1,251 students. Each of the schools had the same number of art teachers, meaning that the student-to-teacher ratio in the first school was nearly four times better than in the second school.
- Each school made its own decisions about time and staff available for art instruction.
- Schools generally had limited space for theatre and dance instruction.
- Of the schools that participated in the survey, 73 percent indicated that planning, preparation, and implementation of the Florida Comprehensive Assessment Test adversely affected art education. They stated that the need to increase time on remedial courses and tutoring caused the decline in the enrollment in art classes. Many art teachers started incorporating test-preparation content in the art class curricula.

The Florida Department of Education's requirements for graduation indicate the somewhat low priority that art instruction receives in public schools. To graduate with a standard twenty-four-credit diploma (a four-year diploma), a high school student is required to have one credit in fine or performing arts, speech, debate, or specified practical arts. There are no requirements to have a similar credit for three-year, eighteen-credit college-preparation program or three-year, eighteen-credit career-preparation program.[3]

As funding for public schools decreased, art programs became the first ones eliminated from the school curricula. Art teachers were among the first to be laid off or transferred to other teaching assignments. The Orange

County Library System staff perceived the need to tie the vibrant art scene with the teen community. Teens may not have means, or often not enough knowledge, to develop the curiosity necessary to become interested in art, understand its value, and become involved. These are the same teens who are enrolled in public schools without enough funding or incentives to develop a meaningful art program. Art nurtures teens' natural needs to experiment with ideas and identity. The availability of after-school programs reduces the incidents of teens engaging in harmful activities. Additionally, these programs support teens' social development through interaction with adults and other teens in a meaningful after-school environment.

PROJECT GOALS AND OBJECTIVES

The goal of the ART: Art Revolution for Teens program series is to enrich the lives of the Orange County teen population by igniting interests in the arts as a way to create lifelong learners. To achieve this goal, we focus on four specific objectives:

1. Implement arts workshops that are attractive to teens.
2. Utilize the programming to supplement what is missing from public education in Orange County.
3. Supplement each workshop with relevant library materials to expand the learning experience.
4. Establish ownership by giving teens opportunities to shape library programming.

PROJECT FUNDING

Money can often be a stumbling block when a library wants to develop programming for teens. We started with identifying a source of funding that would financially support our ideas. When we found the Hot Topic Foundation, it looked like a perfect match for our goals. According to the foundation's official statement, "music and the arts make everyone's life a whole lot better, so we've decided to enrich kids' lives by enabling them to express themselves musically and artistically!" The foundation's goal is to "support programs and organizations that specifically focus on encouraging and educating youth in music, creative writing, painting, photography, film-making and more."[4] We applied for a grant and received the money, and that is how ART: Art Revolution for Teens was born.

Later in the project we also applied for Disney's Helping Kids Shine grant and received additional funding that allowed us to spread teen art programs to more library locations over a longer period of time. Most recently, a local private family foundation funded Art & Sole, a teen art workshop series that focused on recycling old shoes and other reusable objects into art projects.

PROJECT BUDGET

We received a grant from the Hot Topic Foundation for $13,750 and from Disney's Helping Kids Shine for $5,000. We matched the funding with $10,100 in in-kind contributions for staff time and benefits, promotional materials, and additional materials needed to conduct the workshops:

Hot Topic Foundation grant	$13,750
Disney's Helping Kids Shine grant	$ 5,000
Library in-kind contributions	$10,100
Total funding	$28,850

The grant dollars paid for presenter fees, supplies for the workshops, and materials and instructions for teens to take home after each workshop.

MARKETING

Our graphic designer created an edgy logo and postcards that were sent to all middle and high schools; distributed at every library location; and shared with community partners such as YMCA, Boys and Girls Club, Orange County Families, Parks and Recreation's program called the Club, and other organizations. As part of the ART initiative, we invited Orange County Public Schools, youth organizations, foster homes, group homes for youth, and alternative schools to attend the workshops.

The OCLS uses a variety of social media outlets to market programs and contests, recognize sponsors, and provide teens with opportunities to select contest winners. We advertise on Facebook and Twitter, via RSS feeds, and on our Informed Teens website. This benefits the entire community by breaking down geographic barriers and expanding opportunities for teens and community members to participate.

The ART logo, created in-house by the OCLS's graphic designer

PROGRAMMING

We want to expose teens to new art forms and give them the tools they need to sustain interest in those arts. The programming for ART: Art Revolution for Teens focuses on three main areas: performing, visual, and creative arts. Programming includes workshops, contests, and other scheduled activities that involve teen participation. Each workshop is designed to give teens a chance to practice a specific art form during the session and to continue the practice at home.

PERFORMING ARTS

Involvement in the performing arts helps improve self-image and self-control, and it builds teamwork. As part of ART, we have invited local improv and theater groups to host teen workshops designed to build teamwork, develop confidence, and public speaking skills.

Dance programs featuring a range of styles and cultural traditions have been an integral part of the ART program series. They continue to be requested by our active after-school crowd of teens and tweens.

Numerous community dance groups have presented teen workshops, including the following:

- Orlando School of Cultural Dance (African dance)
- Salsa Heat Dance Studio
- Voci Dance (modern dance)
- Yow Dance (modern dance, flamenco, and ballet)
- Orlando Zumba
- Kalena's Polynesian 'Ohana
- A Magi Temple (belly dancing)

We also host events and contests to promote the performing arts. Each year we hold a teen talent show that attracts diverse talents, such as singing, piano playing, dancing, and martial arts. In addition to inviting local performers from the community to participate as judges, we try to include a teen on our judges' panel.

TEEN BATTLE OF THE BANDS

Our most popular teen event is the annual teen battle of the bands, now in its eighth year. Each year, more than three hundred teens, parents, and fans are attracted to this event. At the beginning of summer, we audition local teen bands to perform. The battle of the bands is hosted each June and serves as the kickoff to our teen summer-reading program. We partner with local businesses and music organizations to provide judges for the competition and prizes for the winning bands. For the past two years OrlandoBands.com streamed the event live for those who could not attend in person.

Sean Kantrowitz from Park Avenue CDs has served as a judge for three years. He says, "I think that the teens benefit greatly from this kind of program. Since most venues [and] clubs are catered more towards an [eighteen and older] crowd, being able to perform in a library where their friends and family can attend is a great opportunity. It's also great for them to be able to cut their teeth in the world of performing live and to get a taste of what their peers are doing as well."

The Orange County business community has donated prizes to reward participating bands, such as:

- Recording sessions
- Photo shoots
- Band posters from a local print shop
- Gift certificates to music stores
- Concerts at local venues

VISUAL ARTS

In this highly visual age, teens need to learn to interpret the images they see around them. Through our programming, OCLS actively engages teens in creating and interpreting visual art. Workshops have focused on Japanese calligraphy, Matisse's painting-with-scissors technique, and working with a variety of painting mediums.

In addition to programming, we host at least three yearly contests to promote visual arts: a teen art contest, teen photo contest, and the *animanga* reality-art contest. We partner with local art schools, public schools, community centers, and local teen hangouts to promote the contests. We reach out to local art-supply stores, comic stores, and other businesses to participate on judges' panels and provide prizes for our finalists. We upload submissions to Facebook and ask teens to select their fan favorites. This allows our Facebook community to participate in the judging process. Winning pieces from each contest are featured on our Informed Teens website and highlighted via social media outlets, and some are included on art contest materials for the following year.

The teen art contest and art show are held each spring. We invite an artist from a local art school to be involved in judging the entries. At the conclusion of the contest, we host an art show and awards ceremony. We invite one or more teen musicians to play piano or acoustic guitar at the event, thereby promoting creative arts. All contest entries are displayed at our main library for a month to give the community a chance to appreciate local teen art.

Each summer, in conjunction with the teen summer-reading program, we host a teen photo contest. We ask teens to give us insight into their world by snapping a photo and submitting it online or in print. This contest gives teens the chance to express themselves and gives the world a glimpse into their lives.

The *animanga* reality-art contest is held in conjunction with our annual program Animanga Mini-Con and sponsored by our *animanga* club. This art contest asks teens to think outside of reality and create a fantastical character or share a story through comic panels. The entries are judged on artistic ability, creativity, and originality. The OCLS holds an annual cosplay (costume play) contest at the Animanga Mini-Con, where teens who have created their own costumes dress up as their favorite characters from anime and manga. Winners are selected on the basis of the quality of their costumes and on crowd response.

CREATIVE ARTS

Creative arts span a broad scope of art forms, from culinary and musical arts to poetry, *graffiti,* magic, martial arts, and balloon twisting. Creative arts programming at OCLS reflects this diverse range of artistic expression.

Music workshops can often be heard throughout the library building and draw a large crowd of teens as well as younger kids and adult onlookers. Professionals in the community have hosted drumming, *deejaying,* didgeridoo, and guitar workshops at our libraries. Many teens have not had the opportunity to experience playing a stand-up bass, a violin, or an electric guitar. A local music school brought strings and percussions to the library to give teens an opportunity to touch, play, and learn about the instruments. The didgeridoo workshop introduced teens to this native aboriginal Australian instrument and gave them the opportunity to make and decorate their own instruments. The instructor demonstrated that though didgeridoos can be pricey, it is possible to pursue this art form inexpensively.

Dance workshops fit into both the performing and creative categories of art. The OCLS has invited local high school step teams and a duo of break-dancers into the library to share their styles with teens and get their bodies moving to the beat. Stepping is a kind of percussive dance in which the body is used to make rhythm and beats primarily using footwork with some hand claps. Usually a team of dancers performs stepping, with a team member leading the group through the routine by calling out commands and instigating dance sequences. Team members often create their own routines, develop new moves, and create their own stylized forms of stepping. Teen boys respond well to this stylized form of dance as well as to the more free-flowing style of break dancing.

CULINARY ARTS

Chefs from a local culinary institute and bakery have hosted two of our best-attended teen workshops. These events allowed teens to get creative with food by learning basic techniques for making molded chocolate candies and for decorating cupcakes. Although culinary workshops can seem daunting and messy, they can be successful teen programs if kept simple and focused on one technique per session.

LITERARY ARTS

In honor of National Poetry Month, each April OCLS hosts a teen poetry contest and open-mic night. Teens are asked to submit poetry, prose, raps, limericks, haikus, or any other form of poetry. Winners are invited to read

Products of the OCLS graffiti workshop

their works at the annual Java Lounge, our teen open-mic night. Teen open-mic night is a popular event full of poetry, music, and comedy.

TEEN LIBRARY CORPS

The library has an award-winning teen volunteer program, the Teen Library Corps (TLC), which encourages teens to give back a little TLC to their library and community. The ART series provides opportunities for teen volunteers to assist with programming. Teens supply the library with suggestions for workshop topics. Volunteers also serve as a street team by taking promotional materials to their schools and telling their classmates about upcoming events. In addition, volunteers have created a variety of audio and visual materials:

- Writing and recording podcasts to promote the library
- Storyboarding their ideas, acting, filming, and editing a documentary about being a teen volunteer
- Creating promotional videos for the summer-reading program

A local deejay presents an OCLS workshop

BENEFIT TO COMMUNITY

Providing teens with after-school art-based activities is a highly valued benefit that the library offers to the community. By making connections with local art directors, choreographers, designers, musicians, dancers, artists, and art organizations, the library has become more recognizable as a venue for artistic and cultural programs. Viewing and interpreting teens' artwork collectively builds a sense of community among involved parents, teachers, and other adults.

Our teen art contests allow us to further establish connections with community artists and businesses. Several local businesses sponsor our teen contests and events by donating prizes for our participants. For example, we invite local musicians and performers to judge our annual teen talent show and artists to judge our annual teen art show. Local studios that offer art and dance classes can promote their classes to teens and parents. They pass out coupons for discounts or a free class to bring parents and teens through their doors.

Teens directly benefit on several levels. They are exposed to new art forms and taught life skills that are often not developed in traditional coursework. Participation in the arts promotes self-respect and a positive self-image. Teens who feel that their contributions are important are more likely to become civically engaged. This fulfills one of the library's goals to help create well-rounded, informed community members.

PROGRAM EVALUATION

We have used a youth program survey that asks teens whether they would recommend the program they just attended to a friend. Peer recommendations are especially important for the teen demographic. We can evaluate our success on the basis of teens' responses to this question. In the surveys teens also tell us what kinds of art they would like to learn about, which helps us plan for future programs.

The most frequently used measure of success of library programming is overall attendance. The average program attendance for art workshops is higher than at our regular teen programming. Over a three-year period from January 2008 through January 2011

- We hosted 39 teen art workshops
- 1,163 attendees participated in library art workshops
- 29 participants on average attended each program

In 2009, we surveyed more than one hundred attendees of the teen battle of the bands to assess its value to the library and our community. We discovered that the event is effective at attracting first-time library program attendees, reaching a broad range of the teens, and creating a strong opportunity to promote future library programs. Survey results concluded the following:

- 42 percent of respondents were attending a library program for the first time.
- 77 percent of respondents said that they were likely to attend another library event that summer.
- 57 percent of respondents had an Orange County Library card.
- Twelve of nineteen local public high schools had at least one student attending.
- Attendees came from twenty-nine different local schools, including middle schools, high schools, community colleges, universities, and schools out of our district

Although the majority of attendees had an Orange County Library card, this was an opportunity to distribute library-card applications and register new customers. Our survey results certainly support the idea promoted by the National Art Education Association that "the arts have a great capacity to engage many students who otherwise would be alienated."[5]

PROGRAM LONGEVITY

The initial ART: Art Revolution for Teens grant application to the Hot Topic Foundation was written to cover one year of programming. However, with careful planning and spending, we stretched the grant funding over three years. One reason the funding covered a larger span of time is because of the positive response from local artists. Many artists reduced their regular fees to aid us in bringing this innovative series of programming to local youth, which allowed us to continue hosting workshops and bringing additional art forms and artists into the library. The program continues to receive donations of time and services from supportive community members and businesses.

PLANNING FOR THE FUTURE

We continue looking for additional funding opportunities from organizations whose missions match the goals of the ART: Art Revolution for Teens program. We have a steady track record of successfully engaging teens in meaningful art activities in the library, and interest in art programs remains strong among this age group.

ADDITIONAL MATERIALS

Videos and photos from many programs discussed in this article are available online. This includes highlights from the teen battle of the bands over the years, the Teen Library Corps documentary, and footage of ART workshops:

- Orange County Library System, Informed Teens website: www.ocls.info/teens
- OCLS YouTube: www.youtube.com/oclsvideos
- Facebook: www.ocls.info/clubcentralfb

Notes

1. *Status Review of Arts Education in Orange County Final Report*, February 2004, www.orangecountyfl.net/Portals/0/resource%20library/open%20government/Arts%20Education%20Status%20Review.pdf.
2. Ibid.
3. *Florida's Guide to Public High School Graduation for Students Entering Ninth Grade in 2010–2011*, 2011, www.fldoe.org/BII/StudentPro/pdf/HSbrochure.pdf.
4. Hot Topic Foundation, 2011, http://community.hottopic.com/content/ht-foundation.
5. *Learning in a Visual Age: The Critical Importance of Visual Arts Education*, 2009, www.arteducators.org/learning/learning-in-a-visual-age/NAEA_LVA_09.pdf.

CHAPTER 12

Children in a Research Library?

Creative Projects for K–12 Students at the Rakow Research Library of the Corning Museum of Glass

REGAN BRUMAGEN AND BETH HYLEN

"DID HE HAVE A RECIPE FOR PINK GLASS?" asked an excited third grader, peering at a tiny handwritten nineteenth-century batch book. The unknown factory worker did not keep a pink glass formula in his pocket; instead, we found recipes for green, black, and lead glass. Helping students glimpse the past and learn about local glass art and history is essential to our outreach program at the Rakow Research Library of the Corning Museum of Glass, located in Corning, New York. Seeing these artifacts from past eras firsthand makes the study of history accessible and engaging to even the youngest school-age child.

THE RAKOW RESEARCH LIBRARY AND OUR K–12 OUTREACH PROGRAM

Since our opening in 1951, the library has had a strong public services component, but we have since taken on a more active role to reach out to potential audiences. In 2005, the museum hired an outreach librarian and established a three-year outreach plan that balances achievable objectives with flexibility in planning. The plan's purpose is "to participate fully in the Museum's mission to educate the world about glass and to enhance the local and international reputation of the Library as the foremost library in the world on the art, history, and early technology of glass." All six members of the public services team participate in outreach activities and planning. From 2004 to 2010, the library has quadrupled the number of group visitors, with some years increasing by more than 75 percent.

With collections ranging from medieval manuscripts to exhibit catalogs of contemporary glass artists, we cover fine arts, decorative arts, design, history, and science and technology, and our materials include publications in more than forty languages. Browsing through our stacks, one can find anything from glass you take for granted (lightbulbs, windshields, or wine glasses) to the unexpected (musical scores for glass harmonicas, postage stamps, or life-size stained-glass drawings for windows). Our extensive collection of design drawings by artists such as Tiffany, Lalique, the Blaschkas, twentieth-century Czech designers, and Frederick Carder, as well as archival materials, provide a wealth of primary documents to employ in our outreach programs.

Library exhibitions constitute a portion of our K–12 programming. We may install a small exhibit of materials for the day or focus on the current year's formal exhibition during a group's visit. Library exhibits are planned to include educational components that can be used with groups of all ages.

Our outreach efforts are geared to attract primary and secondary school students. Thousands of students in grades K–12 visit the museum each year during school outings. In past years, the library was not a regular stop for most of those groups, since its collections were viewed as too scholarly for children and teens. One of our goals has been to expand our instruction and outreach to these groups through a stronger partnership with the museum's Education Department.

To this end, library staff began developing more activities that correspond to the New York State curriculum standards, focusing on unique and compelling primary sources in the collection. For example, students have variously analyzed the patent "Preserving the Dead in Glass," discussed working conditions for children in glass factories after studying Lewis Hine photographs from the early twentieth century, and solved math problems based on invoices for glassware and other historical glass-factory records.

To reach the K–12 student population, libraries must make their programs relevant to the school districts' curricula, so we work closely with the Corning Museum of Glass Education Department and the school systems to tailor our presentations to the individual needs of the students. If students are studying chemistry, we may focus on the physical properties of glassmaking or its alchemical history. If students are studying ancient civilizations, we might talk about the origins of glassmaking or its early importance as a traded commodity.

It has taken time and effort to market our library as an educational partner for the K–12 population. We have found that promoting our successful programs and partnerships to our own Education Department and to the school

---

Guidelines to Keep in Mind

- Seek out and find partners with connections to the schools, who know the curricular needs of the district (e.g., education departments in museums and academic institutions; children's librarians in public libraries; school librarians, teachers, and curriculum directors; local arts organizations).
- Make your program fit local curricular standards.
- Customize presentations for your audience.
- Make the activity interactive.
- Market your successful programs.

---

districts has created the greatest dividends. We have worked with the museum's Public Relations and Marketing Department to publicize innovative K–12 programming via public announcements on local television and radio stations, stories in the local newspaper, and articles in the school district newsletter. Library programs are promoted at the semiannual Evening for Educators, a continuing education workshop the museum offers to area teachers.

EXAMPLES

The following are examples of recent K–12 programs.

Corning–Painted Post School System—Third Graders

Beginning in 2008, the library became an integral part of a new museum program for all third grades in the local school district. The program focuses on Frederick Carder, an internationally known glass designer, who worked in Corning's glass industry from 1903 to 1963. Students visit the Carder Gallery to study glass designed by Carder; the hot glass studio, where they see glassmaking techniques used to make his glass objects; and the library, where they see Carder's original design drawings and notebooks as well as a nineteenth-century pictorial map of Corning. The map has been reproduced in puzzle form, and the children assemble it as they talk about what made Corning a good choice for glassmaking industries in the nineteenth century. They are thrilled to see rare books from our collection and children's books on glass, and to participate in a glass-themed matching game, which asks them to identify unusual objects made of glass. In its first year, more than 750 children participated in the program.

Students are quick to catch the connection between the designs Carder was sketching in his notebooks (many of them scrawled haphazardly across the pages) to the glassware they view in the Carder Gallery. We also ask them to find buildings and streets on the 1882 map that are still in existence today, as well as to locate current landmarks on the map. They are amazed to see pastures where the museum and the local YMCA stand today.

Corning–Painted Post School System—Fifth Graders

In 2010–2011, all fifth graders in the school district visited the library to see our latest exhibit on telescope history and the "Glass Giant of Palomar," the Hale Telescope, which uses a two-hundred-inch mirror built locally by Corning Glass Works. The exhibit is on multiple levels and includes memorabilia on the Hale Telescope from the 1930s and 1940s, images of telescopes from our rare-book collection, and large-scale photographs of the mirror being created in 1934 and images of space taken by the Hale Telescope. The library produced a series of trading cards on the telescope that each student receives on the tour. The fifth-grade classes view letters written in the 1930s by schoolchildren across the country who have inquired about the mirror, pictures of the giant ladles filled with molten glass being poured into the massive mold, and a map of the train route that the disk took on its journey to Mount Palomar.

They also view photographs of downtown Corning from the 1930s to the 1950s, and we use the photographs to talk about changes that have occurred in the topography of downtown, as well as the cultural and social climate of the period. This tour was designed to enhance students' visual literacy skills through interpretation and discussion of the images on display.

Charter School of Technology

A regional high school group also visited the library to view the telescope exhibit. Because of the older age of the students, the library refocused the program to highlight the history of telescope making and the scientific importance of the Hale Telescope and other giant telescopes of the era.

With larger groups of forty-five students apiece, finding an engaging activity to introduce them to the exhibit was challenging. We decided on a presentation that incorporated audio, video, and still images to orient them to the story behind the construction of the giant telescope, followed by giving them time to browse through the exhibit with knowledgeable guides.

School of the Deaf

A high school class from the School of the Deaf visited the museum to see our exhibit "Harvard's Glass Flowers" by the nineteenth-century lampworkers

Rudolph and Leopold Blaschka. The library exhibit of the Blaschkas' archives included their design drawings for the glass sea creatures that predated the flowers, as well as letters and business correspondence of the Blaschkas.

In collaboration with the museum's Education Department, the library developed an activity in which students could compare how a scientist, a designer in industry, and an artist might use drawings on paper to develop three-dimensional artworks.

We asked the students to think about the creative process as we showed them examples of the Blaschkas' sea creatures, design blueprints from the Steuben Glass factory, mid-twentieth-century Czech glass artists designs and full-size cartoons, and design sketches by a local glass artist.

Using a signer to help us communicate with the students, we encouraged the students to talk about what they were seeing and how they understood the design process. Afterward, the students drew their own designs for glass. One drawing was chosen for the museum's You Design It, We Make It program at the Hot Glass Show. Gaffers made the piece while the students watched them work.

Glass Detectives

Our focus in instruction has been to find interactive ways to help students garner research skills. With this in mind, we created the Glass Detectives game in which students examine personal artifacts from cut-glass maker Samuel Hawkes and answer a series of questions about him. Students are supplied with magnifying glasses to examine small print on documents and artifacts, such as Hawkes's wallet, checkbooks, and tobacco pipe. They wear archival gloves to handle materials safely and to learn something about the care and preservation of paper-based archives.

In this activity, students had the experience of discovering facts about an individual from a different period through the study of his personal papers and artifacts, thus allowing them to use authentic methods of historical research in a manageable time frame.

Bookmaking—Sixth Graders

Our educational programs focus on glass art or history, or just explore the purpose, activities, and processes of a research library. Approximately two hundred sixth-grade students have traveled to the museum during each of the past several years to visit exhibits and participate in a make-your-own-book activity with library staff. They see rare manuscripts and incunabula, learn a little about the history of printing, and then construct a book from simple construction paper and yarn. The teachers ask them to decorate the books with drawings and text describing their visit to the museum.

In this activity, the students' writing satisfied a language-arts component of the school's curriculum and helped students reflect on what they saw and learned during the day. They were also able to share their books with parents, another valued educational practice.

Paper Arts

The Rakow Library was awarded a community grant (Community Foundation of Elmira-Corning and the Southern Finger Lakes) to hire a local artist to develop and teach a paper arts class for children and adults.

The artist led the two-hour class using traditional paper-cutting techniques and projects appropriate for all ages. Advanced planning was necessary to set our goals, select a local artist, and apply for the grant.

This program was part of a larger celebration of National Library Week planned collaboratively with our staff and with public and community college librarians. Each library developed programming independently and participated in a joint kickoff attended by the state librarian, the mayor, and members of the community.

Design Drawings

A new program will be initiated this spring, partnering with 171 Cedar Arts Center, our regional arts center. A local artist who has expertise in botanical drawings will teach Design Drawing at the Rakow for four Thursday

Hammondsport sixth grade students examine artifacts from the Samuel Hawkes archive at the Rakow Research Library. *Photo courtesy of the Corning Museum of Glass.*

afternoons in the spring. The age group ranges from fifteen years old to adult, so high school students are eligible to participate.

The Rakow Library has an extensive collection of design drawings by artists such as Tiffany, Lalique, the Blaschkas (who created of the Harvard Glass Flowers), and twentieth-century Czech designers and Marinot, among others. These are working drawings that may have functioned as a conduit between the artist's conceptual ideas and the artisans who made the finished piece. Now these historical drawings will serve as inspiration for other artists.

The course description states: "In this four week course we will recreate the process historic glass artists have used, from sketching objects found in nature, like the Blaschkas did, to designing our own forms using conventional drawing techniques. This class will view original drawings from the Rakow archives and will have the opportunity to draw within the Museum galleries. Instruction not limited to glass artists or specifically for glass application."

Partnering with 171 Cedar allows us to offer programs without the burden of administrative tasks. The arts center offers and administers the class: it negotiates with and hires the teacher; markets the class; and collects the fees, all within its well-established system. We provide the inspiration and will work with the teacher to provide content. To protect the original artwork, the drawings will be viewed with the librarian's assistance in the first hour. They will be put away when drawing materials come out! When it is useful, the teacher can continue to refer to our drawings as digitized images in PowerPoint format.

We hope to expand the program in the near future both to offer similar classes taught by other local artists who may interpret the design drawing collection in new ways and to adapt the program for the school system, helping art teachers incorporate design drawing into their classroom instruction.

Stories from the Crystal City

One of our most intensive school-age projects was funded by a Save Our History grant from the History Channel. The grant allowed us to work with the High School Learning Center at Corning Community College, an alternative high school for at-risk students, to produce a documentary and an exhibit about Corning's rich glass heritage. "Stories from the Crystal City" was one of twenty-seven Save Our History grants given nationwide, intended to inspire and motivate communities to actively preserve their past.

Thirty-five students, three teachers, and numerous volunteers participated in the yearlong project during which students interviewed twelve community members with connections to the Corning glass industry during the post–World War II era.

In the process, the students learned about the importance of historical preservation, as well as various ways of studying history. They learned about oral-history collection, research using primary and secondary sources, interviewing methods, camera operation, and film editing. Their teachers designed units in history, math, and English to provide background material for the project, and every part of the curriculum for the year included a component relating to the grant.

Finally, students planned a public reception and exhibition for the community, during which the documentary was premiered and members of the community were invited to see the results of the students' research and labor. The interviews, the documentary, and the exhibition materials are preserved in our library. The documentary is available on the museum's website.

In organizing the reception, students worked with members of the museum's Event Planning and Marketing and Public Relations departments. Students selected a menu, on the basis of their catering budget; designed the invitations; and selected photographs for the exhibit. They also developed lists of community members who received mailed invitations, although the reception was widely publicized and open to all members of the public.

"Stories from the Crystal City" not only provided a pilot for future oral-history projects but also helped the museum and library engage in an in-depth project with students who had the chance to develop new skills and make connections with their local history and, in particular, with members of a different generation.

The grant-funded project also created unique collaborations and partnerships in the community: local glassmakers, photographers, videographers, newspaper reporters, and library and museum staff all provided formal, specialized training.

EDUCATIONAL METHODS

Research Activities

Activities that correspond to the New York State school curriculum include these samples:

Analyze patents using the 1903 patent "Preserving the Dead in Glass."
Use original glasshouse money (money glassmaking facilities issued before 1861 to pay their workers or pay off their debts) for solving math problems.
Compute the current value of children's wages in a 1910 glass factory using statistics found in a US Bureau of Labor Report on the

condition of woman and child wage earners in the United States, from 1910 to 1913.

Calculate shipping costs for sending the Blaschkas' Glass Flowers from Dresden to Boston using original shipping invoices.

Games

Using games engages visitors. It is fun to create questions to challenge a variety of groups with our trivia game. We have developed trivia games for high school chemistry classes to sixth graders studying ancient civilizations.

Trivia: Our *Jeopardy*-style quiz game was developed in PowerPoint. We plan to build a new version using Prezi. We use lively or humorous images on each screen to further engage the students.

Match game: We print images on looseleaf paper, laminate them, and attach the sheets to a felt board with Velcro strips. Students match an object with the appropriate name, for example, "glass fly trap" or "glass knitting needles."

Puzzle: We reproduced an 1882 map of Corning surrounded by illustrations of landmarks (56 × 74 cm), mounted the copies on foam board, and cut them into pieces. Students work in small groups of five or six to assemble the puzzle.

Glass detectives: This is a scavenger hunt–type activity in which students answer a series of questions to solve the research mystery. We provide materials and questions and clues for the students to answer. For example, "Solve the clues below to fill in the missing word in this phrase: Glass is __ __ __ __ __ __," or "Put on the white archival gloves and lift the Plexiglas from the items displayed. This wallet, pipe and toothbrush belonged to a famous Corning cut-glass maker. Using the clues in his wallet, find his weight. Enter his weight here: ____ _____ _____. Copy the highlighted number into Clue No. 4 above." For younger groups, questions may be based on clues found in our reference books. We often lead children from one resource to another with paper footprints placed on the floor.

Language guessing game: "Library Puzzles Guaranteed to Make Your Eyes Glassy" lists terms that mean "glass" in a variety of languages. Students select the multiple-choice answer, for example, is üveg Kurdish, Hungarian, or Serbo-Croatian?

Bookmaking: Using photocopy paper for pages and brightly colored heavier stock for covers, we cut the paper in half and fold it into 4 ¼ × 5 ½-inch pages. Punch two holes in the spine, thread narrow ribbon, string, or yarn through the holes, and tie a bow. Students decorate the covers with tissue paper, colored markers, photocopied images of glass, sequins, and other materials.

Bookmarks: Students create bookmarks with brightly colored and patterned papers, sturdy paper for backing, scissors (in a variety of sizes), and glue sticks. We also provided additional decorative elements (e.g., ribbon, lace). A local artist taught paper-cutting techniques.

Trading cards: We created trading cards from themed images—our latest cards featured the Palomar exhibit—with brief text, sized to 2 ½ × 3 ½ inches, laminated and cut (guillotined) to create a set of six different cards. Ours were designed by the museum's Communications Department and produced professionally. Handmade trading cards can be equally effective and produced inexpensively. We give the cards to groups touring the exhibit at the library.

CONCLUSION

The Corning Museum of Glass has a strong commitment to educational programming. The library's outreach programs help us fulfill the museum's mission: "To tell the world about glass by engaging, educating, and inspiring visitors and the community through the art, history, and science of glass."

Bringing children into a research library has many rewards:

- Our programs enrich the school curriculum.
- We provide content and resources to support the museum's educational programs.
- Our partners inside and outside the museum help us connect with the K–12 community.
- We strengthen the community of Rakow Library users through expanded programming.
- Bringing children and their teachers and parents into the library helps us reach a new generation of potential users.
- The library gains greater visibility in the general community.
- The library reaches greater numbers of people, which helps us remain economically viable.
- The techniques we use with children can be adapted for adult visitors, including Road Scholar programs, college students, and tour groups.
- It is fun! Bringing young people into the research library enlivens our team and promotes creativity.

CHAPTER 13

Gilpin County Public Library Arts Programs

LARRY GRIECO

SMALL, RURAL LIBRARIES do not need to be trailing when it comes to arts programming in the library. With the help of friends-of-the-library groups, along with some creative thinking, any library can offer programs to patrons of all ages that celebrate the arts in a variety of ways.

Gilpin County Public Library, which is located on the open highway about eight miles north of Black Hawk, Colorado, serves a mountain community of about six thousand people, most of whom live in various subdivisions throughout the county. The library is situated between the towns of Black Hawk and Central City and the tiny community of Rollinsville. Until a year ago, when a county shuttle route added the library as one of its stops, most people had to travel to the library by car, with just a comparative few living within walking distance. This reality of geography called for some creative outreach to let the community know what library services and programs are being offered and, of course, to attract new patrons.

The Friends of the Library was (and is) a hardworking group of people who care passionately about the library and its programs. They raise money with book and bake sales, the annual Barnes & Noble Book Night, and through membership dues and donations. A relationship of trust had to be established when the new director took over administration of the library. It is fair to say that a certain pessimism about the potential of library programming existed. Slowly, through some early programs and projects that met with success, the Friends began to trust the director's judgment. Once this partnership is established, which is symbiotic in nature, there is no telling what can be accomplished, and that's when the fun begins:

- We have had up to three five-part film series each year for the past eight years, with a noted film critic leading a discussion about each film.
- We are in our fourth year of having an artist-in-residence in the summer months (we've had a poet-in-residence, a visual-artist-in-residence, and a musician-in-residence already, and in the summer of 2011 we plan to have a theatrical-artist-in-residence.)
- We alternate twice a year between A Midsummer Night's Poetry Reading and A Midwinter Night's Poetry Reading with local poets (an anthology of selected poetry read at the Gilpin County Library, from 2000 to 2010, is in the works).

One of the first ideas that the library director had in relation to arts programming was to augment an ongoing program of showing work by local artists on the library's "art wall."

Since there was occasionally a period between artists' exhibits when the wall would be empty, the director thought to purchase a small collection of fine-art prints by a number of classical and a few well-known contemporary artists:

- A list of twenty-five prints was made, including the likes of van Gogh, Gauguin, Matisse, Picasso, Klee, Rivera, and Cassatt.
- Through a local gallery, an estimate was made for the purchase of the prints and for their framing, which came to $2,500. The director wrote a grant proposal to a local funding source and was turned down.
- The Friends of the Library stepped in and funded the project. For the past ten years, this set of prints has graced the art wall in the library on a number of occasions, usually between live artists' shows, and it always garners excitement and positive feedback from patrons. It was an early success that began to forge a partnership between the Friends of the Library and the director.

Another early success was an American Library Association–sponsored video viewing and discussion series called "Research Revolution," which called for viewing six films over a period of time, with discussions following each one, led by a scholar from the University of Colorado, Denver:

- The library was one of only fifty libraries in America to be selected for this program.
- Rising to the excitement of the occasion, the Friends of the Library group was so proud that it purchased a large-screen television with built-in VCR and DVD players, to better present the videos to our audience of participants. From that point on, the library was on its way to some innovative arts programming.

POETRY PROGRAMMING

The first of three ongoing programs to be presented here is the series of poetry readings that have developed over the years in an interesting way, with some unexpected and desirable results.

The library director asked the Friends to pay for a trip for him to attend the Poetry in the Branches institute, offered by Poets House in New York City. The Friends approved the request and the director attended the two-day workshop. He came back with ideas galore for poetry programming and activities in the library.

A series of poetry readings were offered, inviting local poets to come and read from their works, in a completely open-mic setting. A couple of times a year, the library became the venue for these poets. After several years, the director began featuring a notable poet from outside the area to headline the show. This new format presented a bunch of local poets reading with the featured outside poet, followed by a break and then open mic for anyone else who wanted to read something.

This format lasted for several years, until the library began to schedule a poetry reading once a year that coincided with the birthday of a 1960s poetry icon, the late Richard Brautigan. Brautigan was a poet, novelist, and story-writer who had a fiercely loyal following among flower children through the 1960s and 1970s. (Brautigan committed suicide in 1984.)

Several times the library honored Brautigan on the anniversary of his birthday with a party in which local poets read from their own and Brautigan's works, with an open-mic session rounding out the evening. The library was fortunate enough to find a CD that offered many of Brautigan's own poems and stories, which he read himself, and these were also featured in the celebrations of his life and poetry.

Over the past three years, the director has offered two poetry programs a year, six months apart: A Midsummer Night's Poetry Reading and A Midwinter Night's Poetry Reading.

Seven poets, who have formed the core of the regular poets at the library readings over the past ten years, are now featured in the publicity for each reading and form the first part of the evening's program. After a break for refreshments, we go to open mic for anyone else who has something they want to read.

Now the director is compiling work from these seven poets to include in a poetry anthology, to be self-published in the near future, called *Reality Is Not a Meatball: Ten Years of Poetry from the Gilpin County Public Library.* (The plan is to secure funding for the project, or short of that, to have the seven poets put up the money themselves for the initial publication.) The result of these readings and the potential publication of an anthology is to instill pride in the community in recognition of the literary talent we have right in our midst. Over a period of time, the library has gained a certain reputation for arts programming that is also a source of pride for the community. The cost of this ongoing arts programming over the past ten years has been a small amount of money for refreshments and, on a couple of occasions, honoraria (of about $100 each) for special guest poets from outside the local community.

FILM VIEWING AND DISCUSSION SERIES

After the initial success with the "Research Revolution" film series, the library director contacted the English Department of the University of Colorado, Denver, to seek out a film scholar who would come up to Gilpin County (about an hour's drive from Denver) to introduce, show, and discuss films with library audiences. A film historian at the university recommended an individual who was not on the faculty but who was an excellent film scholar and critic, and whose presentations in front of an audience were engaging, fun, educational, and full of movie-making tidbits and trivia. This was the beginning of an eight-year (and counting) partnership between Walter Chaw and the library.

If memory serves, Walter's first series theme at the library was film noir, which set the tone, standard, and format for a continuing program of film series, consisting of five films each, about three times a year, and running each time for five Saturday afternoons in a row. A number of attendees at the film series became regulars, and through word of mouth, the audience grew over the years.

Our themes have been wide and varied: early Hitchcock, westerns, ghost stories, foreign films, comedies, forgotten classics, forty years of movie musicals, romances, movie adaptations, and the real best movies, just to name a few.

A note on the scheduled day and time for the movies: it could be built into our collective subconscious that Saturday afternoons are ideally suited for movie watching. For many of a certain generation (yes, baby boomers) perhaps we remember as kids the habit of going to the show for Saturday matinees, the smell of the popcorn, maybe even how we'd leave the darkened movie theater to be blinded by the bright sunlight outside, and how that might have made an indelible impression on our minds, as valid as childhood itself. Maybe we're reliving those lost times when we attend Saturday-afternoon movies at the library. Ironically, many of the films selected for inclusion in the varied series themes are from the same era (the 1940s, 1950s, and 1960s) in which we were children.

The cost of this ongoing program is for the purchase price of the movies on DVD, which then are added to the collection anyway, and the average cost is about $20 per film. So with five films in a series, that's around $100. We began paying the film critic an honorarium of $100 for each film, so that's $500 for a five-part series. After a few years we raised it to $125 per film, so that became $625 for each series. Refreshments, usually popcorn and cookies, are a minimal expense.

The Friends of the Library has been ready, willing, and able to finance this program three times a year for the past eight years. Your library may choose to do something different. You may have a person on the staff or in the community who is a film buff and has the skills to facilitate a discussion following a film showing. The nearest college or university to you may have someone on the faculty who would be ideal as an expert and who could frame the series according to themes and talk about the movies in an engaging way. Someone may even do this for free or for less than what we are paying our scholar. You might also be able to get a small grant to pay for this, perhaps as a pilot program, and see how it goes. The community engagement can be enormous, and it is well worth the effort to make it happen in your library.

ARTIST-IN-RESIDENCE

We have hosted some very successful poetry readings with some notable guest poets who have shared their talent and work with an audience of poetry lovers, both writers and nonwriters alike. Also, our use of the art wall in the meeting room, as well as the display case in the lobby, has provided many opportunities over the years for the library community to view some outstanding exhibits by local artists and craftspeople. There are other forms of the arts (and humanities) that we still might tap into, such as theater and dance, if we had the right person around for a period of time to concentrate on his or her field of expertise and talent.

In 2008 we created the honorary position, outside of the library staff and exclusive of the county budget, of artist-in-residence at the Gilpin County Public Library. This is an award given once per year to an individual who is capable of offering to the public, during the months of June, July, and August, some insight into a particular artistic discipline through public programs, workshops, and other activities. We began with a poet-in-residence in 2008, and followed in 2009 with a visual-artist-in-residence and in 2010 with a musician-in-residence. The following guidelines, in general, apply to the artist-in-residence:

- The terms of the artist-in-residence are the months of June, July, and August.
- During those months the artist will engage in activities in the library to promote and further the public's appreciation of a particular art form.
- These activities might include, but not be limited to, the following: lectures, workshops, collection development (e.g., recommending titles on a particular art form to the library director for purchase and addition to the library collection), production of displays and other public relations strategies to promote the art form in the library, engagement in other activities that promote and celebrate the art form.
- The project, funded by the Friends of the Library, includes an honorarium of $1,000, plus expenses to implement the planned activities, not to exceed $500.

We advertise in the spring for an individual whose talents and accomplishments fit the theme of artist-in-residence for that particular year. Nominations (including self-nominations) are accepted and reviewed, along with letters of support and recommendation. These are considered by a five-member panel made up of the library director, two trustees, and two directors of the Friends of the Library, and finalists are then interviewed. The panel selects the winner by a majority vote. (The artist-in-residence must reside in Gilpin County.)

As noted above, the cost of this program, each summer, is $1,500. The Friends of the Library has committed to this as a long-term project, and each year's success adds to the group's excitement as well as its anticipation of what will happen the following year, as we go from artist to artist in the myriad possibilities that make up the broad range of artistic endeavors.

This program was the basis for the library winning the 2010 EBSCO Excellence in Small and/or Rural Public Library Service Award, given its uniqueness of service, the impact on our community, and the fact that the program is ongoing and has a positive effect on the future of the library and its community.

The EBSCO award is given annually by the American Library Association's (ALA) Public Library Association and EBSCO Information Services. The award recognizes a public library serving a population of ten thousand or fewer people that "demonstrates excellence of service to its community as exemplified by an overall service program or a special program of significant accomplishment" (www.ala.org/pla/awards/ebscoexcellencesmallrural award). Besides a plaque presented at the Public Library Association awards ceremony during the ALA's Annual Conference, a $1,000 honorarium is given to the winning library. Nominations (including self-nominations) are accepted in the fall of each year, with the winner determined by a committee that convenes at the ALA Midwinter Meeting.

PUBLICITY FOR ARTS PROGRAMMING

There are a number of successful avenues for publicity that we use at the library. Here are a few of the most effective ones:

- The library director writes a weekly column in both local newspapers, not only highlighting a few newly added circulating items but also discussing current and upcoming programs.
- On some occasions the library has partnered with a local newspaper to present a program or project, which results in free publicity and ongoing coverage of individual events, including interviews with key persons, such as authors, and plenty of photographs.
- Flyers at the circulation desk, and having staff point them out or hand them to patrons, is a good way to get the word out and build anticipation for programs.
- Our county newsletter, which is mailed to every household in the county, albeit only a few times a year, can sometimes be timely enough to publicize an event or program.
- A large sign in the front of the library is used to announce programs to people entering or leaving the parking lot, or even those driving by on the highway.
- The library website, as well as the county website, can be used to publicize events and programs.
- The library maintains an email list of past participants and sends out messages and announcements of future programs.
- As the library is small and rural, the library staff often personally invite individuals whom they know to like particular types of programming.

ONGOING NATURE OF PUBLIC PROGRAMMING

Just as the summer reading program for children in most public libraries is an annual occurrence, with a history of statistics and a future of hopes and dreams, public programming can also take on that sense of consistency from one year to the next. Our poetry programs have become semiannual, marking (roughly) the midsummer and midwinter dates on the calendar. The film series are three times a year, in the spring, fall, and winter. The artist-in-residence program is planned in the spring and presented in the summer. Presenting any one of these programs and allowing it to evolve and develop according to community interest and support raises the bar for public programming in any given community. As expectancy grows, and the library meets it satisfactorily, so does community pride in the library and all of its services. People begin to look from one summer to the next, from one film series to the next, and before you know it, a sense of tradition is established. That makes the library an integral part of life in the community, maybe even the focal point of culture.

CHAPTER 14

The Library as Canvas

Library Larry's Big Day

KEROL HARROD

DENTON IS A THRIVING North Texas arts community with no shortage of artists and citizens who value creativity and imagination. Painters, photographers, poets, and other artists have all taken advantage of our willingness to showcase art in the library. Denton Public Library sponsors contests that allow artists of all ages to compete and display their art. But what if the art that arises from and thrives in the library wanders out the front doors, to include and encompass an entire community?

A BRIEF HISTORY OF LARRY

Library Larry's Big Day is an educational children's television program produced by the Denton Public Library, Denton Television, and the Denton Independent School District. It airs twice a day every day on Charter, Verizon, and Grande cable channels. It's also available online, and we get hundreds of monthly viewers who click on www.librarylarry.com to view the current episode. I created the show format and the characters, write the show each month, and act as coproducer and the puppeteer behind one of the main characters. The show received a first-place award in 2010 from the Texas Association of Telecommunications Officers and Advisors, the 2011 North Texas Regional Library System's Margaret Irby Nichols Award, and a speech I wrote and delivered promoting the show won a 2011 Texas Library

Association Branding Iron PR Award. Winning awards helped us get more publicity, which translated into a larger viewing audience. We also received recognition in the City of Denton's *Annual Citizen Update* and *North Texan* magazine.

Library Larry's Big Day stars three puppets that "live" in the library. There's Library Larry, who is a good old Texas bull; Emmy Lou Dickenson, a word-obsessed pig; and Mr. Chompers, a hippo who might get his words and phrases mixed up but who adds a lot of silly fun to the show. In each episode, which airs for a full month, a librarian reads a book to the puppets, and then they visit a place in the community that relates to that book. Places we've been so far include the central fire station, Denton Airport, the Denton Police Department, the landfill, and L. A. Nelson Elementary School. We toured the Denton Public Library (that was one of our easier episodes to film), the University of North Texas Observatory and Planetarium, and the Denton Animal Shelter. We also paid a visit to the Texas Woman's University gymnastics team, Grammy Award–winning band Brave Combo, the water and wastewater treatment plants, Denton Municipal Electric, the Denia Recreation Center, and Denton City Hall. And more are being scheduled, filmed, and edited as I write this.

PUPPETS UP!

Library Larry's Big Day takes the library directly into people's homes and the community, and that all starts in the library itself. Much of the work is done early in the morning before the library actually opens, but we also film for a couple of hours after we open. This allows children to see the process of how a television show is filmed and to see the art of how puppeteers manipulate the puppets. The majority of the filming is done in the youth section of the library so as not to disturb adult patrons.

Our puppets go all over town, and kids see them interacting with people throughout the community. *Library Larry's Big Day* brings education home and bridges the gap between art and reality. In this way, community and city leaders who act as guides on our visit each month become characters, playing along by interacting with the puppets. Not only is the show an educational outreach program for reading, library promotion, interpersonal skills, and community awareness; it's a tool that teaches the importance of creativity and artistic expression.

THE ART OF GETTING STARTED

I met with Roy, a friend of mine who works in video production at the Denton Independent School District. I told him a little about the situation, that I had pounded out a script, and that I had been given permission from my supervisors to work on the project. For those who aren't experienced writers, try looking at script-writing books if you're concerned about proper formatting or the nuts and bolts of script production. Also, looking at actual screenplays will give you a good feel for things like dialogue, action, and establishing your setting.

Roy said he was interested in helping, but he didn't have any lighting equipment or the types of microphones we needed. What he did have was a camera, an editing bay, and film experience. We still lacked several key ingredients for our project to get off the ground.

That led me to Denton Television (DTV), the city of Denton's cable-access station, where I talked with David, who was in charge of production there. I showed him the script I had written and explained my vision for the show, and at first he thought it might be too much work. But as we kept talking over the following few weeks, he started taking interest. Roy would provide additional equipment and help with editing, and DTV would put the final product on the air. Now we had the equipment, the relationships, and the go-ahead.

We decided to film our first visit at the fire station. What kid doesn't like screaming fire engines, the shiny metal poles firefighters slide down, and the big ladder trucks? I contacted the media spokesperson for the fire department to see if we could film there. Once the location for our first visit was secured, we filmed the in-library segments of the show (the part where the puppets read their book and people tell jokes). This is where we made our first of several mistakes. I had written a lot about sliding down the fire pole, and we filmed the entire intro scene with Mr. Chompers talking about how he was going to slide down one at the fire station.

When we got to the fire station—no pole! But we were able to incorporate this misstep as part of the puppet's character. Every episode now has Mr. Chompers wanting to do something he doesn't get to do, like driving the trash truck or winning a Grammy Award. It worked out well in the end, but it taught us to film the location segment first so we could change the structure of each script to fit what was available on our visit.

We liked the fire station visit so much that we invited "Driver Charlie" to a series of special story times during our Summer Reading Club. He read a book about fire trucks and talked about fire safety, and the puppets were on hand to promote the Summer Reading Club and the television show. The kids loved it, and the turnout was incredible.

GET SET AND CUE THE MUSIC

One of our first big artistic hurdles was in-library set design. We soon found that to design an entire set with large murals and props was going to

Preparing to film Library *Larry's Big Day* at the Denton Police Department

far exceed our meager annual provision of $500. WyLaina Hildreth, who is coproducer and puppeteer for Emmy Lou Dickenson, suggested that we put two flat library carts together and cover them with a board and dark cloth to create a space for the puppeteers to hide behind. It was a stroke of genius. We then garnished the carts with books and different little puppets and other props from our puppet closet that were specific to each episode. And instead of filming on some set that had nothing to do with the actual library, we decided to film out in the library itself to share the process with the children and emphasize the library as our primary setting.

We also wanted good music for the show, so we decided to bring in local musicians on the project. I had written a theme song for the show and played it on guitar for some people at our first production meeting. I am also a musician, but I knew next to nothing about recording and had none of the recording equipment I needed. Everybody seemed to like the song I wrote, but to get a good, quality recording of it would cost money, something we didn't have in abundance. I decided to knock on a friend's door to see if he was interested in contributing his skill in sound recording to the show.

My friend is Fritz Schwalm, and he has a home recording studio. I asked him if he would be interested in donating some of his time and talent to an educational children's television show I was preparing. He agreed. I played guitar, laid down a simple drum track and vocals, and then let him put some slide guitar and bass to it. Chuck Voellinger, another multitalented friend from the library (who is the puppeteer for Mr. Chompers and plays the recurring character Mr. Chuck), put some pedal steel in the mix to finish it out. Fritz mastered it and sent the copy to me. It sounded incredible.

We went on to record other music for the show with Fritz, bringing in still more local musicians. We have used a local accordion player, drummer, and a whole range of children and adult singers on the show. Fritz has been the backbone of many songs and sound effects, and he has proved an incredible artistic partner.

READY FOR YOUR CLOSE-UP?

From the very beginning, there was the question of on-screen talent. Who would want to be in the show? Who would work well in front of the camera? At first, I was looking outside the library to find volunteers who would be interested in playing the main characters, but I was hesitant to use lots of people on a voluntary basis when we had drop-dead production deadlines. Then I realized that most of the people in the library already possessed many of the artistic skills we needed.

I had written the script for three puppets, and the library had plenty of puppets. The script also called for a couple of goofy human characters as well as some book readers. I realized that everyone in the library had done story-time duty at some point, and because of this, they all had experience singing, dancing, working with puppets, playing musical instruments, and generally being silly.

So I asked around all three branches of our library until I found a few willing participants. After some practice, we filmed a trial run with a small handheld camera that the library owned, and it looked promising. My thinking was that by using librarians and library workers for our on-screen talent, kids who watch the show would recognize them when they came into the library. I mentioned that one of the regular characters on the show is Mr. Chuck, who is one of our librarians, and he takes the puppets on their visits around town in his super-awesome, powder-blue 1963 Chevy Impala. He says kids come up to him on a regular basis and recognize him from the show. They know him, they see him as a meaningful part of their community, and that connection brings them back to the library.

We decided to use random citizens on the town square for our "Puppet on the Street" segment in which we ask people what the meaning of that episode's mystery word is. We also use local children who come into the library as dancers on our "Boogie" segment, so we use patrons and non-patrons in the artistic process. And of course we use a different person in each episode to host our visit segment. We've had gymnasts, professors, city department directors, firefighters, and police officers as hosts, to name a few. We have yet to work with an actor, and I really like that. We're encouraging art in others by making actors out of nonactors and using the library as the vehicle for this artistic transformation.

We make art and artists out of the people who work at the library and the people who live and work in the community, and that in turn lets the kids see the library in a different light. We've used library practicum students from the universities in town as production assistants and on-screen talent. Denton Television has used interns from the Radio, Television and Film Department of the University of North Texas to help with editing and filming. We also featured a local kindergarten teacher in a promotional video for the show that the school district produced. It's a library art project at heart and a community art project in every sense of the word.

DENTON GOES HOLLYWOOD

Special-effects editing is also an art form, as I found out in the course of writing and coproducing the show. One of the wonderful discoveries we made while collaborating with DTV was the station's creative use of graphics. It really enhanced the flavor of the production and made it look more like what you would see on a bona fide children's program. It taught us all more about the artistic possibilities at our disposal, and as we all became more familiar with the process, it helped us collaborate on a higher level.

It was incredible to see what DTV could do in the editing process. The mystery word would fly across the screen; question marks would dance when the puppets asked what the mystery word meant. The landfill episode showed cartoon graphics of how a landfill was constructed. The astronomy episode had graphics of constellations and royalty-free video clips from NASA. When we visited the police station and two motorcycle officers rode past the camera, the mystery word (which for that episode was *uniform*) blew away into the wind. It was so much more than we expected, and so much more than we could have done on our own.

I eventually started writing my scripts with these editing tricks in mind. Mr. Chuck would disappear with a snap of his fingers, or props would magically appear in people's hands. An invisible drinker drained a glass of water on the episode about water. I wrote in dream sequences and thought bubbles above Mr. Chompers' head. We all became better artists as the show matured, which translated into a more dynamic and compelling product, and a larger viewing audience.

WRITING

Script writing as an art form is not just about writing with dialogue or action in mind; it is also about writing for the camera. I wanted to include the audience in writing the script but struggled at first to figure out how to manage this. After a few episodes, I created a segment called "Mr. Chompers's Mailroom," which invites kids who watch the show to write letters to Mr. Chompers. This enables viewers to ultimately develop and define the character of Mr. Chompers by having him interact with their feedback. In a sense, the kids who write the letters are also helping write the script, which gives them a stake as artists in creating the show.

Children are also encouraged to draw pictures for Mr. Chompers's mail room, and we've had some great art featured on that segment. Some kids send their letters by snail mail (a lost art, to be sure), and others drop theirs into one of the artfully constructed "mailboxes" with the picture of Mr. Chompers at each library branch.

I also discovered the downside of script writing. Each script is ten or more pages long, and several scripts, as well as cue cards, have to be printed for each show. Since we produce so many scripts each month, I wanted to share the art of writing while being as "green" as possible with the program. Each time we're done with an episode, I collect all the cue cards and scripts. I then cut them up into fourths and put them out by our catalog computers as the scratch paper for patrons to use. In addition to recycling, this helps bring the art full circle, highlighting the fact that writing is a critical part of the art of producing our show.

ART AND THE AUDIENCE

Art includes all the avenues of promotion we do for the show. Colorful posters, bookmarks, and thoughtful library displays are just the start. Before the show even aired, we sent out press releases and got some good coverage with pictures of the puppets in local papers and on the Web. And after the show started, we continued our marketing campaign by doing things like participating in the Fourth of July parade (with Chuck driving the puppets in that super-cool, powder-blue 1968 Chevy Impala) and partnering with Denton Airport (which we visited on one of our episodes) to make an appearance at the Denton Airshow. We participated in career days and school outreach programs, set up booths at local art festivals, and produced DVDs of the show to hand out as prizes and media incentives. As I mentioned earlier, we scheduled special Library Larry storytimes during our Summer Reading Club and had viewings of the show in the library.

We applied for grants from the Denton Rotary Club and our Friends of the Library organization, which both gave us funding. We not only received grants from the local Rotary Club chapter for marketing supplies; the club also made the marketing of our show its community service project. The Rotary Club has been instrumental in connecting us with more community organizations and in getting more teachers in Denton and the surrounding areas to air the show in their classrooms. Rotary eventually gave us a grant earmarked for a billboard, which we are in the process of implementing. Grant writing was something I had to learn from scratch, but I talked to people around me who had written grants and read books on the subject. What you don't know is often at your fingertips, and you might be surprised who will help you if you just ask and be politely persistent.

PICTURE PERFECT

What artistic canvas do you want your library to be? It may not be a television show. It may relate to some other collaborative outreach program or collective endeavor. Most municipalities have all the elements in place for a television show, but also for many other projects. The trick is to make the project unique, to make it fill a need, and to make it beneficial for all involved and for the community as a whole. Take chances and see where those chances take you.

What talents do you or the people around you have that you can use on your project? You don't have to know how to do everything picture perfect when you start. When you can't do it yourself, locate people who can and don't be afraid to learn something totally new. Ask yourself what existing organizations would be willing to help realize the goals of your project. Find out what type of artistic medium will make your big day, and let it shine!

Part V
Management and Administration

Art Works

Strengthening Downtown with
Library-Arts Partnerships

ELIZABETH GOLDMAN AND SARA WEDELL

THE SMALL TOWN OF Chelsea, Michigan, like many neighboring areas of Michigan, has felt the impact of the decline of its base, both agricultural and manufacturing. As part of a broadening of its economy, the town has invested in the arts, supported by the presence of actor and local resident Jeff Daniels's Purple Rose Theatre Company. This foundation helps support a well-regarded theater program in the local schools, numerous art galleries, and the Chelsea Center for the Arts. An extended partnership with the Chelsea Center for the Arts has led to several successful initiatives, including the Midwest Literary Walk and an artist-in-residence program.

Since moving into a new building in 2006, the library has focused its efforts on community engagement, outreach, and partnerships. The library's mission is "is to provide equal access to quality resources that serve the lifelong cultural, educational, and informational needs and interests of all people." The library has a staff of twenty-seven and was recognized as the "Best Small Library in America" for 2008 by *Library Journal* and the Bill and Melinda Gates Foundation, in part for its innovative partnerships and programs.[1]

The Chelsea Center for the Arts is among the only professionally staffed arts center in its county and supports a number of communities through traditional programs like music and dance lessons, as well as providing support services to area organizations producing community cultural events and public art projects. Like the library, the arts center is housed in a historical building in the downtown area, and the library and the arts center share a commitment to the economic health of the region. Among the arts center's major projects is support for Sounds & Sights on Thursday Nights, a summertime series of musical performances in outdoor venues around the downtown. The library's outdoor amphitheatre, along Chelsea's Main Street, has often been one of the venues for this program.[2]

WHY PARTNER?

Partnerships are the foundation of the successful public library today. Libraries have traditionally been quiet and internally focused, counting on the users who come through their doors and a general feeling of goodwill for continued funding. In an era of increasing competition for public funds, however, libraries must look outside their walls and prove that each tax dollar is being well spent. Working with other organizations in the community allows both the library and the partner to offer improved services to a wider range of people in a more economical way. The programs outlined in this chapter demonstrate how the initial act of networking in the community can lead to an awareness of needs not being filled, which in turn results in the creation of successful programs that support downtown vitality.

Creating partnerships doesn't have to be complicated or time consuming. Once they are established as a willing community partner, libraries will often have more interest from potential partners than they can handle. But a smart library will take the initiative of creating those initial partnerships. By following a set of easy steps, libraries can establish partnership and outreach initiatives that will work well for everyone involved.

The best way to begin is with a little brainstorming: think about programs or services that you would like the library to be able to offer. Once you have prioritized this list, draw up the outlines of a concept for a specific project or program that will accomplish your goals. Next, look at who would make a good partner. You might start with people or organizations already known to the library, but other good sources are groups known to be working in the community in a relevant area. Partnerships can be with nonprofits, other government agencies, businesses, nearby libraries, schools, and others. Before approaching a potential partner, work out some of the details of your proposal: what the library can provide; what else is needed; and how money, staffing, and other logistics might be handled. It's important to be able to approach your partner ready to point out how the partnership will benefit both organizations.

With this preparation, you can approach your potential partners confidently, knowing that the library will look professional and present a strong case for the merits of the project. You may already have a contact at the target organization or know of someone through networks, but there's nothing wrong with cold-calling either. In fact, establishing a relationship with an organization or group with whom the library has had no previous ties does even more to expand the library's presence in the community. At the initial meeting, while presenting the library's concept, remain open to the partner organization's feedback. Once the partners have agreed to move forward with the project, it's important to keep those lines of communication open. A written project plan outlining expectations and responsibilities for each partner is key, as are regular meetings to evaluate the progress of the initiative. The partners should agree on the parameters of the project, as well as how it will be evaluated. All partners should also contribute to publicity and marketing, as the extended network created by the partnership is one of the major motivations for working together. Remaining flexible and letting your partners know that you appreciate their contributions will go a long way toward creating partnerships that you can extend and build on for future projects.

The benefits of partnerships go well beyond the results of the initiative itself. By partnering, libraries expand their reach and increase their advocates. Advocacy is still often thought of as the purview of library directors and board members, but in reality, it extends to all staff and even all users of the library. The key to sustainable funding is making the library known, making the work of the library known, and building a case for the library as an essential piece of a healthy community. Partnerships serve this goal in multiple ways. First, they show that the library is not complacent or unwilling to think beyond traditional services. They show that libraries are good community partners, interested in broadening the number of people they reach by working with other groups and optimizing time and money spent by taking advantage of different organizations' strengths and areas of expertise. Finally, each partner organization has its own constituency. Improving the library's image in the eyes of these constituencies exponentially expands the number of advocates the library has, and each time each of these people speaks positively about the library, it enhances the library's secure place in the community's priorities.

FUNDING THE PARTNERSHIP: WRITING SUCCESSFUL GRANTS

In the ideal world, either the library or its partner organization would have the funding to support any project imagined. But in reality, other sources of funding are often necessary. The ability to write successful grants is a key part of creating strong partnerships, and the existence of partners often strengthens the case on a grant application.

Common funders of grants for libraries in many areas include the state library, state cultural or heritage divisions, local community funds, bank or business foundations, and the federal government. Each of these funders has different schedules and different requirements. In some cases, the library may not qualify for the grant funding while the partner organization does, thus giving the library access to additional sources of money. Most grant funders have staff members who are able to meet with potential applicants in advance and/or review applications in progress, offering guidance on how to frame the proposal in order to find better success.

The keys to successful grant writing are no more complex than the keys to creating successful partnerships. Those seeking grants should research their funders' priorities and goals, making sure to apply for grants that make sense with the project. Read the instructions carefully—many a grant has been lost because of administrative errors, such as not including a required document. Letters of support for the grant demonstrate how widely the proposed project will affect the community. Established partnerships create a base of references for the library, and partners on previous initiatives can provide evidence that the proposed project is likely to be successful. What really sets one grant application apart from a mass of others, however, is how the library tells the story. If a project is well planned and based on a true vision of how the partnership and resulting service will have a positive and concrete impact on the community, that will come through in the grant application. The narrative explaining the need for funding should couch the specific project in the larger picture of its potential impact, including follow-on projects that could result from the partnership.[3]

With partnerships and grants in hand, projects can get under way. The following sections present two successful grant-funded partnerships between Chelsea District Library and the Chelsea Center for the Arts.

THE ARTIST-IN-RESIDENCE SERIES

The Midwest Literary Walk and the Artist-in-Residence series are events that center on bringing arts and culture into the Chelsea community and encouraging creativity in the everyday lives of area citizens. The partnership between Chelsea District Library and Chelsea Center for the Arts has been an innovative way for both organizations to spread cultural literacy, increase their visibility in the community, and demonstrate the value of interorganizational cooperation. The programs serve the residents and business community of Chelsea and the surrounding area by creating sustainable programming and services that expose users to various forms of music, visual arts, film, literature, and other arts. This project reaches beyond the boundaries of the service areas of the each organization to attract out-of-town visitors.

The Artist-in-Residence program intends to place a local or regional artist in the community spotlight for a year. The definition of *artist* is intentionally broad, to include potential candidates from all art forms from visual arts to literature to performance. Thus far, artists-in-residence in the series have ranged from poets to memoirists to cartoonists, all of whom have successfully brought their artistic passion and encouragement of creative expression into the community. Artists-in-residence are given a great deal of freedom in designing engaging programs for all age groups. They also attend community events, such as Rotary Club meetings and fund-raisers in an ambassadorial capacity, representing the shared cultural missions of the library and arts center.

The Artist-in-Residence program began in September 2008 with M. L. Liebler, a Wayne State University English professor and well-known Detroit-area poet and performer. Liebler facilitated a poetry-writing workshop and a songwriting workshop, performed his poetry at a live jazz event, assisted in the planning and execution of the first annual Midwest Literary Walk, hosted a series of open-mic events featuring readers from the local writers' group, and invited guest poets to facilitate a writing workshop. Subsequent artists-in-residence have also hosted workshops and participated in the Midwest Literary Walk, but they have also expanded program boundaries with events in the schools, senior living centers, and local businesses. Jerzy Drozd, the 2010–11 artist-in-residence, is a cartoonist and graphic novelist and an organizer of an annual convention called Kids Read Comics. In June 2011, Chelsea will host this event, featuring dozens of nationally known comic-book artists and animators teaching workshops and encouraging the art of storytelling to hundreds of kids ranging from kindergarteners to high school seniors.

The library and arts center partnership is responsible for gauging community opinion, selecting an artist, identifying and providing opportunities for the artist-in-residence to contribute programs or skills, and facilitating the administrative aspects of the overall series. Each spring, representatives from the library and arts center poll community members—including contacts at the schools, senior centers, arts organizations, and local businesses—to gather artist nominations and develop a sense of which area of the arts should be highlighted. A committee of partnership representatives ultimately selects and meets with an artist before finalizing the decision to offer the position. Individual librarians and program coordinators plan and host most of the artist-in-residence events throughout the year, and the artist's participation in larger events, such as the Midwest Literary Walk, involves further cooperation between the organizations.

THE MIDWEST LITERARY WALK

The Midwest Literary Walk aims to highlight the power of literature and poetry in everyday life, and it underlines this by staging readings at various locations throughout downtown Chelsea. By taking the event outside the library walls and selecting multiple venues, the Midwest Literary Walk provides an opportunity to further relationships with local businesses and community partners while simultaneously exposing a larger segment of the population to the literary arts. The target audience is the region's lovers of literature. The partnership hopes to draw poetry and literature enthusiasts from nearby academic institutions and to attract people seeking a cultural event from the surrounding cities and towns, as well as any locals or visitors in Chelsea on that day who may stumble upon the event.

Past Midwest Literary Walk participants include the beat generation playwright Michael McClure, the Oprah Book Club author Brett Lott, the critically acclaimed poet and essayist Thomas Lynch, and the Pushcart Prize–winning novelist and poet Laura Kasischke. The event starts off at the library's Main Street location and progresses to downtown venues, which have included local art galleries, cafés, restaurants, and bookstores.

The library–arts center partnership is at the core of this event, which is planned by a committee consisting of local business owners, authors, and artists and is led by library and arts center representatives. This committee, which includes the artist-in-residence when appropriate, selects authors and poets and identifies businesses in the downtown area that may be interested in participating as venues. The committee is also deeply involved in marketing the event—inviting mailing list members and promoting the walk in newsletters and through press releases—to help spread the word and ensure a good crowd.

Funding for the 2008–9 Artist-in-Residence program and the 2009 Midwest Literary Walk was provided by the library's programming budget. To establish these events annually, the arts center and library together wrote and submitted a grant proposal to the Chelsea Community Foundation, and the proposal was generously funded in the amount of $25,000 over two years. Although the grant was written in tandem, the arts center acted as the fiduciary and is responsible for handling the grant's administrative and monetary duties. The grant has given both organizations time to experiment with fundraising possibilities to make these popular annual events sustainable.

Establishing sustainable funding is the most challenging aspect of this partnership and these events. Because of the size and enthusiasm of the crowds drawn to the first Midwest Literary Walk, the second Midwest Literary Walk was planned with bookend events that required a purchased ticket. This attempt at fund-raising proved difficult because placing events in the late morning and early evening around the four-hour-long afternoon event made it a tiring day for participants. Interest was also limited, most likely as a result of the amount of free entertainment available throughout the day. Fund-raising attempts, like auctions of work or private lessons by the artist-in-residence or VIP receptions at the Midwest Literary Walk, are ideas that we are currently exploring.

There have been several instances of demonstrated positive economic impact as a direct result of these partnership events. Saleem Peeradina, one of the 2009–10 artists-in-residence, conducted a poetry workshop hosted at a local art gallery and used some of the gallery's visual art as inspiration pieces from which the participants wrote poems. The gallery owners enjoyed the event and the resulting poetry so much that they have commissioned exhibit-inspired poems for every show they have scheduled in 2011. The poems will be a part of the marketing process for the gallery shows and will hang on the walls alongside the art to enhance the viewing experience.

Another local arts organization, the nationally renowned Purple Rose Theatre Company, has also connected with the Artist-in-Residence program. The theater's upcoming production is a world premiere of a new play whose protagonist has an obsession with comic books. To underline this major plot point, the Purple Rose Theatre has invited graphic novelist Jerzy Drozd, the 2010–11 artist-in-residence, to help promote the production.

The Midwest Literary Walk has a simpler and more obvious connection to local business as an annual event that draws more than 250 people to town and guides them directly into participating stores. Restaurants and cafés also benefit from hungry and thirsty literature fans refreshing themselves between readings. The increased foot traffic in Chelsea's downtown is a direct result of the mobile nature of the Midwest Literary Walk.

Public author readings go hand in hand with selling and signing books, which is another way the Midwest Literary Walk has been able to have a positive impact on local small business. The library has partnered with a nearby independent bookstore to manage the sales of Midwest Literary Walk authors' books. This simplifies the event for committee members and event volunteers and gives a small bookseller an opportunity to reach a large audience of potential buyers.

LIBRARY-ARTS PARTNERSHIPS: A WINNING COMBINATION

As the success of the Artist-in-Residence and Midwest Literary Walk programs demonstrates, library partnerships with arts organizations can prove fruitful for both the sponsors and local business. By developing strong community connections, the library was able to get involved with projects that otherwise might have passed it by. Both the Artist-in-Residence and Midwest Literary Walk programs would have been substantially more difficult to achieve for either small institution on its own. Financially, the partnership and commitment to outreach benefited both programs. The existence of a partnership goes a long way toward obtaining grant funding and getting the programs going. In terms of turning that funding into a successful event, the benefit of outreach to local businesses that supported the Midwest Literary Walk is clear. For a small town the size of Chelsea, drawing several hundred people to an event and getting them through the doors of independent businesses can make a big difference.

In a community with a strong arts presence, the library looking to arts groups for collaborative projects makes sense, but there is value to these partnerships in any setting. The arts can form the basis of programs related to fine arts, filmmaking, storytelling, theater, and more. These types of programs support a variety of interests and needs among patrons and can lead to the creation of original works that are meaningful to the community. Working with partners strengthens both organizations and allows the partners to think big and develop programs and services with the potential to have a major impact.

Notes

1. For more, see the Chelsea District Library website, at www.chelsea.lib.mi.us.
2. For more, see the Chelsea Center for the Arts website, at www.chelseacenterfor thearts.org.
3. A starting place for grants open to libraries is the blog *Library Grants,* at http://librarygrants.blogspot.com, and the associated book by Pamela H. MacKellar and Stephanie K. Gerding, *Winning Grants: A How-to-Do-It Manual for Librarians with Multimedia Tutorials and Grant Development Tools* (New York: Neal-Schuman, 2010).

CHAPTER 16

Behind the Scenes

The Legal and Contractual Aspects of Booking Exhibits and Presenters in a Library

NORA J. QUINLAN AND SARAH CISSE

PUTTING ON A LIBRARY EVENT, be it an exhibit or a program, entails a great deal of preparation and work behind the scenes that involves many people and groups. Many logistical steps before and after the actual event takes place need to be executed.

EXHIBITS

First, the purpose and needs of the exhibit must be determined—what is the exhibit about, who is the audience, and where is the material coming from? The easiest exhibit to prepare is internally developed using materials from the library's own collection. Objects are checked out and displayed with the appropriate security and environmental conditions that meet the exhibit's needs.

Letter of Request
If the library needs to borrow material from individuals or other institutions, the process can be more complex. The type of the material being borrowed can also make a difference.

Out-of-the-box, or prepackaged, exhibits sent out by such organizations as the American Library Association, the Smithsonian Institution, and the Gilder Lehrman Institute of American History usually have basic

requirements. These traveling exhibits rotate through a number of libraries. They come with a standardized agreement form that is easily completed.
Many of these exhibits are panel exhibits and are of minimal value. If they do
include original material, the agreement specifies more detailed requirements
for security and environmental conditions.

If a library is developing its own exhibit and borrows items from other
institutions for display the first step should be to prepare a *letter of request* to
the lending institution. The Rare Books and Manuscripts Section of the Association of College and Research Libraries has developed guidelines. This letter
should be written with sufficient time for the lender to receive and respond.
The letter, addressed to the appropriate staff member of the lending institution, should be signed by the director or designee of the borrowing institution. When coordinating international loans, a minimum of a one-year lead
time is recommended.

The letter of request should include the following:

- exhibition title
- name and credentials of curatorial staff
- brief description of the exhibition purpose and scope
- inclusive dates of the exhibition and proposed loan
- full description of each item to be borrowed (citation, classification
  or catalog or inventory number, and source information identifying
  the lending institution as owner of the item)
- whether or not the catalog will accompany the exhibition
- whether the borrower plans to create an accompanying web version
  of the exhibition
- borrower's willingness to conform to the conditions of the loan
  determined by the lender
- a request that the lender state the requirements for safe transporta-
  tion of the item

Similar requirements can be used for borrowing from individuals. It may
differ depending on the institution's relationship with the individual. The initial contact can be more informal, but documentation should be prepared to
ensure that the lender understands what they have agreed to do. This process
is discussed later in the chapter.

Facilities Report

The exhibit space that is being used should meet a number of criteria. Many
institutional lenders require a site-specific facilities report to be submitted before an exhibit is loaned particularly if the display contains original

artifacts. A very detailed form is available from the Registrars Committee of the American Association of Museums.

A recently revised and more user-friendly form is also available for sale from the American Association of Museums. The facilities report includes general institutional information, such as location and contacts, accreditation information (from the association usually), and the type of institute borrowing the material. Libraries are designated as being either a university or a cultural organization facility. A geographic profile is required. Does the library lie in an earthquake, brush fire, or flood or extreme weather zone? Local risk management agencies can answer this.

Information about the history of the construction and the configuration and maintenance of the library building will be required. The following should be included:

- year the building was constructed
- materials the building is constructed of
- how fire resistive the building is
- the size of the building
- whether the building is currently being renovated
- The latter is a concern as accidents and fires caused by workers can occur during building renovation when fire alarms and other protection are disconnected.
- Specific information should be provided about the use and maintenance of the actual exhibit space and the building as a whole. The following will need to be addressed:
- food and drink policy in the exhibit area
- whether and by whom pest control is done, and if not, why not
- whether there is routine custodial work; who performs this; and if not, why not

How the library handles shipping and receiving of materials is also important. The library should have a contract with a moving company that has experience moving art or museum objects. One person or department should be responsible for handling shipping and receiving.

It is important to know where shipments are received. Do items come directly to the library or to a central receiving area? During shipping, the location of exhibit items should be tracked. Only authorized persons can sign for a shipment. One does not want an exhibit item to arrive and have it left in an open, public area or out on a loading dock exposed to weather! Staff, trained to handle valuable or fragile material, should be assigned to unpack and check-in items as they are received. Items should be placed in a dedicated and secure storage space. Access to this space should be closely monitored and securely controlled.

Environmental conditions can influence a lender's decision to part with treasures. The lender will want to be reassured that appropriate environmental conditions are maintained in the exhibit space and that light, temperature, and humidity levels will be monitored. An exhibit area should be evaluated to make sure that environmental standards can be met. Damage can occur if the item is not exhibited in a controlled environment. To determine whether the library has proper environmental conditions, one will need to check the following:

- Does the air system run 24/7, or does it routinely shut down when the library is closed?
- What type of system is in use?
- Are temperature and humidity monitored and recorded in the exhibit area and/or in the library?
- Is there documentation of the monitoring?
- What type of lighting is installed?
- Is the light exposure being measured?
- Where are the sources of light in the exhibit space (including windows and skylights)?

Fire protection is an important consideration as well. A fire and smoke alarm and fire suppression system should be installed in the building. One should know what type of system is installed and who is notified when the alarm goes off. Staff should be able to identify the location of the nearest fire hose, fire hydrant, and fire station.

Security is crucial. Trained and bonded public safety officers or guards should be in the building. They may be required to patrol or be stationed in the exhibit area. There should be a checklist of who controls access or has keys to the space. An electronic monitoring and alarm and video surveillance system should be installed in the exhibit area. This system should be connected to either a central station or a local law enforcement agency. A security system should be in place at the entrance and exit of the building. Patrons entering the building should be required either to check their bags or to have them searched on exit. When installing an exhibit, attention should be given to the security of how items are displayed. Lockable, secure exhibit cases should be used for fragile, small, or valuable articles. Artwork hung on the walls should have a built-in secure hanging system or be hung in a manner to deter theft.

Finally, and most important, is the library insured? Find out who the institution's insurer is and what type of coverage is provided. It is important to be able to show that there is an art rider that is more than the value of the building the exhibit space is in. Insurance coverage for borrowed items must be spelled out clearly, stating the following:

- the kind of coverage for the borrowed material
- the name of the insurance provider
- whether there have been any damages or loss of property in the library's care in the previous three years, regardless of whether a claim was filed

In addition to being able to provide all this information, a floor plan of the exhibit space should be provided. The plan or map should show the layout of the exhibit space to scale and should include dimensions and square footage of the display area. The placement of outlets, windows, doors, and security and fire systems should also be identified on the plan.

How well these questions are answered will determine how loan ready the library is, especially if it wishes to display original and valuable materials.

Loan Agreement between Institutions or Individuals

According to *Black's Law Dictionary*, *bailment* is "a delivery of personal property by one person (the bailor) to another (the bailee) who holds the property for a certain purpose, usually under an express or implied-in-fact contract." *Bailment* derives from the French word *bailor*, which means "to deliver."

In loaning an object, the lender retains the ownership of it. The borrower obtains only temporary control or possession of the property with the permission of the lender. Bailment exists during the loan period in which the borrower's interest in the property is above all others, including that of the lender, unless the borrower violates a portion of the agreement. Once the exhibit is over, the item is returned to the lender or otherwise cared for on the basis of the lender's instructions. A bailment is only an exchange of possession or custody, not ownership. A rental or lease of exhibit can be a bailment, depending on the agreement of the parties.

It is very important that any loan be accompanied by a loan agreement. This document legally protects both the lender and the borrower. The loan agreement should have the contact information of the loaner and a description of the piece(s) being loaned, including size. Height, width, and depth, if needed, should be given in inches or centimeters. A physical description along with a photograph should also be included. The lender should sign and date this information.

Ideally, there should also be an exhibition loan agreement prepared that identifies all the obligations of the lender and the borrower. This agreement will help eliminate confusion or possible disagreements. The name and addresses of the participants should be clearly spelled out. Contact information from a lender should include street mailing address, e-mail, and landline and cell phone numbers.

The lender will agree to provide a list of all items being loaned, with sizes, descriptions, and assigned values. The lender should describe how the material is being sent (e.g., framed, unframed, whether it needs to be unpacked and assembled). Each item loaned should also be accompanied by a photograph to help identify it. The list and images should be received in a timely manner before the exhibit is installed. If the lender is sending a stand-alone show, the borrower must have the lender's agreement to allow the redesign of the layout and/or to add anything to it. The agreement should clearly describe who is responsible for arranging and paying for packing and shipment both to and from the exhibit venue. The borrower must notify the lender of any changes in dates or setup plans. Condition reports must be provided by the lender and completed by the borrower. Exhibits are much like renting a car: one would never drive the car out of the lot before inspecting it for damage. The same is true for borrowing material.

Reports noting material conditions should be dated and signed by both the lender and borrower at receipt and return of the exhibit. If damage or loss occurs during a display, the lender must be immediately notified. An agreement on installation and security should also be included—what the lender is expecting and what the borrower is capable of providing.

Detailed information, clearly spelled out, should be given on how credits should appear; how identification of sponsorship should be done (including sample logos); and what the loan fees, if any, should be. A cancellation clause should be included. It is better to sort it out in the agreement than later after a problem occurs. Responsibilities for photography or reproduction of images and publicity should also be detailed.

Finally, a force majeure should be included. *Black's Law Dictionary* defines this as "an event or effect that can be neither anticipated nor controlled" from the French for "a superior force." Force majeure can include acts of nature and people such as floods, fires, hurricanes, riots, strikes or war. It protects both the lender and the borrower from acts of God.

Exhibiting valuable materials requires an appraisal of items. This can be done in several ways—self-appraisal by the owner, outside appraisal, or appraisal done by the borrower. Be aware that an insurance company may contest an appraisal, so it is best to have the most accurate information when assigning a value. Sources can include sale or purchase receipts, auction records, and published sources such as *American Book Prices Current* for books and manuscripts.

A letter of receipt for any items that are picked up from individuals or from another institution should be prepared and signed at the time the items are obtained. Most insurance includes door-to-door coverage, and this receipt will help document date and time of pickup and protect the person transporting the items from liability. This letter can be as simple as a signature and date and a note indicating "received," with a list of the borrowed items. Both the owner and the person doing the pickup should sign the letter.

An exhibit has multiple stages, all of which have their own particular needs or concerns. From the gestation stage to the planning, implementation, setup, maintenance, takedown, and return of an exhibit, one is involved in a complex endeavor with many potential legal implications and consequences. If one keeps in mind at all times that the exhibit is an expression of the institution and that the institution works as a organizational entity with all the myriad legal complexities that entails, then one will be successful in putting up an exhibit that is long remembered for its aesthetic or intellectual contribution to the community rather than the legal problems that occurred.

WORKING WITH PRESENTERS

Just as in preparing for an exhibit, one should also prepare for any possible programming. In developing programs, outside presenters and performers who are considered independent contractors may be brought in. An independent contractor is any person who is not an employee of the library or its parent institution who is hired to perform services. The independent contractor controls the means and methods of accomplishing the results of the work and not the library. For example, the library hires Tillie the Clown to do a children's program. Tillie and the library agree to have the performance include a play on a certain theme. How Tillie prepares for the play and what Tillie buys to build the set and create costumes is Tillie's responsibility as an independent contractor. The library is not responsible for these costs unless they are detailed in the contract. The library has paid only for the performance.

The initial contract for programming needs is usually made by phone or e-mail. But a letter or e-mail documenting expectations and compensation (if any) should be sent in a timely manner once the presenter has agreed to participate. If the person conducting the programming is outside of the institution, there should be a formal independent contractor agreement as well. If grant funding is being used, there may be additional paperwork as well. The agreement should cover the following:

- performer's full name
- citizenship status
- description of services performed
- date(s) of service

- total fees for services
- payment schedule (e.g., one lump sum before or after the presentation or prorated over a series of programs)
- reimbursable expenses (e.g., mileage, performance fee, honorarium, equipment, supplies)

In addition, the independent contractor may be asked to abide by certain rules involving background checks (which can include having a name search done in a sexual predator and local criminal database) if children are to be present at the program, insurance coverage, the right to make travel arrangements or substitution or transfer of services, employment status (employment status may mean the presenter is not eligible for worker's compensation insurance or fringe benefits), and responsibility for state and local income taxes. An agreement should also include a payment schedule. Some presenters will want payment on the day of performance or upon completion of services rendered.

The independent contractor will also need to provide either a social security number; an employer identification number (also known as a federal tax identification number), used to identify a business entity; or an individual taxpayer identification number, which is available for certain nonresident and resident aliens who cannot get a social security number. In addition, the independent contractor will need to submit a signed W-9 or W-8BEN form. Both forms are available from the Internal Revenue Service. The library submits the W-9 to the IRS to document taxable payments to the independent contractor. The W-8BEN is used by foreign nationals for the same purpose.

In preparation for the actual event the library and the presenter should be in frequent communication so that no misunderstandings occur. If any questions or problems come up, each agent should be notified promptly. There should be, if there is time, a walk-through of the presentation venue to make sure that the presenter's needs are met. This can include a check of the sound system, technology, and environmental conditions, as well as amount and placement of seating. The library should have backups for all requested equipment. It is best to be prepared with some redundancy to avoid any problems that could cause a breach of contract.

CONCLUSION

Developing exhibits and bringing presenters to the library can be a rewarding experience for anyone—if done properly! By thinking and preparing for any possible liability, one can protect oneself and his or her institution from costly litigation. Legal counsel is important to have when drawing up any contract or agreement. If the institution does not have access to an attorney on staff there are alternatives that can be explored. In many communities there are pro-bono legal programs that may be willing to take on reviewing a contract. One can also check to see whether a local law school clinic can provide advice or assistance. Another source is *Lawyers for Libraries,* a project of the American Library Association's Office for Intellectual Freedom. This program was developed to create a nationwide network of attorneys committed to the defense of the First Amendment freedom to read and also for the application of constitutional law to library policies, principles, and problems. By working behind the scenes in a legal environment, one will be a better-prepared, better-protected developer of library exhibits and programs.

Resources

American Library Association Office for Intellectual Freedom. "Lawyers for Libraries." www.ala.org/ala/aboutala/offices/oif/oifprograms/lawforlib/lawyerslibraries.cfm.

Association of College and Research Libraries. "Guidelines for Borrowing and Lending Special Collections Materials for Exhibition." 2005. www.ala.org/ala/mgrps/divs/acrl/standards/borrowguide.cfm.

Brown, Mary E., and Rebecca Powers. *Exhibits in Libraries: A Practical Guide.* Jefferson, NC: McFarland & Company, 2006.

Garner, Bryan A. *Black's Law Dictionary.* St. Paul, MN: West, 2009.

Lind, Robert C., Robert M. Jarvis, and Marilyn E. Phelan. *Art and Museum Law: Cases and Materials.* Durham, NC: Carolina Academic Press, 2002.

Lipinski, Tomas A. *Libraries, Museums and Archives: Legal Issues and Ethical Challenges in the New Information Age.* Lanham, MD: Scarecrow Press, 2002.

Malaro, Marie C. *A Legal Primer on Managing Museum Collections.* Washington, DC: Smithsonian Institution Press, 1998.

Registrars Committee of the American Association of Museums. "Standard Facility Report." http://sceti.library.upenn.edu/dreyfus/docs/Standard_Facility_Report.pdf.

CHAPTER 17

Collaboration as Outreach in the Twenty-First-Century Academic Library

ALLAN CHO

ALTHOUGH ACADEMIC LIBRARIES have traditionally been the nexus of the campus experience, and focused on building collections, providing research support to students and faculty, and offering information literacy instruction, they are increasingly integrated into the broader aspirations of the institution, especially in terms of community engagement and outreach. As one expert argues, outreach should be central to the mission of academic institutions and, by extension, a library's mandate.[1] In recent years, there has been a call in higher education for more collaboration between universities and their surrounding communities.[2]

At the Irving K. Barber Learning Centre (IKBLC) at the University of British Columbia (UBC), the library's historic Main Library was reconceived as a 250,000 square foot space and an enduring symbol of the university's commitment to community engagement. The IKBLC opened in 2008 as an innovative model that integrates existing collections with teaching and learning spaces; it includes classrooms, academic departments, a learning common, and informal learning spaces. Since its inception, community initiatives have evolved from traditional academic outreach to one that acknowledges the contributions of the community motivated by its needs and priorities.[3]

In particular, this model attempts to bring community to the university campus. The Learning Centre is the centerpiece and the conduit for the planning and coordination of events including lectures, seminars, and symposia.

As program services librarian, I work closely with individuals and departments across the library, university, and other communities in the province. However, defining *community* is a challenge for academic libraries interested in outreach, as it has traditionally been limited to the general campus community, faculty, and academic departments in response to collections and services.[4]

With its highly popular Robson Reading Series, which showcases Canadian authors and poets, and the art gallery, which merges its open foyer space and its popular Ike's Cafeteria, the Learning Centre is an innovative place where the academic library can collaborate with local artists in repurposing library space for public art consumption. In particular, engagement with the artist community has been a successful example of how writers, artists, and musicians can all partner with the library while also attracting community to use library spaces.

ARTISTS IN THE LIBRARY

In many ways, the Learning Centre is about inspiring a sense of learning, research, and beautiful spaces for users to contemplate, socialize, and relax. In offering spaces that provide a place to view art, the Learning Centre also encourages a "visual literacy" that takes place outside formal educational activities by engaging individual artists and groups from broader communities. As Crit Stuart points out, space-use trends in academic research libraries are responding to these demands by integrating art, lectures, displays and performances as assets and "showcas[ing] the intellectual outpouring of the university and celebrating the creative mind."[5]

With the highest percentage of visible minority and immigrant populations in Canada, 51 percent of Vancouver's total population is of visible minority background. People in the city speak a multitude of languages; in 2006 census figures, 50 percent (286,175) identified a language other than English as their mother tongue.[6] Along with the fact that 20 percent of the university's student body is international students, UBC is a place of diversity in and of itself.[7]

In engaging this culturally vibrant and diverse arts community, one of the main opportunities for the Learning Centre is to bring such works to a campus that simultaneously reflects the city's diversity. One such exhibit was "Exquisite Corpse" in 2010, cosponsored by the Mexican Consular General's Office of Vancouver. In celebration of the bicentennial anniversary of Mexico's independence and the centennial of the Mexican Revolution, Mexico Fest was a series of cultural and artistic events in Vancouver during 2010. With Vancouver's growing Mexican and Latino population, Mexico Fest was prominently featured in local English and Spanish television, radio, and newspapers. For the Learning Centre, it was an excellent decision to collaborate with the Mexican consulate to bring to UBC a number of Vancouver-based Mexican artists, including Richard A. Kent, Alfonso L. Tejada, Miriam Aroeste, Claudia Segovia, Sergio Toporek, Adriana Zúñiga, and David Merino.

Also known in English as "Exquisite Cadaver" or in Spanish as "Cadáver exquisito," the exhibition's art featured a unique technique of painting mastered by surrealists in the 1920s. As a collaborative exhibit among the seven artists, each artist added to a composition in sequence, by being allowed to see only a small section of what the previous person contributed. As such, the exhibit blended beautifully three themes throughout the gallery: the first section represents life, the middle section represents love, and the last section represents death—all three aspects constantly present in the Mexican culture.

On the theme of culture, Asian Heritage Month celebrates the long history and contributions of Asian Canadians in Canada year in May. As a way to engage its Asian student populace, approximately half of UBC's student body, the purpose of the Learning Centre's art programs is not only to be relevant and responsive aesthetically; they also reflect the cultural heritage interests of its audiences.[8] As Asian Heritage Month is a series of events important to the cultural fabric of Vancouver, it made sense for the Learning Centre to partner with explorASIAN, the annual festival sponsored by the Vancouver Asian Heritage Month Society for an art exhibit. This proved a tremendous opportunity to reach out to artists who otherwise might not be aware of the public spaces at the university.

The exhibit "Generation One" featured work from the local art scene, including Vancouver artists Raymond Chow, Ron Sombilon, Ray Shum, and Rubina Rajan. Internationally renowned, Raymond Chow's artwork has gone from art galleries across Canada to as far as the Royal Palace of India in Rajasthan. With paintings reaching serious private and corporate collections worldwide, Ron Sombilon's experience in the animation industry for more than twelve years has honed his abilities to employ new media in his body of work. Having exhibited in community galleries in Vancouver and Tokyo, at the embassy of Japan in Ottawa, and at the Ottawa School of Art, Rubina Rajan's Zen calligraphy paints in the moment, spontaneously, without revision, harmonizing brush, breath, and body. In all, the monthlong exhibit proved one of the library's most successful attempts to bring the artist community to campus.

Although many academic libraries offer gallery space in the traditional sense of enclosed walls, the Learning Centre, after an assessment of its space, decided early on that its art exhibits would spill out into the learning spaces and be integrated with the rest of the building.[9] One of the most engaging exhibits held at the Learning Centre has been seventy-three-year-old Ilsoo

Kyung McLaurin's "The Beauty of Nature" exhibit. With a large Korean-immigrant population in Vancouver and on the UBC campus, Kyung McLaurin's works from a first-generation Korean-Canadian standpoint blended in with the intercultural engagement of the university.

With references to the tradition of landscape painting that captures the beauty of the land and trees, Kyung McLaurin's art pieces have a surrounding landscape that serves as a backdrop to her daily life within her adopted homeland of Canada. Through her works, she also illustrates the darker side of the landscape and reveals the troubling aspects of environmental pollution that threatens nature. The exhibit at the Learning Centre, spread throughout the open foyer and continuing into Ike's Café, challenges both philosophical and physical contours of a traditional art gallery.

Consistent with the rest of the building's art, ongoing art work is positioned in areas of the building that attract most attention from users of the Learning Centre. Before its official opening, Learning Centre donors Irving K. and Jean Barber had both attended an exhibition of glass works held by the Architectural Institute of British Columbia, which led to their interest in the artistry of local Vancouver artists Jeff Burnette and John Nutter. Impressed, the couple commissioned both artists to create their installations for permanent display at the Learning Centre to accompany its future gallery.

Owner of Vancouver studio glassblowing studio called Joe Blow Glassworks, Jeff Burnette's *Belle Verre*, two hundred blown-glass plates, form a multicoloured beacon in the southeast stairwell, drawing people into the building to marvel at the glowing spectacle. This installation, which reaches a height of sixty feet, took nearly four months to complete and three days to install.

Magic of Discovery, by John Nutter, who was first approached by Jean Barber to create an installation for the Learning Centre's silent reading room, the Ridington Room, is designed with forty-five panel-glass sculptures to "flow like the Northern Lights," and is centered on the intricate etchings around a series of compasses. As Nutter himself describes this metaphor, the art is like a compass, in which a library needs to be used "as a tool of discovery."[10]

Nutter's other piece, *The Atrium*, is a chandelier-type piece that fills the Learning Centre's atrium with a spiral of fifty-seven panels of star-fire glass. Lead-free and low in iron, star-fire glass is less green in hue than ordinary glass. As Nutter reveals, "Of all the work I've done, this piece exceeds what I thought was possible."[11] Using sandblast carving and stained-glass detailing, Nutter's work incorporates symbols, runes and excerpts from such ancient texts as the Gutenberg Bible, *Beowulf*, and the Dead Sea Scrolls. Nutter applies a dichroic coating to each panel, which lends a luminescence to the work, and LED lights are embedded in metal panels accompanying each glass piece to add to the ambience of the art and building.

Gyung bok gung Great Roof by Ilsoo Kyung McLaurin

Magic of Discovery by John Nutter

The Atrium by John Nutter

ROBSON READING SERIES

Events programming at IKBLC represents a rethinking of the traditional academic library. Holding a reading series is a natural evolution of community outreach, as it is argued that the very act of reading "along with the desire to talk about the reading experience" invites a sense of community into libraries.[12]

What began as an informal reading series in one of UBC's satellite campus bookstores at downtown Robson Square has evolved into one of the longest-running weekly reading series in Canada. Through collaboration with Robson Square, the Learning Centre has integrated a number of these reading events into its building on campus. This Canadian government–sponsored multigenre series brings new and established Canadian authors to the UBC campus, using the Learning Centre's academic space as a venue to attract students and classes that have relevant content in their coursework.

When the IKBLC first opened in 2008, a challenge the events programming staff had to overcome in coordinating events was not only confronting the psychological barrier of distance and isolation of campus from the city but also finding opportunities to capture the cultural diversity of its community—not an easy task, for programming is still a new area for the library. As such, the university's commuter campus is a hurdle for community engagement as many from the Greater Vancouver area tend not to participate in campus events, as UBC is somewhat isolated from the rest of the city.

For the Learning Centre, one of the opportunities in community engagement is to draw on existing campus resources with existing connections with organizations and groups off-campus. Rather than reinventing the wheel with every new event, the Learning Centre partners with a number of campus units that directly work with community and uses the building's space as a physical gathering point for events. With the Robson Reading events, the Learning Centre actively seeks out partners that already have existing connections and mandates to serve the Greater Vancouver off-campus community.

Partnering with an inner-city-located partner like the UBC Learning Exchange not only affords the Learning Centre an opportunity to outreach to the external campus community but also allows access to residents from the Downtown Eastside, one of the poorest neighborhoods in Canada.[13] This partnership proved large dividends with the increased number of audience participants coming from the Learning Exchange. Through a combination of readings, conversation, multimedia presentations, and socializing, the Robson Readings appeal to a number of residents who might not otherwise have an opportunity to travel to campus. This is all made possible through this partnership: the Learning Exchange subsidizes travel costs through reimbursement for bus fare in return for the marketing provided by the Learning

Centre and UBC Library. More important, the value of having these readings through community-university collaboration ultimately supports the university's overall community engagement strategic initiative to facilitate public dialogue on issues of public concern while actively encouraging community participation.

One of the most heartwarming events took place in 2008, when Gabor Maté, a physician based in Downtown Eastside and renowned for his creative nonfiction, came to the Learning Centre for a reading from his new book, *In the Realm of Hungry Ghosts*. In all, the reading drew more than one hundred audience members who filled the room, the majority of people coming from off-campus.

Another example of a community-driven author reading at Learning Centre was Madeleine Thien's event in 2008. Vancouver-born Madeleine Thien, a Canadian of Malaysian-Chinese descent, read from her debut novel *Certainty*, which had already captured positive reviews from the Canadian literary community. Although we knew that searching for partners for this event would not be too much of a challenge, for Thien was already well known, the programming staff kept in mind that finding the appropriate partners would be challenging. As Hood and Rogers argue, community co-programming needs to be more specific than general when anticipating what potential partners might be able to offer.[14]

As the librarian liaison responsible for this reading series, when making inquiries to community organizations familiar with Thien's work, I was careful to select groups that would have membership interested in attending the event. Although Thien resided in Laos, her local roots in Vancouver worked in our favor, as there were community groups excited to partner with us, including *Ricepaper* magazine, for which Thien had written and worked; the Chinese Canadian Historical Society, which promotes Chinese Canadian culture; and UBC Alumni Relations. As an alumnus of UBC, Thien was a natural fit for collaboration between the Learning Centre and UBC's Alumni relations network, which helped promote the reading to alumni around the city.

Finally, another factor in the Learning Centre's programming selection is the suitability of content for the campus' surrounding community. The UBC campus is in close proximity to the traditional territory of the Musqueam peoples, a West Coast First Nations group. Moreover, one of UBC's three main strategic initiatives is on First Nations cultures, and not surprisingly, First Nations are heavily emphasized in UBC's curricula and teaching.

Another exemplary Learning Centre event featured Michael Yahgulanaas, a First Nations artist and storyteller, who presented on his latest work, a graphic novel. What was appealing in bringing an artist as eclectic and unique as Yahgulanaas is that his work—taking traditional Haida stories and turning them into manga (Japanese-style comics)—appeals to a wide range of audiences. From artistically inclined individuals interested in manga art, First Nations peoples, Asian studies majors, and youths interested in graphic novels, there is no shortage of interest in Yahgulanaas's work. Moving away from traditional rectangular boxes and voice balloons associated with North American comics, Yahgulanaas's graphic novel integrates Haida art and history with Western motifs. Indeed, Yahgulanaas's reading became one of the most celebrated events at the Learning Centre, with more than one hundred audience participants. Two classes from the local Bayview Elementary School also attended the reading.

DODSON MUSIC SERIES

A recent development at the Learning Centre has been the revival of a musical tradition of the Learning Centre's earlier incarnation as the UBC Main Library. What began in 1999 as the Friday Noon Hours at Main concert series has evolved into the current-day Dodson Music Series. It could be said that the music series preceded the Learning Centre's collaborative spirit, as it had begun before the reconstruction of the current building began. Initiated by the UBC Music Department in 2001, the goals of the music series were to give students studying music an opportunity to perform for a new audience in a new setting. The Dodson Music Series is very much driven by these student-artists, and students perform for public audiences in the Learning Centre's Dodson Room. In 2011, the series marked its new start with the event "Global New Year: New Year's Music from around the World," which featured music from different national and religious traditions from Bali, Russia, Korea, Ireland, and North America—another reminder of the vibrancy of the campus's ethnic and cultural makeup. Students from the UBC School of music, including students from the voice and opera divisions of the school, organized and performed the entire show.

CONCLUSION

It has been said that universities are, for the most part, walled-off cities with narrowly defined concerns and interests.[15] As such, the examples in this chapter of collaborating with artists to bring community into an academic library space are some general but telling experiences about how to approach this area of librarianship that is perhaps still unfamiliar to many.

First is mutual gain. As Miller and Hafner argue, there should be a mutual accord to work for mutual gain for both the artist and the library.[16] Although not all artistic projects worked as successfully as expected, the ones that did work well met the interests of both the artist and the Learning Centre. Our case studies reveal that mutual collaboration not only engaged and entertained audiences but also ultimately allowed for the artist to reach out to a segment of a university audience that he or she might not have otherwise had access to.

Second is collaboration. Academic libraries' community engagement should be much more than library outreach; rather, libraries should view their engagement as "collaboration as dialogue."[17] As artwork and readings are free-flowing spontaneous processes in which the artist improvises, the librarian is there merely to facilitate discussion between audience and artist—whether in a reading or an art presentation. Because much of the programming is artist driven, the themes and decor of the exhibits and readings are largely established with the interests of the artists in mind. The duration of the exhibits and the length and focus of readings are all set by the artists themselves.

Third is a culture of constant assessment. We decided the gallery space needed to be in an open space of the building, to further integrate it into the experiences of patrons. As a result of this flexibility, the gallery has been able to be responsive to audience's and artists' preferences. For the Learning Centre, engaging stakeholders—students, faculty, community members—in assessment was a key factor in the decision to relocate the gallery space to the open foyer area and to Ike's Café.[18]

Fourth is more civic engagement and less outreach. Although the term *outreach* has been used most often in the academic libraries literature regarding collaboration with external campus partners, it can be restricting in that it denotes a one-way relationship in which the library actively seeks one-off events to fill a programming need. In taking a civic engagement approach, we feel that relationships need to be nurtured and that we are on a continuous journey with community and library.

Notes

1. Nancy Courtney, "Breaking Out of Our Shell: Expanding the Definition of Outreach in Academic Libraries," in *Academic Library Outreach: Beyond the Campus Walls*, edited by Nancy Courtenay (Westport, CT: Libraries Unlimited, 2009), 4.
2. Peter Miller and Madeline Hafner, "Moving toward Dialogical Collaboration: A Critical Examination of a University-School-Community Partnership," *Educational Administration Quarterly* 44 (2008): 68.
3. Sandra Singh, "Librarians as Information Providers and Facilitators: The Irving K. Barber Learning Centre as a Model for the Expansion of the Role of Academic

Libraries in University-Community Engagement" (paper presented at the conference "One Road In, Many Roads Out; Education as a Catalyst for Regeneration," University of Limerick, Ireland, June 2–4, 2010), 7.

4. Thembi Hadebe, Robin Kear, and Paula M. Smith, "Cultural Lessons: Academic Outreach across Borders," in *Academic Library Outreach: Beyond the Campus Walls*, edited by Nancy Courtenay (Westport, CT: Libraries Unlimited, 2009), 38–39.

5. Crit Stuart, "Learning and Research Spaces in ARL Libraries: Snapshots of Installations and Experiment," *Research Library Issues: A Bimonthly Report From ARL, CNI, and SPARC* (June 2009): 7–8.

6. City of Vancouver Planning Department, "Mother Tongue (single responses) 1991–2006," CityFacts Census Data Series, February 4, 2009, http://vancouver.ca/commsvcs/planning/census/2006/languages.pdf.

7. University of British Columbia, "UBC Profile," 2010, https://you.ubc.ca/ubc/htmlemailupload/File/ubcprofile.pdf.

8. Henry Yu, "Global Migrants and the New Pacific Canada," *International Journal* (Autumn 2009): 1019–20.

9. Crit Stuart, "Learning and Research Spaces in ARL Libraries: Snapshots of Installations and Experiment," *Research Library Issues: A Bimonthly Report From ARL, CNI, and SPARC* (June 2009): 14–16.

10. Irving K. Barber Learning Centre, "Through the Learning Centre Glass, *Connects Newsletter*, 7 (2009): 3, http://blogs.ubc.ca/libnews/files/2009/03/connects-spring-2009.pdf.

11. Ibid.

12. Stephanie Mathson, Robin Sabo, and Joyce Salisbury, "Growing Grassroots Collaboration between Academic and Public Libraries, in *Academic Library Outreach: Beyond the Campus Walls*, ed. Nancy Courtenay (Westport, CT: Libraries Unlimited, 2009), 77–78.

13. Patricia Shaw, "Language and Identity, Language and the Land," *BC Studies* 131 (2001): 39–55.

14. Yolanda Hood and Emily Rogers, "The NEA Big Read Comes to Valdosta!" in *Academic Library Outreach: Beyond the Campus Walls*, edited by Nancy Courtenay (Westport, CT: Libraries Unlimited, 2009), 166–68.

15. Gar Alperowitz, Steve Dubb, and Ted Howard, "The Next Wave: Building University Engagement for the 21st Century," *Good Society* 17 (2008): 69.

16. Ibid., 74.

17. Peter Miller and Madeline Hafner, "Moving toward Dialogical Collaboration: A Critical Examination of a University-School-Community Partnership," *Educational Administration Quarterly* 44 (2008): 74.

18. Barbara Holland, "Different Worlds and Common Ground: Community Partner Perspectives on Campus-Community Partnerships," *Michigan Journal of Community Services Learning* (2006): 55–58.

CHAPTER 18

Java City

Developing A Successful Cultural Center

JACK G. MONTGOMERY

DEFINING SPACE

Western Kentucky University (WKU) Library had a large two-level but largely unused lobby that had once been the library's entrance but had been closed after a new entrance was created. By 2002, the lobby sat empty and all but devoid of human traffic just outside our reference area. Reference statistics were down, as were circulation and library usage in general. Dean Michael Binder believed that with the renovation and development of the former lobby, the library would realize an increase in campus visibility and library usage would increase.

Binder partnered with the campus food-service provider to establish a café with comfortable and attractive seating area on both levels and to reopen the former entrance, which opens onto a large patio and heavily used thoroughfare and community space between the Fine Arts Center and the library. As Binder began working on logistics with the various organizations on campus to bring his vision to reality, he also conceived of an ongoing series of live entertainment and cultural events in the café. The library could become, in a way that it had not before, a center for culture and university life. To this end, he formed a committee to develop a vision for the cultural program and an organizational plan for its management. He recruited several faculty and staff from the library and solicited members from WKU academic departments who were likely to participate in and benefit from such a program. I was appointed committee chair, because in addition to being a faculty member and librarian, I am a working musician with a background in nightclub management and connections to the local and regional entertainment community. We developed a mission for Java City: "To provide adequate and appropriate planning, networking and implementation required for the establishment of a regular schedule of live entertainment programs and events in the 'Java City' coffee shop in the Helm-Cravens Library Complex."

Our initial planning sessions were lively, and our discussions and brainstorming were very valuable, which created an atmosphere of a collective effort. Among the topics we discussed were the following:

What kinds of entertainment did we want to offer?

When and where would these events take place?

Who would provide the initial funding for materials like sound equipment, a stage, and staff?

How would we be able to support an ongoing series if it became successful?

Were we going to offer money for these performances?

Who was going to manage the events and bookings?

Should we have a performance contract? Who should sign these contracts with agents?

How were we going to publicize these events?

After several meetings, we decided that the library would essentially fund and manage the entire process with input from other departments. The result was the Java City Noontime Concert Series, and over the past few years the series has become an exclusive library-managed operation. Input from multiple departments was initially valuable in inaugurating such a program, but anyone planning a similar program should consider that, in the end, a small, cohesive, dedicated group of people will conduct the actual work.

The Java City Café opened in August 2002, and we began the concert series in October. Western Kentucky University has historically been, and essentially still is, a regionally based "suitcase" institution, with most of its students returning to their homes each weekend. As a result, we decided we would offer the one-hour performances in the middle of the week during lunch hours, from 12 P.M. to 1:30 P.M.

There is now a tremendous amount of foot traffic into and past the library. The opening of the Java City Café was responsible for much of this traffic, as people go there to buy food and beverages. The library decided to allow covered beverages into the library in recognition of the presence of the Java City Café and the changing dynamics of our patron population. I must admit, as a book preservationist, I expressed real concerns about damage to our books and facility. Patrons have been very respectful and seem to understand and value the privilege of bringing beverages into our facility.

ORGANIZATIONAL STRUCTURE

As we progressed in the planning process, we soon realized that we needed a core of reliable, available people to manage the concert series. Our former dean of libraries appointed a committee of library employees, with me as chair, one professional colleague from Public Services, and two staff members from Public and Technical services who responded to our call for interested people. The Java City Live Entertainment Committee initially met to plan logistics, approve performers, and purchase sound equipment. We were initially funded from discretionary monies from the Office of the Dean. Today the committee rarely meets in a formal manner but instead functions like a well-oiled machine around the concert events. Everyone knows what to do and how to do it, and we are a very cohesive group. In addition, everyone is cross-trained so that if someone is sick or absent, someone else can cover his or her position. One piece of advice to anyone planning an event like this would be to keep the working group small and to use great care in selecting who is to be involved.

LOCATION

Initially, we decided that our concerts would be held inside the entrance lobby of Helm Library (inside the Java City Café) to be able to control the effect of the noise on the surrounding area. We had to install and maintain an additional security gate in this lobby, as a new library entrance and exit had been created. This arrangement worked well until warm weather drew our audience outside. We soon realized that we could have an expanded audience for the events by moving the concerts out onto the patio just outside the library entrance. As a result, some outside concerts have had estimated audiences of up to five hundred people.

SOUND MANAGEMENT

We quickly realized that few of our performers had the ability to manage their own sound, and so we decided that we would employ a library staff member to operate the sound system. Fortunately, we have another employee who is also a professional musician and understands how to set up and balance sound. He is paid a small fee per event for this service.

BOOKING MANAGEMENT

I took over the task of booking the performers because of my personal connections in the local entertainment community. Our original decision was to solicit performers who would perform without charge. We also decided to allow performers to sell their music CDs, T-shirts, or other promotional materials as an inducement to perform. The college circuit is a very lucrative one for traveling performers, and many aspiring artists really want to get into this market.

Over the years, we have gradually been able to offer a small stipend to performers. We still do not offer what would be considered an attractive amount of money, but we can offer the value of self-promotion and publicity. On occasion, agents call me only to dismiss our venue because of the small stipend, but most realize that it is better for promotional value to book a low-paying event between more lucrative ones.

To make our low-paying venue more attractive, I began to make personal connections with cafés and clubs in the area that book live entertainment. I offer to send people I book for Java City to their venue so the performer can possibly get two low-paying gigs while passing through Bowling Green. Sometimes, acts perform for us at noon and then do a second performance that night before going out on the road again. I also keep a list of venues with contact information to e-mail to aspiring performers or agents so that they can arrange another event for themselves. I provide the potential for additional performances in the area, but I leave the details to the performers or their agents. I have, on occasion, called a club owner and made a recommendation, but I do not act as anyone's agent.

In the early years of Java City concerts, we had more performances by faculty and students of the WKU Music and Theater departments, but within a few years, those types of performers became the exception rather than the rule. We maintain good relations with both departments, and our door is always open to their performances. One of the major reasons for the decline in student and faculty performances is schedule conflict with midday classes. Our one exception is an ongoing series of evening poetry slams by the Department of English. These are our one event at night. We provide the setup and sound system, and the department manages the acoustics. We come in the next morning and break down the equipment. We also host sales by the Art Department, occasional student events, and selective lectures by approved speakers and community groups.

We still have an occasional performance without cost to us, usually by university faculty and staff, whom we are not allowed to pay. The majority of our performers, however, play for a set fee, so we can stay within our annual budget. As we progressed into hiring paying performers, we enlisted several other people to the committee from the office of the dean of libraries, to help with promotion and payment processing, but they do not actively manage the events themselves.

As our popularity as a venue grew, we found ourselves in the enviable position of being besieged by people wanting to perform. For a couple of years we tried two to three performances a week, but that proved too costly and too much additional work for the committee to manage. All members of the committee have full-time jobs in the library, so we have returned to booking a single performance per week. If a performer should cancel, I keep a list of folks I can call on short notice who are willing to perform.

We soon realized that the Java City Café was a good vehicle for outreach to the local community and to the campus. To this end, I have always made a special effort to seek out and recruit performers from the southern Kentucky region.

From the earliest years of the Java City Café concerts, I used social networking resources and electronic booking services to locate potential performers. I have used Facebook, Myspace, Sonicbids, and ReverbNation to explore local and regional talent. After nine years, I no longer have to search for performers; they come to us largely, and by word-of-mouth recommendations and through our social networking presence. The social networking sites are excellent showcases for performers' information, photos, video clips, music samples, and touring schedules. All this information is very valuable in evaluation and promotion of those selected.

When performers or booking agents contact me about performing at Java City, I look them up and listen to their musical samples. I then forward the information on likely performers to the Live Entertainment Committee members for their input before scheduling a performance. If the committee approves the selection, I use performers' information available online to promote them after confirming the booking.

I also seek out committee and library administration input when booking an act that may be controversial. Good communication must go in both directions. On rare occasions, we have denied access to our space because of an act's content and the possible negative impact on our library.

Free speech is an important right, especially on a college campus, but we do not see Java City's role as a speaker's corner, and we have clarified that in our performance policy. It is important to clearly state the role of your performance venue and other policy objectives in the mission statement and working documents. The mission statement and policy documents provide protection for you as organizer and for your organization. The value of clear policies cannot be overstated. Our statement is as follows: "The events scheduled for 'Java City' are for entertainment purposes only and hence the committee shall not approve presentations which include partisan political rhetoric or speeches espousing political, racial or religious agendas. This does not include the presentation of religiously oriented music but refers to polemical or evangelizing oratory. The 'Java City' events are also not a forum for public debate."

During our planning process, we had a university attorney review the wording and overall policy documents related to Java City before we booked the first concert. Generally, we book acts only one semester in advance and do not book during summer or holiday seasons. Booking too far in advance becomes problematic in terms of cancellations and changes in touring schedules. In addition, we do not book acts the week before final exams or during the week of graduation. On average, we book eleven to thirteen concerts per semester.

SPONSORSHIP

Many small public, college, or university libraries do not have the discretionary funds to set up and maintain a performance venue. Sometimes start-up monies are available through competitive internal grant programs. Seeking funding from a local sponsor or sponsors is a way to partner with local businesses with an interest in supporting community projects. Here are some tips for preparing for meeting with a potential sponsor:

Have the project working documents ready: policy, mission statement, goals and objectives.
Negotiate in good faith regarding potential sponsors' logos, name recognition, and so on.
Try to be flexible about the types of support offered. Keep an open mind and work with administrators to build a potential long-term sponsorship program.

Several years ago, a local bank willing to sponsor our concert series for a five-year period approached us. We gladly accepted the offer and made certain that we recognize the bank's generosity in all our promotional efforts.

The key to our success has been in selecting those acts appropriate to our particular venue and audience. Our most popular indoor concerts are often a singer-songwriter, duets, trios, and small acoustic bands. Outside on the patio, larger bands and dance troupes are the most popular acts.

I try as much as possible to present a wide variety of musical styles. Over the years we have presented all types of music, from classical, contemporary Christian, rap, hip-hop, soul, Celtic, folk, old-time, bluegrass, rock, and jazz. We have had comedians, poetry groups, theatrical productions, percussion groups, belly-dance troupes, and performers from all over the United States, Canada, the United Kingdom, and from as far away as Peru.

Every once in a while, we book a performer whose work or style just does not resonate with the crowd, and the audience members always let us know their feelings on this matter. As an example, I often book rap artists for the patio. Knowing that rap and hip-hop can have lyrics that are challenging to some people, before the performance I counsel performers on what language is acceptable, and most of the time they comply.

Our mission statement contains the following statement:

> Presentations which contain questionable lyrics or language. The committee reserves the right to request transcripts of presentations in advance of the performance and reserves the right to refuse or terminate a performance that violates the above-mentioned standard or violates established community standards for public behavior. Part of the standard for appropriate language shall include the guidelines of the [Federal Communications Commission] for words which may not be said on broadcast radio or television.

Usually, if performers get really negative reviews or reactions from the audience or fail to appear for a show without contacting us, we do not ask them back to our venue. Often when they contact us for a rebooking, I always defer to a kind refusal because this is a word-of-mouth business. Ill will and condemnations can cause problems for all parties involved. In a small community, relationships are close knit, and it is important to use great tact and diplomacy in all types of communication.

PROMOTION

Promotion of the events is a critical element of our success and requires a multiple-step approach by several people. A few strategies we have developed involve the following: we send out campuswide e-mail announcements a few days in advance of the event. Those e-mails are carefully worded to promote the performer, to brand the library as the host, and to give credit to our community sponsor. Logos and branding are key elements with all our promotional materials. We post photos of the concerts to the library's blog after the event.

Our library marketing coordinator supplies me with monthly group and individual performer posters, which are uniform in design and size, complete with our logo and the logo of our sponsor. Once a week before each concert I distribute them in high-traffic areas on campus.

We also promote the events though local radio announcements. I send copies of our performance schedules to local DJs and post the schedule online in the regional online entertainment paper and the library's website.

As a part of our community outreach, I often interview a performer before or after the performance, and the interview is published in the monthly regional entertainment newspaper in a column called "Music from the Hill." "The Hill" is a well-known nickname for the university, and the column has been read and accepted by the local community. Finally, when I go out for an evening, people often approach me with new ideas for a performance or performer. In addition, when I see performers who will fit our venue, I am always quick to introduce myself and recruit them for Java City.

EVENT MANAGEMENT

Before each performance I personally go and greet the performer, making sure they have what they need to be able to start on time. If problems arise, I am there to ensure that the performer finds a quick resolution. During each performance, after collecting the necessary information for paying our performers, I stay for a while to do the sound check with our technician, and then I take photos of the performer. Within an hour of the performance, our assistant posts those photos with a promotional blurb and uploads them to the library's blog. The request for the performer's payment, along with the W-9 tax form, is delivered to the library's accounts manager for payment. I often reappear at the end of the concert to be certain the performer can easily pack up equipment and get back on the road. This personal touch has helped create a very positive impression of Java City as a desirable venue.

CONCLUSION

The growth and development of the Java City Noontime Concert Series and facility is a case of evolution from humble beginnings to the phenomenon it is today. To date, we have hosted more than 250 events and hundreds of performers. A number of those who have achieved national recognition have passed through our venue. One immediate effect of the series was a sharp rise in our library gate-count and, surprisingly, a measurable increase in the amount of traffic to our reference desk. The table below shows the rise in inquiries at our reference desk over four-month periods in two years. The higher numbers reflect an increase in foot traffic in large part as the Java City Noontime Concert Series grew.

Reference	2002–3	2001–2
August	1,514	500
September	2,528	988
October	2,259	1,231
November	1,994	1,331

We have, without question, achieved our mission and become a cultural and community center for the university. We have also increased our public awareness as a cultural venue within the greater community of south-central Kentucky. I am grateful that the Java City Noontime Concerts and other events have been a part of the library's overall successful outreach mission, and I am sincerely grateful to all the people that have worked so hard to make it happen.

CHAPTER 19

Raising Money to Support the Arts in Your Public Library

FLORENCE F. CADDELL

THE FRANKFORT COMMUNITY Public Library (FCPL) in Frankfort, Indiana, began as a twelve-thousand-square-foot Carnegie building in 1906. In 1973, Claude W. "Bill" Caddell assumed the position of library director. In the 1980s, patron Mary Gorham Herrick asked Caddell if he would like her husband's art collection for the library. Caddell responded that he would love to acquire the art, but there was neither space to exhibit nor store the collection. Inspired by the potential gift, he asked Herrick if she would like to build the library a new wing. She responded affirmatively. In her will she bequeathed the library $1.3 million.

Caddell gained countywide library service in 1984, which brought the library district population up from 16,800 to approximately 30,000. In 1989, the $2.5 million Mary Gorham Herrick Wing opened to the public. Additional funds for the new wing came from a $486,000 Library Services and Construction Act grant, a $250,000 municipal lease, and a $350,000 local fund drive chaired by then state attorney general Linley Pearson; the remainder came from library savings.

Under Caddell's leadership, and thanks to the support of Mrs. Herrick, donors, the board of trustees, and staff, FCPL grew to a spacious fifty-one-thousand-square-foot library and cultural center that includes a two-hundred-seat theater, art and music rooms, art galleries, art storage, annex with woodworking shop, theater rehearsal and prop-storage space, and a parking lot. The Frankfort Library's Herrick Wing, as well as the Helen Shanklin Children's Department and Garald and Toni Gill Lower Level remodeling projects and three branch libraries, were all built without bond issues.

In 1995, the Friends of the Library formed the Anna and Harlan Hubbard School of Living as the structure behind the library arts programming. The Hubbard School is based on the philosophy "we can make our life a work of art," and it is dedicated to the memory of Anna and Harlan Hubbard, who made their life together a work of art on a daily basis.

In 1999, Bill Caddell and the Friends of the Frankfort Library received the Indiana Governor's Arts Award. In 2006, the library received an award from the Institute of Museum and Library Services, presented by First Lady Laura Bush in Washington, DC, for outstanding library service and support of the arts. In 2006, Caddell received the Indiana Arts Administrator Community Arts Leadership Award. In 2007, he was named a Distinguished Hoosier by Governor Mitch Daniels. Currently a library consultant and fundraiser, Bill Caddell presents motivational fund-raising workshops on how to turn libraries into cultural centers.

The following sections discuss helpful steps for raising money for the arts at the Frankfort Library.

CREATE A FRIENDS-OF-THE-LIBRARY ORGANIZATION

Friends groups can become a legally recognized charitable organization by filing forms for 501(c)(3) nonprofit status. Donations and membership dues

Library Director Bill Caddell receives a 2006 Institute of Museum and Library Services Award from First Lady Laura Bush for outstanding library service and support of the arts. L-R: Dr. Anne-Imelda Radice, Julie Miller, Claude W. "Bill" Caddell, First Lady Laura Bush.

Photo courtesy of the Institute of Museum and Library Services

to your Friends group, in many cases, can then be considered charitable contributions and are tax deductible. Income can be deposited with the Friends group and gifted to the library for projects outside of the library budget.

The library director oversees the operation of the Friends and manages the budget. It is beneficial to recruit Friends board members who share an interest in the arts. Those whom you recruit to serve on your Friends board may move into positions on the library board of trustees. Most goals cannot be accomplished without board support. Board members should be asked to support the library financially.

CREATE SPACE IN WHICH THE ARTS CAN THRIVE

Meeting, work, performance, and exhibition space are all important to artists. If your library can provide a venue for these activities, you will be on your way to a partnership that could prove mutually profitable.

When FCPL added a cultural center wing, it was important to bring arts groups into the library. The Friends hosted programs on topics including quilting and gardening. Workshop participants were invited to form

A member of the Tuesday Night Inkers Printmaking Group, high school student Elias Garza carves a block for printing in the Mae Conard Art Studio, Frankfort Library.
Photo by Tammie Farrell

organizations that meet at the library. This led to the formation of the Frankfort Quilt Guild, the Frankfort Garden Club, the Clinton County Art League, the Clinton County Civic Theatre, and others. As groups become established, they may start giving back in ways such as sponsoring classes, performing, exhibiting, volunteering, and making donations.

The Frankfort Quilt Guild makes a quilt every year for an auction. Proceeds benefit the library in the form of cash, workshops, furniture, lighting, and support for other projects.

The Frankfort Garden Club helps with the library gardens. Library director Bill Caddell grew flowers for the club. The members harvested the flowers, created arrangements, and sold their creations at the library's Christmas Art Exhibition and Sale. The proceeds from the garden club sales helped pay the gardener's salary, purchase plants, and provide gardening programs for the public.

The Clinton County Art League sponsors art exhibitions and programs that are free and open to the public. The league also purchased paint and painted the gallery walls.

The Clinton County Civic Theatre performs three times per year at the library. Ticket sales and grant dollars helped purchase lighting and curtains for the theater. In the past, the theater has donated more than $1,000 a year to the library.

HIRE STAFF WITH A PASSION FOR THE ARTS

If you can hire staff members who have a passion for the arts, they will work hard to make the arts successful. Start these positions as part-time and move them to full-time as funds become available.

The FCPL's head of maintenance also is the director of the Clinton County Civic Theatre. This ensures that the theater is staffed by someone familiar with library procedures, such as locking up and keeping the building clean and in good repair.

The children's theater director dreamed of leading her own children's theater. Bill Caddell offered her the position if she could find ways to fund it. She enthusiastically asked friends, family, and local businesses to help out. She raised enough money to put on shows and pay herself a salary.

The arts director Flo Caddell was a Clinton County Art League member who planned art programs at FCPL for the league. She was interested in taking art classes and was happy to plan occasional workshops as a volunteer. When the library was ready to take a more comprehensive approach to arts programming and exhibitions with the formation of the Hubbard School, it was natural that she step into the role.

HOST ART PROGRAMS

With the Anna and Harlan Hubbard School arts programming, there are fees charged for some programs. In most cases, the Frankfort Library programs operate on a breakeven basis, charging just enough to cover instructor and material fees and a little extra for library costs, such as publicity and a fraction of the arts director's salary. The arts programming helps support the Friends group as well as artists in the community. We need to provide artists with a venue in which they can meet, create, perform, teach, and sell their work. If having the arts woven into the fabric of the community is desired, then the community must support the artists financially, enabling artists to create and make a living doing what they love.

When Bill Caddell first started arts programming at FCPL, the library hosted belly-dancing classes at the request of a group of ladies working at an auto-parts factory. The trustees approved hosting the classes on the condition that they were held elsewhere. With the modest profit made from the classes, the library was able to purchase handsome exterior signage.

Integrate the arts into your existing literature-based programming. Story hours can include time for crafts. Children's concerts can incorporate a musical story. Likewise, art programs may include an appealing display of books about the current project.

Library coffee shops are brimming with programming potential. Aside from being an inviting place to peruse library materials over an aromatic cup

Participants in gourd art workshop at the Frankfort Library. *Photo by Florence Caddell*

of freshly ground coffee, the coffee shop is an excellent venue for author visits, brown-bag lunches, and live musical performances. Pass the hat at each performance for donations to musicians. With arts activities happening in this engaging space, the Friends group may be able to break even or see a profit through sales of coffee, pastries, and art available for purchase.

With arts organizations meeting at the library and Friends-sponsored art programs taking place, the library becomes a beehive of activity. This creates an atmosphere that is magnetic. People want to be a part of something positive. People have traveled many miles to take classes or to see an exhibit at the Frankfort Library.

SPECIAL EVENT FUND-RAISING—ART EXHIBITIONS

The Frankfort Library has hosted art exhibition fund-raisers for more than thirty years. In 2010, the Friends of the Frankfort Library's Christmas Art Exhibition and Sale included more than artists and sales of more than $52,000 in a three-day weekend. The artists keep 70 percent of their sales. The Friends keep a 30 percent commission on all work sold. This surplus of about $15,000 a year helps pay the arts director's salary and supports arts programming and exhibitions for the coming year.

Before the cultural center addition at the Frankfort Library, Bill Caddell started bringing the arts into the library in small ways, having art exhibitions with just two artists, hanging paintings from the end panels of the book stacks while a string quartet played in the entryway in front of the circulation desk. Start small. What you need is probably at hand. Look closely at your local community and patrons. There may be hidden talents and gifts as close as your front door.

Hosting art exhibits provides a means of furnishing the library with original art. Examine your budget and find ways to purchase original art from some of the exhibitors. The nonprint budget may be a source of funds. Since your Friends group retains a commission on work sold, you can purchase this work at the reduced price and build an art collection for the library. Some libraries have a circulating art collection that has works of art available for checkout just like a book but with a longer loan period. It is also a fine idea to build a permanent art collection. Artists may consider it prestigious to have their work in the library collection and offer the library a larger commission. Some artists may be willing to donate their work. Artists may also be commissioned to create a work of art for a specific location. Having art in the library promotes interest in art and art education. It can also be a source of inspiration for patrons and artists in your community.

Some patrons may not have wall space for art at home but still want to support the art exhibit fund-raiser. These patrons may donate toward the acquisition of a work of art for the library collection.

Hosting exhibitions can be a form of economic development. While guests are in town for your exhibit, they may shop, eat, purchase gas, and spend money locally. Downtown businesses collaborate with FCPL events to capitalize on the influx of people.

You can also host student art exhibits. Collaborations with schools help improve students' art education and familiarity with the library. Parents come to the library for student exhibit receptions. While the family is at the library, they may register for library cards and check out books or other materials, thus promoting literacy and continuing education outside of the classroom.

Have fun! Make your events a party. Have great refreshments, flowers, and music. Let your volunteers do what they enjoy doing. For all the points mentioned above, hosting a big event fund-raiser like an art exhibition can build a sense of community at your library. More than a hundred volunteers help with the November Christmas art show. Many have been involved year after year.

At your art exhibit, have a guest book that designates space for contact information such as home and e-mail address and phone number. Gather this information from all purchasers as well. With this guest register and sales receipts, you can build a mailing list for future exhibitions, events, and fundraising appeals.

Invite private art collectors to have an exhibit at your library. Many collectors are honored to share their collection and quite willing to talk about it publicly. This is another way to build community and stimulate immediate or future donations of art or funds.

CULTIVATE GRANTS, DONATIONS, DEFERRED GIFTS, AND ENDOWMENTS

Seek Private and Corporate Gifts and Grants for Current Projects

Ask the local newspaper if it is interested in a column written by library staff about upcoming programs, exhibits, and new materials available for checkout. When funds are needed for a special project or an arts acquisition, insert a plea for this special project in the column and in the friends-of-the-library group's newsletter. This is a way to reach a broader audience and discover new patrons with interest in the arts and the library.

In Frankfort there was a very kind and generous lady who loved art. Whenever she saw a plea in the paper for a library art project, the very next day there would be a check on Bill Caddell's desk. When this thoughtful lady passed away, she remembered the library in her will and endowed the children's art enrichment classes with a gift of $54,000.

Send news to local radio and television stations for public service announcements. Send the newspaper and the radio station news releases about upcoming events. Ask the paper to come to take a picture of the artist setting up an exhibit or the musician rehearsing. Schedule television interviews. Post information in the newsletter and on your website and social networks. This publicity before your event helps ensure an audience, ticket sales, and community support in a variety of forms.

There was a local artist who loved taking classes and exhibiting at FCPL. In fact, this artist and her husband donated money to name one of the library art galleries and financed gallery lighting. After she passed away, a friend created an art-class scholarship fund to honor this generous lady's memory and share her love of the arts.

High school alumni are good candidates to approach about funding special projects. Alumni are often proud of their roots and happy to see good things happening back home. As a group, they may wish to have their class year listed as a benefactor for a special project. At the branch library in Mulberry, Indiana (population 1262), the high school alumni and Friends of the Library raised more than $200,000 toward a new five-thousand-square-foot building.

Look at who is attending your arts programming. People who attend musical performances in the coffee shop may be good candidates for sponsoring those programs via a donation for music-licensing fees, other associated costs, and regular donations for the musicians. Private collectors and their friends who loan art to be exhibited or who attend library art exhibits are prospective donors of either art or funds.

Don't stop with just the library patrons for your mailing list. When you go to other nonprofit organizations' facilities such as the hospital, theater, or symphony, look at their donor list in the program or on the donor wall. Who is the building named after? Add these names to your mailing list. Chances are that if they support other nonprofits, they may also be interested in supporting art and music at the library.

Corporate sponsors support the concert series, the Friends annual meeting, the children's art enrichment classes, and other projects. Sponsors are recognized publicly in the programs, newsletters, newspaper articles, radio public service announcements, and on the website. Local Japanese-owned businesses sponsor the Japanese Festival in conjunction with the Friends annual meetings, complete with *taiko* drums, *sumi-e* paintings, and sushi. This is a rich source of cultural exchange set in a venue that is open and inviting to all.

There are corporations in Indiana and others states that fund arts projects or organizations. Look at their past giving history, read up on their interests, and then prepare a query or grant proposal. The Indiana Arts Commission provides grants for operating support for arts organizations. The arts director at the Frankfort Library writes grants yearly to the Indiana Arts Commission to pay a portion of her salary.

When buying a grand piano for the library, at the request of a patron who was willing to donate $5,000 seed money, the piano manufacturer had an innovative fund-raising plan to secure the additional funds needed. A large piano keyboard was posted at the front entrance. Patrons could "note" the progress each day as they entered the building. Opportunities were available to purchase a note or an entire octave, and then the patron's name would be written on the keys that he or she purchased. There was quite a flurry of activity to buy middle C! The original donor doubled his pledge to $10,000, and $14,000 was raised from the community. In no time, all keys had been paid for, and the new piano was on its way to the Elizabeth O'Rear Skanta Theatre stage.

If a patron is interested in making a gift to the library that must be used right away, the money is placed in the gift fund. The patron receives a charitable contribution deduction, and the library can use the gift immediately. In Indiana, the donation of stock may be accepted. The library may hold or sell stock, but in Indiana the library cannot buy stock.

In-kind donations may be requested when special skills are needed but funds are short. Excavating, digging trenches, moving books, landscaping, and many other services were donated for Frankfort and branch-library-building projects such as the cultural center wing. One man donated thousands of dollars worth of cherry and walnut lumber for furniture and paneling in the Frankfort Library's art gallery and theater. These in-kind donations can save the library tremendous amounts of cash.

Solicit Deferred Gifts to Build an Endowment for Future Funding

Make an endowment plan. Decide what you want and how much it will cost per year. Determine the amount of endowment needed to generate enough income per year to sustain your plan. Be generous in your estimates of what you need. Things always cost more than expected. The economy can change overnight.

It is important to build an endowment for your library so that you will have money in the future to continue funding the programs and activities that are established and valued. When the economy takes a downturn or income decreases, it is a lesson in logic that you should not have all your eggs in one basket. Don't rely just on tax money. If you wish to embrace the concept of library as cultural center, you must search for a variety of income streams.

Figure 19.3. The Anna and Harlan Hubbard Gallery, Frankfort Library. *Photo by Florence Caddell*

Spread your investments over stocks, bonds, and certificates of deposit. Don't spend your principal, only the interest.

Remember those board members, volunteers, and members of arts organizations now meeting at your library? These patrons have a vested interest in your library's future. These are the people to ask to become donors for special programs such as free children's art classes or music lessons. These people should be moved to the top of the list to be asked to make a deferred gift.

Be sure to have staff take down the names and addresses of people donating books or anything of value. Donors have an interest in the library. Ask these patrons to make a deferred gift and name the library in their will, estate plan, or trust. It is very important to ask people for the gift. If you don't ask, you are not likely to receive any money.

Some patrons may be interested in remembering a loved one in a way that supports the arts. The FCPL's Elizabeth O'Rear Skanta Theatre was named after a local lady involved in theater. Bill Caddell wrote Mr. Skanta a letter that stated he could memorialize his wife forever by donating money for the library theater in her honor. Skanta agreed. A childhood friend of Elizabeth O'Rear Skanta left $88,000 to the library to endow theater maintenance.

In Indiana, community foundations are another avenue for patron donations. If you do not have a library foundation, you may wish to start one or join an existing community foundation. Different funds for your library can be established with your local community foundation. The Frankfort Library has several funds that endow arts programming, including the Eleanor Ryan Youth Theatre Fund ($50,000), the Nancy N. Fullerton Fund for the Anna and Harlan Hubbard School of Living ($29,000), the John Chandler Fund ($64,000) to endow the library gardens, and many more. The patron may donate cash, real estate, or stock to the community foundation.

The community foundation can also help your patron establish a charitable remainder trust, which gives donors an immediate tax deduction and a source of income for the rest of their lives. Donors may fund the trust with cash, stock, real estate, or a paid-up life insurance policy. The patron's money is put into a fund that the community foundation invests and manages, and the patron receives the interest earned. After the patron passes away, the remainder goes to the library.

Think big. Ask big. People may be far more generous than your greatest expectations.

CHAPTER 20

Where to Find Programming Ideas and Resources for the Arts Online

ALA PUBLIC PROGRAMS OFFICE

WHEN PLANNING FOR arts programs in your library, there's no need to start from scratch. Plenty of organizations have created program models and resources that are available free of charge to libraries. The American Library Association's (ALA) Public Programs Office has compiled the following list of online resources for programming ideas as well as some potential sources for funding. Visit ALA's programming resource website, www.programming librarian.org, for articles about innovative library cultural programming written by programming librarians and other experts. The website also features the Brainstormer, a tool designed to get library programmers started planning cultural and community programs. Updates to the list below can be found by searching "Arts."

PROGRAMMING RESOURCES

Creative Arts—General

Art 21 Inc. "Art 21 on PBS—Online Lesson Library, Visual and Performing Arts," www.pbs.org/art21/education/visualarts.html

The Art in the Twenty-First Century short-film series introduces audiences to a diverse group of visual and performing artists, including painters, photographers, sculptors, and performance and video artists.

The series explores "what it means to be an artist and an imaginative thinker today," and the Art 21 website provides myriad discussion questions and lesson plans for younger audiences.

Johanna Misey Boyer, "Creativity Matters: The Arts and Aging Toolkit," http://artsandaging.org

A comprehensive guide to creative arts programming for older adults, with information on how participating in the creative arts can benefit older adults, as well as tips and best practices for generating creative arts programming. The tool kit is available in both English and Spanish.

John F. Kennedy Center for the Performing Arts, "ArtsEdge," http://artsedge.kennedy-center.org/educators.aspx

A dynamic and thorough website featuring resources and information relating to the arts and education, with how-to guides, tip sheets, lesson and project plans, and a large multimedia library. Definitely a great place to start for those interested in exploring arts programming but having trouble coming up with a topic.

National Endowment for the Humanities, "EDSITEment! The Best of the Humanities on the Web," http://edsitement.neh.gov

A vetted and reviewed collection of humanities-based resources for lesson and program planning. The website features customizable searches—including "arts and culture" and "literature and language arts" categories—and a yearlong calendar for program planning. EDSITEment was selected as one of the top twenty-five websites for 2010 by the American Association of School Librarians.

Smithsonian Center for Education and Museum Studies, "Smithsonian Education: Educators," www.smithsonianeducation.org/educators/index.html

Educational resources presented by the Smithsonian Center for Education and Museum Studies. Users can search by broad subject-based lesson plans, by resource name, and by state standards of learning.

Visual Arts

Art Institute of Chicago, "Art Institute of Chicago Collection Interpretive Resources Search," www.artic.edu/aic/resources

This site has a search feature on the Art Institute of Chicago's website that allows users to search for interpretive resources on collection materials. Users can narrow search to include only educator resources and/or multimedia items, and they can retrieve resources including commentary on a work and the period of its creation, an audio lecture on the artist, teacher manuals, and suggested activities based on Art Institute-housed works, and more.

Mid-America Arts Alliance, "Exhibits USA Traveling Exhibitions," www.eusa.org/home

A good resource for programming librarians interested in hosting a traveling arts exhibit in their library, with exhibits covering fine art, studio craft, folk art, design, and history and culture. Although interested libraries pay a fee for hosting, additional funding from foundations and humanities agencies may help subsidize exhibition rental fees, and Exhibits USA includes educational resources and support with all exhibitions.

The Museum of Modern Art, "MoMA Online," www.moma.org/learn/teachers /online/

A collection of online resources for teaching children and teens, all involving works in the museum's collection and aimed at teaching children and young adults about modern art.

National Endowment for the Humanities, "NEH on the Road," www.nehontheroad .org

Another good resource for libraries looking to host a cultural exhibition, with expertly curated smaller-scale versions of the National Endowment for the Humanities exhibitions. The exhibitions cover a broad range of topics in the arts, history, and culture, and are available on a first-come, first-served basis. Libraries pay a flat fee for hosting and shipping of the exhibitions, and programming grants of $1,000 are also available following a competitive application process.

The National Endowment for the Humanities and the American Library Association Public Programs Office, "Picturing America," www.programminglibrarian .org/pa/

An initiative of the National Endowment for the Humanities, Picturing America brings American art into classrooms and libraries nationwide, presenting a great opportunity for creating programming centered on the nation's artistic heritage. The Picturing America website on the ALA's Programming Librarian website provides links to Picturing America, programming suggestions, model program templates for all audiences, a downloadable teacher's resource guide, and more.

National Gallery of Art, "NGA Loan Materials Finder," www.nga.gov/education /classroom/loanfinder/

An online database of all arts education materials available for loan from the National Gallery of Art in Washington, DC. Librarians and educators can borrow slide teaching programs, multimedia programs, videocassettes, CD-ROMs, and DVDs for a two-week loan period and pay only the return postage. The available materials cover a large span of visual arts topics, from fifteenth-century European art to postimpressionism, textiles, and much more.

Literary Arts

The Academy of American Poets, "Poets.org," www.poets.org

Created to "foster the appreciation of contemporary poetry," the Academy of American Poets and its website, Poets.org, is an excellent resource for poetry program planning. The site features several ways to search for poets and poetry, including regionally, thematically, chronologically, and more.

The National Endowment for the Arts and Arts Midwest, "The Big Read," www .neabigread.org

Created to "restore reading to the center of American culture," the Big Read program provides resources and support for hosting programs centered on the discussion of a selected work of literature. Selected organizations receive grants ranging from $2,500 to $20,000 to support Big Read projects, which can include book discussions, lectures, public readings, related film discussions, and more. Participating organizations also receive readers, teachers, and audio guides, and numerous online resources to help them host community Big Read events. The Big Read application and guidelines are typically posted to the website in October, with an application deadline in February.

Poetry Foundation, "Poetry Foundation," www.poetryfoundation.org

Another excellent poetry resource, the Poetry Foundation website provides not only a thorough listing of poets and poems—which can be further refined by school/period, region, poet gender, and more—but also multimedia poetry resources such as audio and video. Additionally, the Poetry Foundation website features a poetry "Learning Lab," which dissects celebrated poems and provides related lesson plans and writing ideas, among other activities.

Poetry Foundation and the National Endowment for the Arts, "Poetry Out Loud," www.poetryoutloud.org

Although the Poetry Out Loud contest is limited to high schools participating through their state's arts agency, the Poetry Out Loud website is an excellent resource for programming librarians looking to incorporate poetry recitation and/or slam-style poetry readings into their programming calendar. The site contains lesson plans and teacher's guides that can easily be adapted for programming, as well as a large list of poems and poets for participants to explore and recite.

Poets & Writers, "Directory of Writers," www.pw.org/directory/featured/

An excellent resource for planning author events at your library. Poets & Writers provides a current list of registered authors, which includes contact information, biographies, recent publications, reading preferences, and more.

Poets & Writers, "Guide to Presenting Readings & Workshops," www.pw.org/ sites/all/themes/pw/guide_to_presenting.pdf

A useful step-by-step guide for planning an author event at your library, with information on finding authors, negotiating fees, publicizing your event, budgeting, funding sources, and more.

Performing Arts

National Endowment for the Arts and Arts Midwest, "Shakespeare in American Communities: Educational Resources," www.shakespeareinamericancommunities.org/education

The Shakespeare in American Communities project is an initiative of the National Endowment for the Arts, with the goal of creating the largest Shakespeare tour in the United States. The touring project is targeted at educators of middle and high school students, and the Educational Resources page offers extensive information on Shakespeare and his plays—it also provides, free of charge, the *Shakespeare Toolkit* to junior high, high school, and college librarians.

National Endowment for the Arts and Jazz at Lincoln Center, "Jazz in the Schools," www.neajazzintheschools.org/home.php

A great resource for libraries interested in jazz education programming for children and young adults. The site lists programming resources on several eras of jazz and includes streaming songs that best represent those eras.

National Storytelling Network, "National Storytelling Network," www.storynet.org

Promoting storytelling as a performing art, the National Storytelling Network offers several helpful resources on their website to assist storytelling advocates in planning a colorful and memorable program. The site includes an event calendar along with a storyteller index that users can search for storytellers by state, region, and age level.

Smithsonian National Museum of American History, "Jazz Appreciation Month," http://smithsonianjazz.org

Another excellent resource on jazz music, focusing particularly on programming resources for Jazz Appreciation Month (JAM) in April. Resources include a national JAM events calendar, JAM logos for promotional materials, the list "112 Ways to Celebrate Jazz," archived performances and blogs, and more.

Funding and Support Resources

ALA Public Programs Office, "Programming Librarian," www.programminglibrarian.org

Programming Librarian is an online resource center for library cultural programming, featuring program planning and implementation resources, a blog with grant announcements, featured libraries, guest bloggers, and the Brainstormer—a searchable database where programming librarians can search for programming resources by keyword or type. Recent features on Programming Librarian have provided copyright tips for programming librarians, program marketing and funding resources, community collaboration for successful programming, strategies for conducting successful author programs, and more.

American Library Association, "Public Programs Office," http://ala.org/public programs/

With a mission of promoting "cultural and community programming as an essential part of library service," the ALA Public Programs Office helps libraries define themselves as a cultural center of the community through programming grants, traveling exhibitions, discussion programs, and more. Programming librarians can sign up for regular e-mail updates on available programming grants at the ALA Public Programs Office website, www.ala.org/publicprograms/.

Institute of Museum and Library Services, "Grant Applicants," www.imls.gov /applicants/applicants.shtm

The Institute of Museum and Library Services awards grants to libraries to enhance the quality of library services nationwide. The "Grant Applicants" page of the website is an excellent resource for navigating available institute grants and their eligibility requirements, with sample applications and other tools.

National Assembly of State Arts Agencies, "State Arts Agency Directory," www .nasaa-arts.org/About/State-Arts-Agency-Directory.php

A map listing all state arts agencies, as well as regional arts organizations, including full contact information and website addresses when available. State arts agencies are a good starting point for libraries wishing to bring arts awareness and education to their communities—they may be able to provide best practices, programming resources, and funding.

National Endowment for the Arts, "Apply for a Grant," www.nea.gov/grants /apply/index.html

The National Endowment for the Arts is a potential source of funding for arts education, as it provides direct grants to those conducting standards-based arts education programs as well as initiating program solicitation for arts programming for older adults with their Creativity and Aging in America program. In addition, the National Endowment for the Arts provides direct grant support to all types of libraries for arts programming in literary, visual, and performing arts.

National Endowment for the Humanities, "State Humanities Councils," www.neh .gov/whoweare/statecouncils.html

An alphabetical listing of state humanities councils, including full contact information and website addresses when available. State humanities councils are often a great source of information and funding for programming initiatives.

Contributors

The American Library Association Public Programs Office (PPO) promotes cultural and community programming as an essential part of library service. Through professional development activities, programming resources, model programs, grant opportunities, and the library programming website programminglibrarian.org, PPO supports libraries as they fill their role as community cultural center, a place of cultural and civic engagement, where people of all backgrounds gather for reflection, discovery, participation, and growth.

Regan Brumagen, a member of the Rakow Library's public services team, answers reference questions; coordinates e-reference; and provides expertise and leadership in the identification, assessment, and recommendation of emerging technologies and electronic resources that enhance and expand library services and instruction. Her chapter on institutional planning for outreach appeared in *Art Museum Libraries and Librarianship* (Scarecrow Press, 2007). Brumagen received her MLS in 1996 and her MA in 1993, both from the University of Kentucky.

Robert Craig Bunch has been a librarian for twenty years at the middle school, high school, and school-district levels. He has published more than two hundred reviews and articles in *Booklist, Art Book, Folk Art, Kyoto Journal, St. James Encyclopedia of Popular Culture, Encyclopedia of Recorded Sound, Dictionary of American History* (3rd ed.), and other publications. He is working on a book of interviews with Texas collage and assemblage artists. Bunch lives in Houston, Texas, with his wife, Delana.

Florence F. Caddell, arts director for the Frankfort Community Public Library in Frankfort, Indiana, from 1995 to the present, studied art at Hanover College, in Hanover, Indiana, and earned a master's degree in museum studies at Indiana University/Purdue University, Indianapolis, Indiana. Caddell cares for the library art collections and schedules art programs and exhibitions for the Anna and Harlan Hubbard School of Living at the Frankfort Library, which is based on the philosophy "we can make our life a work of art."

Lance R. Chance, assistant professor of library science and instructional services librarian at Edith Garland Dupré Library, University of Louisiana at Lafayette, has a BA in English from the University of Louisiana at Lafayette and an MSLIS from Louisiana State University. He has written reviews for *Louisiana Libraries* and has contributed to the *Bayou State Periodical Index*. Chance was a coprincipal investigator for the grant establishing the Cajun and Creole Music Collection and has been involved with the collection's development, digitization, and promotion.

Allan Cho is program services librarian at Irving K. Barber Learning Centre at the University of British Columbia in Vancouver, Canada, where he helps design and deliver programs and services to support the broader community and a variety of learners and instructors, as well as integrate other virtual resources and services to support a broad range of users at the Learning Centre and UBC Library. He serves as editor of the Special Libraries Association Western Canadian Chapter's *Wired West* and as book reviewer for *Library Journal* and *Choice Review.*

Sarah Cisse is a reference librarian at the Alvin Sherman Library Research and Information Technology Center at Nova Southeastern University in Fort Lauderdale, Florida. She received her MSLIS from Pratt Institute in 2005. Cisse began her library career at the Metropolitan College of New York as an information specialist. Previous experience includes positions as information assistant in the museum at the Fashion Institute of Technology and as records manager at the New York City Department of Consumer Affairs. Cisse also holds a BA in English literature and an AAS in advertising and marketing communications.

Jeri Weinkrantz Cohen, assistant department head of the Young Adult/Audiovisual Department at the Patchogue-Medford Library in Patchogue, New York, obtained her MSLIS from the Palmer School of C. W. Post, Long Island University. She is a member of the American Library Association and currently serves on YALSA's Amazing Audiobooks for Teens Committee. She is also a member of the New York Library Association and the Suffolk County Library Association. Her writing has appeared in *VOYA,* and she was editor of the Suffolk County Library Association newsletter for five years.

Stacey R. Ewing is an assistant university librarian at Library West, the humanities and social sciences branch of the George A. Smathers Libraries at the University of Florida. She coordinates the Information Commons and specializes in outreach, instruction, and emerging technologies. Ewing received her MSLIS from the University of North Texas, where she was an Institute of

Museum and Library Services fellow in the digital-image-management program. Her most recent publication, "Building a Participatory Culture: Collaborating with Student Organizations for 21st Century Library Instruction," appears in *Collaborative Librarianship.*

Carol Luers Eyman is the outreach and community services coordinator at the Nashua Public Library, in Nashua, New Hampshire. She does publicity and marketing, plans adult programs, works with community groups, and books meeting rooms. She has a master's degree in education and a certificate in technical communication. Before joining the library staff, Eyman was a computer programmer, technical writer, editor, and teacher. She is the author of *How to Publish Your Newsletter* (Square One Publishers, 2006) and the editor of *The Nashua Experience: A Three-Decade Upgrade, 1978–2008.*

Elizabeth Goldman is chief executive officer of the Perth & District Union Public Library in Ontario, Canada. She previously worked at Kingston Frontenac Public Library in Ontario and at Chelsea District Library in Michigan, where she was part of the team that won the award for Best Small Library in America from *Library Journal* and the Bill and Melinda Gates Foundation in 2008. An active writer, presenter, and consultant, she can be found online at www.theblackrivergroup.com. She is a graduate of the University of Michigan School of Information.

Larry Grieco, library director of the Gilpin County Public Library, in Black Hawk, Colorado, obtained his MSLS from the State University of New York at Buffalo. Larry's memberships include the American Library Association and the Colorado Association of Libraries, and he serves on the board of directors of the Association for Rural and Small Libraries. He is chair of the American Library Association's Loleta D. Fyan Award Jury and is an adviser for Dartmouth College's Pushing the Limits project (to bring math and science programs to rural libraries), funded by the National Science Foundation.

Vera Gubnitskaia, youth services manager at the Orange County Library System in Orlando, Florida, obtained her library degrees from the Moscow Institute of Culture (Russia) and Florida State University. Gubnitskaia has worked as librarian, manager, and library consultant in public and academic libraries. She has published in *Librarians as Community Partners: An Outreach Handbook and Florida Library Youth Programs* newsletter. Gubnitskaia has presented at several conferences, including the Florida Library Association and Florida Literacy conferences. She is currently serving on the Florida Library Association Awards Committee.

Kerol Harrod (MA, University of North Texas) works at the Denton Public Library in Denton, Texas. He writes and coproduces the television show *Library Larry's Big Day,* which won a first-place award in 2010 from the Texas Association of Telecommunications Officers and Advisors and received the 2011 North Texas Regional Library System Margaret Irby Nichols Award. Harrod also won the 2011 Texas Library Association Branding Iron PR Award for Speechwriting. He is currently coediting a book for McFarland Publishing titled *Marketing Methods for Libraries.*

Sandra M. Himel, associate professor of library science, is head of research and government information services at Edith Garland Dupré Library, University of Louisiana at Lafayette. She holds a BA in history and an MSLS from Louisiana State University. Himel is coordinator of the Cajun and Creole Music Collection and was the principal investigator for the grant establishing the collection. She has been a principal investigator for other state and national grants and an indexer for the *Bayou State Periodical Index.*

Natalie Houston is currently youth outreach coordinator for the Orange County Library System in Orlando, Florida. She received an MSLS from the University of South Florida and a BA from the University of Miami. Houston has worked as a young adult librarian and has contributed to the *Florida Libraries Youth Programs* newsletter and blog. Natalie is a member of the Young Adult Library Services, American Library Association, and the Fabulous Films for Young Adults Committee 2009–11.

Beth Hylen is reference librarian at the Rakow Research Library of the Corning Museum of Glass, where she provides leadership and expertise for library outreach to national and international communities and oversees the library's oral history activities. She earned her MSLS at UNC, Chapel Hill. Hylen has been a featured speaker for Art Libraries Society of North America, Glass Art Society, and other glass associations. She has published articles in a variety of glass-related publications, and in 2010, she served as president of Art Libraries Society, Western New York.

Greg MacAyeal, assistant head of the Northwestern University Music Library, is an active member of the Music Library Association. He has contributed reviews to the journals *Notes and Music Reference Services Quarterly.* MacAyeal holds an MLIS from University of Wisconsin–Milwaukee, and in 2008 he received the GOLD Award from the university's alumni association. In addition, MacAyeal teaches in the Graduate School of Library and Information

Science at Dominican University, in River Forest, Illinois, and in the School of Music at North Park University, in Chicago.

Jennifer Mayer is the fine arts and women's studies librarian at the University of Wyoming Libraries, in Laramie, Wyoming. She received her MSLIS from the University of Oklahoma. Mayer is an active member of the Association of College and Research Libraries (ACRL) and the Art Libraries Society of North America (ARLIS/NA). She recently served as chair of the ARLIS/NA Mountain West Chapter and currently serves as chair for ACRL's Women and Gender Studies Section Publication Committee. Her writing has appeared in *College & Research Libraries; Art Documentation;* and most recently, in the *Handbook of Art and Design Librarianship* (Facet, 2010).

Jack G. Montgomery, professor and collection services coordinator at Western Kentucky University Libraries, obtained his MLS at the University of Maryland–College Park. Montgomery's memberships include the Kentucky Library Association, and he is a conference director for the annual Charleston conference "Issues in Book and Serial Acquisition." Montgomery is a column editor for *Against the Grain;* also, he coauthored with Eleanor I. Cook *Conflict Management for Libraries: A Strategy for a Positive, Productive Workplace* (ALA Editions, 2005). In 2007 Montgomery received the Vicky Speck Memorial Leadership Award.

Sarah Naumann is a library literacy instructor for Berkeley READS Adult and Family Literacy program, Berkeley Public Library, and a circulation assistant for the Academy of Art University Library. She holds a BA in liberal studies from California State University, Hayward, and an MLIS from San Jose State University. Naumann also holds a certificate in art gallery and museum studies from California State University, East Bay Extension. She is a member of the American Library Association, Association of College and Research Libraries, California Library Association, California Academic and Research Libraries, and Special Libraries Association.

Heather Payne was director of library services at the Art Institute of Fort Lauderdale, Fort Lauderdale, Florida, for twelve years. She now works for City College in Fort Lauderdale, where, among other responsibilities, she is the corporate liaison to the libraries. Payne obtained her MLIS from Florida State University and her MBA from Argosy University. She is a member of the American Library Association and the Special Libraries Association. She is an alumnus of the Harvard Leadership Institute for Academic Librarians.

Nora J. Quinlan is the director of reference at the Alvin Sherman Library, Research, and Information Technology Center at Nova Southeastern University in Fort Lauderdale, Florida. In addition, she oversees the library's gallery and is responsible for identifying possible exhibits, developing programming, and installing shows. In addition to her work at the university, Quinlan has previously worked in rare books and special collections. She was previously head of special collections at the University of Colorado at Boulder.

Molly Raphael, 2011–12 president of the American Library Association, is the chief elected officer of the oldest and largest library organization in the world. A public librarian for forty years, Raphael directed two urban public libraries: Multnomah County Library (Portland, Oregon) and the District of Columbia Public Library. In 2009, Multnomah County Library received the Institute for Museum and Library Services' National Medal, the nation's highest honor for libraries. Raphael earned her MLS from Simmons College and her BA from Oberlin College.

Sue Samson, professor and humanities librarian at the University of Montana, Missoula, received her MA from the University of Missouri, Columbia. Her research has appeared in *College & Research Libraries, Journal of Academic Librarianship,* and *Reference Services Review,* among others, and she contributed to *The Teaching Library* (Haworth Press, 2007), *Books, Bytes and Bridges* (ALA Editions, 2000), and *Document Delivery Services* (Haworth Press, 1999). Samson received the 2010 Outstanding Faculty Mentoring Award, the 2008 Department Assessment Award for Information & Research Services, and multiple merit awards.

Carol Smallwood, MLS, is featured in *Best New Writing in Prose 2010—Compartments: Poems on Nature, Femininity and Other Realms* (Anaphora Literary Press, 2011), nominated for the Pushcart Prize. A chapter of *Lily's Odyssey* was short listed for the Eric Hoffer Prose Award. Smallwood is a Federation of State Poetry Societies winner. Her nearly three dozen books have been published by Scarecrow Press, American Library Association, and others; *Women Writing on Family: Tips on Writing, Teaching and Publishing* is forthcoming from Key Publishing House in 2012. Smallwood's experience includes academic, public, school, and special libraries as librarian, consultant, administrator.

Sara Wedell joined the Chelsea District Library as head of adult services in August 2009. Along with programming, community partnerships, and collections and supervisory duties, her position involves projects such as the Stories of Chelsea documentary series (www.storiesofchelsea.org). She presented at the 2010 Public Library Association conference and the 2008 and 2009 Michigan Library Association conferences. Wedell previously served as the adult services librarian at the Delta Township District Library. She received her master's degree in the science of information from the University of Michigan's School of Information.

Heather Pippin Zabriskie, youth programs coordinator, Orange County Library System, Orlando, Florida, holds a bachelor's degree in linguistics from the University of Florida. Zabriskie routinely works closely with her local community to bring innovative programming to the youth of Orange County. During her career, she has presented poster sessions at the Public Library Association and Florida Library Association conferences, and she has represented the State of Florida at the Collaborative Summer Reading Program conference. Zabriskie is a regular contributor to the *Florida Library Youth Programs* newsletter.

Index

A

Abita Music Company, 95
Abrams, Marjorie, 8
abstract images, writing prompts, 13–14
Academy of American Poets, 211–212
    Accordions, Fiddles, Two-Step and Swing
      (Brasseaux and Fontenot), 95
administration
    Java City and, 187–195
    poetry corner and, 26–27
    programming, resources and, 209–214
    raising money and, 197–207
advertising, 5–6
Aerie Big Sky (publication), 29
after-school programs, 119, 126
Aguas, Raven, 13, 15, 21
Aguirre, Ann, 7–8
Alachua County Public Library, 5–6
Alpha-Numeric System for Classification
    of Recordings (ANSCR), 92
American Association of Museums, 167
American Book Prices Current, 170
American Routes (radio program), 95
analog formats, 91
Andrews, Ilona, 7
animanga reality-art contest, 122–123
Anna and Harlan Hubbard School of Liv-
    ing, 198
Annual Citizen Update (magazine), 148
Aponovich, James, 57
Appalachian Spring: Suite (Copland), 99
Apply for a Grant (resource), 214
archival materials, 91
Aroeste, Miriam, 177
art
    audiences and, 153–154
    classes for, 41

collection difficulties, 56–57
commissions and, 76
contests for teens, 122–123
demonstrations, 50, 54
Design Art program, 134–135
education requirements, 117–118
exhibiting, 43–44, 47–48
finding instructors, 41–42
hanging systems, 48
hosting programs, 201–202
invitational, 80–81
loan agreement example, 83
museums and, 39–40
partnerships, 163–164
purchase awards, 73
Art 21 Inc. (resource), 209–210
Art Institute of Chicago, 210
Art Revolution for Teens (ART)
    additional materials for, 128
    battle of the bands, 122
    community and, 126
    creative arts, 123–124
    culinary arts, 124
    evaluation of, 126–127
    future of, 127–128
    goals, 119
    literary arts, 124–125
    marketing, 120
    performing arts, 121
    project funding, 119–120
    Teen Library Corps, 125
    visual arts, 122–123
Art Walk Nashua, 54–55
article resources, 68
artist-in-residence series, 160–161
artistic scope, 80

Arts Administrator Leadership Award, 198
ArtsEdge (website), 210
Asian Heritage Month, 177
assignments, 69
Association for Recorded Sound Collections, 93
The Atrium (glass sculpture), 178, 180
audiences, 153–154
audio recordings, 91
awards
    Arts Administrator Leadership, 198
    Branding Iron PR, 148
    EBSCO Excellence in service, 144–145
    Indiana Governor's Arts Award, 198
    Margaret Irby Nichols, 147
    purchase awards, 74, 77
    student purchase types, 73
    Teen Library Corps, 125
    Traditional Enhancement Grant, 88

B
Baca, Michaela, 13, 15, 18
background checks, 172
bailment defined, 169
Barber, Jean, 178
Bartel, Marvin, 61–62
Battle of the Bands, 122
Baxter, Dezarea, 22
Bay Area Library Information System (BALIS), 40
Belle Verre (glass sculpture), 178
Berkeley Reads Adult and Family Literacy, 37–38
The Big Read (online resource), 212
bilingual productions, 108
Bill and Melinda Gates Foundation, 157
Binder, Dean Michael, 187
Black's Law Dictionary, 169
blogs
    advertising using, 5
    event management and, 194
    literary arts and, 8
    music collections and, 105
    visual arts and, 78

book resources, 68
booking management, 190–192
bookmaking, educational method, 137–138
bookmarks, educational method, 138
Boyer, Johanna Misey, 210
Branding Iron PR award, 148
Brasseaux, Ryan, 92
Brautigan, Richard, 141
break dancing workshop, 124
Brett, Jan, 57
briefs, 60–61
brochures, 5
budgeting
    Cultural Arts Literacy, 42–43, 45–46
    hosting art exhibits and, 202
    Nashua expenses, 55–56
    promotions, marketing and, 5, 10
Burbank collection, 56–57
Burnette, Jeff, 178
Burns, R. Michael, 4
business collaboration examples, 94

C
Caddell, Bill, 198, 201–202
Caddell, Claude W., 197
Caddell, Flo, 200
Cage, John, 104
Cajun and Creole Music Collection (CCMC), 87–96
Cajun Breakdown (Brasseaux), 95
Campbell, Graeme, 17, 20
camps, 109
Canticle of the Sun (Sowerby), 97, 99–102
Cantu, Jessica, 18
Castillo, Javier, 16
Cedille Records, 102
Certainty (Thien), 182
Charter School of Technology, 132
chat technology, 7
Chaw, Walter, 142
Chelsea Center for the Arts, 157
Chen, Yong, 50
Chicago Symphony Orchestra, 100

Chinese Canadian Historical Society, 182

Chow, Raymond, 177

Cisneros, Violeta, 15, 23

City Arts Nashua (CAN), 54–55

classes, creative writing, 11–23

Coe Library (WY), 80

collaboration

    Cajun and Creole Music Collection,
      89–90

    examples of, 93–95

    outreach events, 3–10

    poetry corner, 26–27

collections

    Burbank Fund, 56–57

    keeping records, 102–103

    mixed arts, 130–131

    music, 87–96

    Poetry Corner, 28–29

    users and, 103–104

commissions, 76

community

    Art Revolution for Teens, 126

    grants from, 134

    PML players and, 114

complications, 56–57

composers, 100

concepts as clients, 60–61

concerts

    attending, 97–98

    children types, 201

    Noontime Concert Series, 195

    special performances and, 102

contact information example, 82

contracts, 165–173

contributors, 215–221

Copland, Aaron, 99

Corning Museum of Glass, 129–138

Corning-Painted Post School, 131–132

corporate gifts, 203–205

Cortez, Stephanie, 18

creative arts

    Art Revolution for Teens, 123–124

    resources, 209–210

creative brief, 60–61

creative writing

    Poetry Corner programs, 25–26

    teaching classes, 11–23

Creativity Matters (Boyer), 210

The Creole Gumbo Show (radio program),
    95

critiques

    creative briefs and, 60, 62

    inner, 9–10

    lessons learned, 62–63

    student poster work, 61–62

culinary arts, 124

Cultural Arts Literacy (program), 38–46

cultural centers

    booking management, 190–192

    defining space, 187–189

    event management, 194

    location of, 189

    organizational structure, 189

    promotion, 193–194

    sound management, 189–190

    sponsorship, 192–193

curriculum

    funding and, 117–118

    program relevance, 130–131

D

damage, materials and users, 103–104

dance groups, 121

dance workshops, 123–124

Daniels, Jeff, 157

Daniels, Mitch, 198

Davis, Hannah, 14, 18–19, 21–22

deferred gifts, 203–205

Delacoma, Wynne, 102

demonstrations, 50, 54

Denton Public Library, 147

design drawings, 130, 134–135

development

    Art Revolution for Teens and, 117–119

    artist-in-residence and, 144

    Burbank Fund and, 57

    economic benefits, 203

    music collections and, 90–91

development (cont.)
    PML players and, 111–112
    poetry corner and, 27–28
Dewey Balfa Cajun and Creole Heritage
    Week, 94
digital formats, 91
Directory of Writers (resource), 212
discussion lists, 5
Disney's Helping Kids Shine, 120
display cases, 77
Dodson Music Series, 183
donations
    Friends groups and, 139, 198–199
    fundraising and, 203–207
    publicity and, 92
    requests for, 5
Doucet, Michael, 95
Drozd, Jerzy, 161, 163

E
e-newsletters, 5
EBSCO Excellence in Service award,
    144–145
economic development, 203
Edith Garland Dupré Library (LA), 87
EDSITEment! (resource), 210
education
    methods for, 136–138
    requirements for, 117–118
El día de los niños / El día de los libros, 108
Eleanor Ryan Youth Theatre Fund, 206
electronic marketing, 5–6
Elizabeth O'Rear Skanta Theatre, 205
Embree, Jerry, 95
endowments, 203–205
environmental conditions, 168
Escriba!/Write! (magazine), 31
events
    Dewey Balfa Cajun and Creole Heritage
        Week, 94
    fundraising types, 202–203
    Grant Park Orchestra, 98–99
    management of, 194
    music types, 54

    outreach types, 3–10
    special performances and, 102
exhibits
    adult literacy and, 43–44
    art walks, 54–55
    art wall, 140
    Burbank collection, 56–57
    economic development and, 203
    environmental conditions and, 168
    expenses, 55–56
    expertise and infrastructure, 55
    "Exquisite Corpse," 177
    facilities report, 166–169
    fundraising events, 202–203
    "Generation One," 177
    labeling, 49
    legalities and, 77–78, 165–173
    letter of request, 165–166
    Nashua Public Library, 47–48
    opening receptions, 50
    procedures of, 82
    public preferences, 51–53
    publicity, 50–51
    sales and security, 49–50
    selecting artists, 48
    temporary, 74–76
    "The Beauty of Nature," 178
Exhibits Etc., 94
expenses
    See budgeting
"Exquisite Corpse" (exhibit), 176

F
Facebook, 8, 120, 191
facilities
    art installation and, 76–77
    report of, 166–169
Federation of Musicians, 98
feedback
    Art Revolution for Teens, 126–127
    NaNo event, 6–7
Fenwick, Ray, 12, 20–22
field trips, 39–40
Figueroa, Chris, 65

films
  film festival, 54
  viewing, 142–143
Finding Joy (Coste), 50
fire protection, 168
First Nations, 182–183
flyers, 5
Fontenot, Kevin, 95
force majeure defined, 170
formatting, 91
forms, presenters and, 172
Frankfort Community Public Library
  (FCPL), 197–207
A Free Song (Schuman), 99
Friends of the Library, 139, 198–199
Frost, Jeanine, 7
fundraising
  Art Revolution for Teens, 119–120
  creating spaces, 199–200
  friends-of-the library organizations,
    198–199
  grants, donations, gifts, endowments,
    203–207
  grants and, 159–160
  hosting art programs, 201–202
  poetry corner and, 26–27
  public school curricula, 117–119
  resources, 213–214
  special events, 202–203
  special events for, 202–203
  staff and, 200
furnishings, Poetry Corner, 27–28

G
Galway Public Library (NY), 31
Garald and Toni Gill Lower Level, 197
Garza, Elias, 199
Gator Times (newsletter), 5
"Generation One" (exhibit), 177
gifts, private and corporate, 203–205
Gilpin County Public Library
  about, 139–141
  artist-in-residence, 143–145
  film viewing and discussion, 142–143

  future of program, 146
  poetry programming, 141–142
  program publicity, 145
glass detectives (activity), 133–134, 137
glassmaking, 130–131
goals, ART program, 119
Gonzales, Rebecca, 14, 19, 21
Gonzalez, Sandra, 14–15, 17
Goulet, Wayne, 53
grading criteria, 70–71
graffiti workshop, 124–125
GRAMMY Foundation, 89
Grand Réveil Acadien, 94
Grant Applicants (resource), 214
grant funding, 43, 88–89
Grant Park Orchestra (GPO), 98–99
grants
  Art Revolution for Teens, 119–120
  community sponsored, 134
  Library Services and Construction Act,
    197
  partnerships and, 159–160
  private and corporate, 203–205
  Save Our History, 135
Great American Downtown (GAD), 54–55
guards, 168
guest speakers, online, 8
Guide to Presenting Readings & Workshops (resources), 212
guidelines
  letter of request, 166
  programs and, 41, 131
Gyung bok gung Great Roof (McLaurin),
  179

H
Hafner, Madeline, 183
Hafner, Marilyn, 57
Haida stories, 182
Hall of Best Knowledge (Fenwick), 12,
  20–22
Hamilton Middle School (TX), 11
Hammond, Bruce, 64
hands-on art class, 41

hanging art, 48
Harrison, Lou, 100
Hart, Roger, 112
Hawkes, Samuel, 133
Helen Shanklin Children's Department, 197
Helm-Cravens Library Complex, 188
Herrick, Mary Gorham, 197
Higashi, C., 31
Hildreth, Wylaina, 150
Hillsboro Branch line, 51–52
Hine, Lewis, 130
Hood, Yolanda, 182
hosting programs, 201–202
Hostos Community College (NY), 31
Hot Topic Foundation, 119
Hubbard, Anna and Harlan, 198
Hubbard School, 200–201
Hutchins, J. C., 8
Hyakunin Isshu (Fujiwara), 14
Hyman, Trina Schart, 57

I
idea jars, 9
in-kind donations, 205
In the Realm of Hungry Ghosts (Maté), 182
independent contractors, 171–172
Indiana Arts Commission, 205
Indiana Governor's Arts Award, 198
industry information resources, 68
Inextricable Fusion: The Poetry of Patricia Goedicke, 28
InfoCommons, 9
Informed Teens (website), 120
inner critics, 9–10
innovative model, 175
instructors, finding, 41–42
insurance coverage, 169
invitational, 80–81
Irving K. Barber Learning Centre (IKBLC)
    about, 175–176
    artists at, 176–178
    Dodson music series, 183
    Robson Reading Series, 181–183

J
J. D. Miller Recording Studio Museum, 94
Jackson-Alvarez, Isabel, 20
jailing the inner critic, 9–10
Java City, 187–194
Jazz Appreciation Month (resource), 213
Jazz in the Schools (resource), 213
Joe Blow Glassworks, 178
John F. Kennedy Center for the Performing Arts, 210
Jones, J. V., 8
Jordan, Claire, 21
juré music, 90

K
Kalmar, Carlos, 99
Kantrowitz, Sean, 122
Kasischke, Laura, 162
Kelley, Pierce, 8
Kent, Richard A., 177
Kids Read Comics, 161
Klinger, Jade, 18
KnowLA, 94
Konicek, Dakotah, 75
Konkel, Anna, 75

L
la-la music, 90
Lacouture, Marce, 95
Ladder of Youth Participation, 111–112
Lafferty, Mur, 8
Lambert, Sandra, 4
language guessing games, educational method, 137
Lawyers for Libraries (resource), 173
Lazarus, Emma, 111
legalities
    facilities report, 166–169
    letter of request, 165–166
    loan agreements, 169–171
    visual arts, 77–78
    working with presenters, 171–172
letter of request, 165–166
liability waiver example, 83

Library Journal, 157
Library Larry's Big Day (TV program), 147–154
Library Services and Construction Act grant, 197
Liebler, M. L., 161
literacy programs, need for, 37
literary arts
    Art Revolution for Teens, 124–125
    librarians as teachers, 11–23
    outreach event, 3–10
    poetry collaborations, 25–32
    resources, 211–212
loans
    agreements, 83, 169–171
    duration of, 80
location considerations, 189
Loisel, Nicki, 19–20
Lott, Brett, 162
Louisiana Folk Roots, 94
Lynch, Thomas, 162

M

Magic of Discovery (glass sculpture), 178–179
management and administration
    art works, 157–164
    collaboration as outreach, 175–184
    Cultural Arts Literacy program, 42–43
    cultural center development, 187–195
    fundraising, 197–207
    Java City and, 187–195
    legal and contractual aspects, 165–173
    locating resources, 209–214
    programming, resources and, 209–214
    raising money and, 197–207
manga, 182
manuscript score, 101
Margaret Irby Nichols Award, 147
marketing
    Art Revolution for Teens, 120
    NaNo event, 5–6
    PML players and, 114
Martinez, Gustavo, 18

matching game, educational method, 137
Maté, Gabor, 182
materials
    Art Revolution for Teens, 128
    balancing users and risk, 103–104
    conditions of, 170
    PML players and, 112
    promotional, 193–194
    recycled, 53
    selection criteria, 91
    Teen Library Corps and, 125
McClure, Michael, 162
McKnight, Mark, 92
McLaurin, Ilsoo Kyung, 178–179
measures of success, 42
Meebo (chat program), 7
Mejia, Luis D., 66
Merino, David, 177
methodology, 38, 136–138
Mexican culture, 177–178
Mid-America Arts Alliance, 210–211
Midwest Literary Walk, 157, 161–164
Mikkleson, Martha, 107, 113
Miller, Peter, 183
mixed arts
    Gilpin County Arts Program, 139–146
    library as a canvas, 147–154
    research projects and, 129–138
    teens and, 117–128
MoMA Online, 211
The Museum of Modern Art, 211
museum visits, 40
music
    collection selection, 91
    Dodson Music Series, 183
    events and, 54
    heritage collections, 87
    Library Larry's Big Day, 149–151
    workshops, 123–124
Music Buddies (program), 109
Music Classification Systems (McKnight), 92
"Music from the Hill" (column), 194
musicals, 108–110
MySpace, 191

N

Nancy N. Fullerton Fund, 206
NaNo (National Novel Writing Month),
    4–6
Nashua Public Library (NH), 47–57
National Endowment for the Humanities,
    210
National Poetry Month, 29, 124
National Storytelling Network (resource),
    213
NEH on the Road (online resource), 211
networking, 6
The New Colossus (statue), 111
New York State Student Music Association
    (NYSSMA), 109
NGA Loan Materials Finder (online
    resource), 211
non-English poems, 11–23
Noontime Concert Series, 195
Northern Texan (magazine), 148
Nutter, John, 178

O

On Road (painting), 74
on-screen talent, 151–152
171 Cedar Arts Center, 134–135
One Community/Many Stories, 110–111
One Hundred Poets, One Poem Each (Fuji-
    wara), 14
online guest speakers, 8
online resources, 209–214
opening receptions, 50
Orange County Library System (OCLS), 117
orchestras, 97–98
organization collaboration examples, 94
organizational structure, 189
outreach events
    Corning Museum of Glass, 129–131
    Cultural Arts Literacy, 44
    National Novel Writing Month, 3–10
Oval (publication), 29

P

paper arts, 134
partnerships

artist-in-residence series, 160–161
    Cultural Arts Literacy, 44
    Education Department, 130–131
    grant writing and, 159–160
    libraries and art, 163–164
    Midwest literary walk, 162–163
    reasons supporting, 158–159
Patchogue-Medford Library, 107
payment, 43
Pearson, Linley, 197
Peeradina, Saleem, 163
performing arts
    Art Revolution for Teens, 117–128
    developing music collections, 87–96
    Dodson Music Series, 183
    expenses, 55
    Grand Park Orchestra, 98–99
    legalities, 171–172
    music collections, 97–106
    PML players, 107–114
    resources, 213
    special performances, 102
Perpetuate (sculpture), 75
Petrillo, James C., 98
photographs as prompts, 18–20
Picturing America (online resource), 211
planning
    Art Revolution for Teens, 127–128
    collections and, 56–57
    Java City, 189
    NaNo event, 4–5
    research libraries and, 136
poetry
    contests, 124–125
    design and development, 27–28
    funding, administration, collabora-
        tion, 26–27
    non-English, 11–23
    readings, 141–142
    serendipity and, 28–30
    space for, 30–31
Poetry Corner, 25–32
Poetry for Lunch, 29–30
Poetry Foundation (resource), 212
posters, 59–71

presenters, working with, 171–172
press releases, 50–51
private gifts, 203–205
Programming Librarian (resource), 214
programs
    Art Revolution for Teens, 117–128
    Berkeley Reads Adult and Family
        Literacy, 37–38
    Cajun and Creole Music Collection,
        87–96
    Corning Museum of Glass, 129–131
    Cultural Arts Literacy, 38–46
    hosting, 201–202
    ideas for, 209–214
    Library Larry's Big Day, 147–154
    Midwest Literary Walk, 157, 161–164
    Music Buddies, 109
    One Community/Many Stories,
        110–111
    PML players, 107–114
    poetry, 141–142
    The Poetry Corner, 25–42
    You Design It, We Make It, 133
promotion
    Cajun and Creole Music Collection,
        92–93
    Java City, 193–194
    NaNo event, 5–6
prompts
    abstract images and, 13–14
    photographs as, 18–20
    sketches as, 22–23
    woodblock prints as, 17–18
proposal submission, 81
public preference, 51–53
Public Programs Office (ALA; resource),
    213
public relations, 78–79
public safety officers, 168
publicity
    academic libraries, 82
    Cajun and Creole Music Collection,
        92–93
    Gilpin County Public Library, 145
    Nashua Public Library, 50–51

Pulitzer Project, 102
puppets, Library Larry and, 148
purchase awards, 73–74, 77
Purple Rose Theater Company, 157, 163
puzzles, educational method, 137

Q
Quirk, Jennifer, 113

R
Rajan, Rubina, 177
Rakow Research Library, 129–138
Ranganathan, S. R., 102
readings, 141–142
Reality Is Not a Meatball, 142
receptions, 50, 54
recycled materials, 53
Reeves, Gabrielle, 74
Registrars Committee, 167
release example, 83
research libraries
    educational methods, 136–138
    examples of programs, 131–136
    K–12 outreach program, 129–131
research materials, 91
Research Revolution, 140–143
resources
    legal counsel types, 173
    programming and online, 209–214
    student list, 68
ResTV, 5
ReverbNation, 191
Ricepaper (magazine), 182
risk management, 80, 83
Robson Reading Series, 176
Rogers, Emily, 182
Rolling Flower (sculpture), 77
Rome Prize, 100
Rooftop Poetry Club, 31

S
sales, terms of, 80
Sandmel, Ben, 92
Santa Fe College, 6
Save Our History (grant), 135

Scary Theater, 110

School of the Deaf, 132–133

schools

after-school activities, 111–113

schools (cont.)

Art Revolution for Teens, 117–128

assignments for, 69–71

teaching classes at, 11–23

Schuman, William, 99

Schwalm, Fritz, 150–151

screenings, film festivals, 54

scriptwriting, 153

sculptures, recycled materials, 53

Search Institute, 111

Seattle Public Library (WA), 31

security, 49–50, 168

Segovia, Claudia, 177

selection criteria, music collections, 91

set design, 149–151

Shakespeare in American Communities (resource), 213

Shalhoup, Mike, 51

Shelton, Michael, 101

Shoja, Jafar, 57

Shum, Ron, 177

Sibelius, 101

sketches, prompts as, 22–23

Smithsonian Center for Education and Museum Studies, 210

smoke alarms, 168

Sombilon, Ron, 177

Sonicbids, 191

sound, managing, 189–190

South to Louisiana (radio program), 95

Sowerby, Leo, 97, 99, 101–102

spaces

art installation and, 76–77

defining, 187–189

example of, 81–82

fundraising and, 199–200

The Poetry Corner, 30–31

speakers, online, 8

special-effects editing, 152

special performances, 102

Spitzer, Nick, 95

sponsorship, 192–193

staff

attitudes of, 103–104

passion and, 200

PML players and, 113

State Arts Agency Directory (resource), 214

State Humanities Councils (resource), 214

Stories from the Crystal City, 135–136

Stuart, Crit, 176

students

adult literacy programs, 37–38

art purchase awards, 73

critiques, 61–62

hosting exhibits for, 203

Poetry Corner and, 30

poster creation and, 59–71

Subject Authority Cooperative Program, 92

subject scope, 80

success, measuring, 42

Successful Art Class Critique (website), 61–62

summer productions, 108–110

Sunday Gumbo (radio program), 95

Super, Paula, 51

support resources, 213–214

Surls, James, 77

surveys, Cultural Arts Literacy program, 38–39

symphony orchestras, 97–98

T

Taste of Chicago festival, 101

teachers

creative writing class, 11–23

finding, 41–42

technology, 7–8

Teen Library Corps, 125

teens

Art Revolution for Teens, 117–128

PML players, 107–114

Tejada, Alfonso L., 177

television shows, 147–154
terms of sale, 80
Terrizzi, Olivia, 67
"The Beauty of Nature" (exhibit), 178
theater productions, 110
Thien, Madeleine, 182
Thompson, Tara, 16
Tinney, Mercedes, 16, 18, 22
Toporek, Sergio, 177
trading cards, educational method, 138
Traditional Enhancement Grant, 88
trivia, educational method, 137
trustees, plan development and, 57
Twitter, 5, 120
Two Lines: A Journal of Translation, 11

U

university collaborations, examples, 93–94
University of British Columbia, 175
University of Florida (Gainesville), 4
University of Louisiana (Lafayette), 87–96
University of Montana (Missoula), 25–32
University of Wyoming, 73–83
users, 103–105

V

Valentine, Barbara, 11
Vara, Raquel, 16, 18
video recordings, 91
View from Jackson Falls (painting), 57
Violin Concerto (Sowerby), 100
visual arts
    academic libraries and, 73–83
    adult literacy programs, 37–46
    Art Revolution for Teens, 122–123
    promoting, 47–58

resources, 210–211
    student talent and posters, 59–71
visual literacy, 176
Voellinger, Chuck, 150–151

W

W-8BEN forms, 172
W-9 forms, 172
waiver of liability example, 83
website resources, 68
Weebly (website), 43
Western Kentucky University (WKU), 187
Winnat, Marc, 51–53
woodblock print, 11, 17
word war contest, 8–9
workshops, 109, 123–124
Writer's Alliance of Gainesville (WAG), 6
writing
    scripts, 153
    teaching, 11–23
writing prompts
    abstract images as, 12–13
    photographs as, 18–20
    sketches as, 22–23
    woodblock prints as, 17–18

Y

Yahgulanaas, Michael, 182
You Design It, We Make It (program), 133
YouTube (social media), 30

Z

Zúñiga, Adriana, 177
Zydeco/Zarico music, 90